INSIDE OUT
Developmental Strategies
for Teaching Writing

INSIDE OUT

Developmental Strategies for Teaching Writing

Second Edition

DAN KIRBY and TOM LINER
with Ruth Vinz

BOYNTON/COOK PUBLISHERS
HEINEMANN
PORTSMOUTH, NH

Boynton/Cook Publishers
A Division of
Heinemann Educational Books, Inc.
70 Court Street, Portsmouth, NH 03801
Offices and agents throughout the world

Library of Congress Cataloging-in-Publication Data
Kirby, Dan.
    Inside out : developmental strategies for teaching writing / Dan
Kirby and Tom Liner with Ruth Vinz.—2nd ed.
        p. cm.
    Bibliography: p.
    ISBN 0-86709-225-4
    1. English language—Composition and exercises—Study and teaching
    (Secondary) I. Liner, Tom. II. Vinz, Ruth. III. Title.
LB1631.K53 1988
808'.042'0712—dc19   88-26308
                                                                   CIP

Printed in the United States of America
91 90 89 88   9 8 7 6 5 4 3 2 1

Preface

Things have changed in the world of teaching writing since the late '70s when we first conceived and wrote *Inside Out*. Kids are doing more writing (it seems to us) in elementary and middle schools; and many of the approaches and attitudes we argued for in the first edition are standard practice in many (if still too few) high schools. Even in some very traditional places, writing is seen as something more than grammar drills or a few formulated essays and a research paper per semester for the English teacher's dispatch.

It might seem that Nirvana approacheth. But wait...as we discussed in a recent *Phi Delta Kappan* article (June, 1988), there are some scary developments out there. Some teachers act as though there is only *one* process, teaching it as a new kind of gospel. They speak in self-assured tones of *the process* and label students' writings as *process writings,* and sometimes those writings don't look any different from the old formulated essays. Publishers have gotten into the process game by offering texts which "teach the process without sacrificing basic skills." Most chilling of all, however, is the way some school districts have installed process approaches into their curriculum guides. Often super-imposed over Hunteresque models of effective teaching, these business-like, industrial-strength curricular documents mandate classroom activities, teacher roles, and sometimes page numbers in texts that convey *the process* of writing as though it were some kind of content in and of itself. God knows, what *they* mean by "process" is not what we mean by "process."

As we worked to revise this edition, we were shocked to find how many times we had said *the process* eight years ago. Maybe we really did think of "process" as mostly steps and stages. We left most of that in the book, but we're concerned about the industrialization of process in the schools and a view that process is a neat, sanitary monolith. It's hard to know what to change when you revise a book. It's hard to represent what you're thinking and working on right now with your students. The first edition of *Inside Out* was basically a story about how two amateurs try to teach writing. You read their book and it's clear that they don't always know what they're doing and why, but they are determined to figure it out and have a good time doing it.

The new *Inside Out* may have lost some of the winsome innocence of its parent. We have learned and grown and changed since the early '80s. Most of that growth is the result of continued work with young writers.

Our questions have changed; our uncertainties have become more complex, less easy to articulate. We are still passionately interested in teaching writing, but more tentative about how that instruction ought to unfold and what our own roles in that unfolding ought to be. After a speech one day in Wyoming, a friend came up to me and said, "Now, let me see if I have this straight: you don't know anything at all for sure anymore." If this more tentative tone is mistaken for ignorance, I'm sorry. It's just that the more we know about teaching writing, the longer we work in classrooms with kids, the more complex and profound the task seems. I think that better questions increase my chances of learning the things I need to know, and a healthy dose of what Charles Kettering called "intelligent ignorance" insures that I will continue to be a learner in my own classroom.

Revising a successful book has proved to be hard, sometimes undoable work. Maybe we should have written a new book, with new stories. Maybe we should have stuck in many new activities for teachers to use. Instead, we have decided to talk back to ourselves in the book, to leave many things unchanged and to argue with ourselves about other things. We offer this revision to our teacher friends who have warmed to *Inside Out,* those of you who have expanded your teaching repertoires by reading this book and those of you who have met us on the road and told us the book has brought support for your efforts. And we offer it to the thousands of soon-to-be teachers who will read it in methods classes, and dream about classrooms of their own.

And so we have tried. We have brought Ruth Vinz, a high school teacher, close friend, and wonderful writer, into the dialogue. You will hear her strong, literate, teacherly voice in the book. We asked Ruth to join us because we wanted the touch of a high school writing teacher in these pages. Tom is now a supervisor, and Dan is in and out of too many classrooms. Ruth is our participant-observer, reality-checker, and super-teacher.

A few readers still grumble about the "I" and "we" switches throughout the book. Since there are now three of us "I's"—if still only one "we"—there might be more grumbling or even confusion. But we've found that most readers find no problem with the shifting persons—that, in truth, we speak as one—and we've felt all along that the third person impersonal would make a mockery of our message. For those who want ready reference to who wrote what, here's a breakdown: Tom wrote Chapters 2, 4, 6, 9, 11, 12, 15; Dan (with Ruth's collaboration is this edition) wrote Chapters 1, 3, 5, 8, 10, 13, 14; Ruth wrote Chapter 16; we all did Chapter 7.

We hope this new edition works for you. We know you will tell us when we meet you in Casper and Melbourne and Grand Rapids and

Sioux Falls and Irvine. We know you will feel free to tell us what you think. We cherish that; and we will tell you things too, tell you how we're still trying to help students seize the power that writing can bring to them when they own it. We will share our latest ideas about how to bring reading and writing and thinking together in meaningful contexts. We will share student writings and stories of successes and failures. We will commiserate with each other, and we will laugh together, reminding ourselves once again that the real reason we keep teaching is because it's fun.

Dan Kirby

in the autumn
the does always come down
from the high meadows

pointing their tracks in the new snow
and pointing the way
for the antlered bucks following

in the autumn
I always watch for their pointings
and their brown eyes

big with watching from the shadows

—TOM LINER

Contents

Chapter One: Where It All Comes From   1

Chapter Two: Notes on the Process   11

Chapter Three: The Classroom Environment   23

The Way the Room Looks,   23
The Way the Room Feels,   25
A Writing Preserve,   25
Beginnings,   26
Beyond the Classroom,   36
Summary,   37

Chapter Four: Getting It Down   39

Personal Writing,   39
The Journal,   43
Personal Writing Exercises for the Beginning Writer,   44
A Note on Topic Finding and Getting Them Started,   52

Chapter Five: The "J"   57

Why the Journal Works,   58
What's in It for You?   60
Four Journals,   60
Reflections on the "J,"   66
Suggestions for Using the Journal,   66
Responding to and Evaluating the Journal,   67

Chapter Six: Writing Poetry   72

Teaching Slow Kids to Write Poetry,   78
Teaching the Exceptional Student Poet,   88
Teaching Younger Kids to Write Poetry,   93
Three Prose Exercises,   101
More About Poetry,   103

Chapter Seven: What Is Good Writing?   107

The Kirby-Liner Working Criteria for Good Student Writing,   110
What Makes Good Writing Interesting?   111
What Makes Good Writing Technically Skillful?   118
Making Up Jokes About Bicycle Spokes and Red Balloons,   124

Chapter Eight: Responding to Student Writing   126

Responding as a Person,   127
Looking for the Good,   129
Teacher's Response,   131

Chapter Nine: Different Voices, Different Speakers   137

Tuning Your Voice,   140
Mad Talking, Soft Talking, Fast Talking,   142
Talking Back to Yourself,   145
How to Say "I Love Thee"—Let Me Count the Ways,   146
Trying On Other Voices,   146
Contrasting Voices,   147
Getting into Another Speaker,   148
Collecting Dialogues,   148
On the Phone,   148
Who Owns the Voice?   149
Multiple Self-Portrait,   152

Chapter Ten: Growing Toward a Sense of Audience   154

Talking Directly to an Audience,   159
Anticipating Audience Response,   160
Profiling an Audience,   161
Rewriting for Different Audiences,   161
Writing for Younger Children,   162
Audience Adaptation,   162
Real Audiences,   163
Endnote,   164

Chapter Eleven: Writing About Literature   165

Things to Think About When Your Students Write
    About Literature,   166
Other Things to Think About When Your Students Write
    About Literature,   168

Writing Responsively About Literature: Backwards and
    Sideways Exercises, 168
Alternatives to the Book Report, 172
A Literary Conversation: One More
    Literature/Writing Lesson, 178

Chapter Twelve: Revision: The Student as Editor 181

Keeping It Going, 194
Elaboration: First Revision Options for Personal Narrative, 194
Crafting: Second Revision Options for Personal Narrative, 195
The Computer and Revision, 196

Chapter Thirteen: Expository Writing   200

Problems with Expository Writing, 202
What's to Be Done? 204
Planning Expository Assignments, 205
Comparison and Contrast Assignment, 210
Action Research Project, 211
Writing About an Author, 212
Thinking It Through, 213

Chapter Fourteen: Grading and Evaluating   215

First—Confession Number One, 216
A Little Self-Evaluation, 218
The Nongrading Approach, 219
A Performance System, 220
Holistic Grading Strategies, 221
Analytic Scales, 224
Checkpoints, 227
Evaluation by Peers, 230
Conferencing, 235

Chapter Fifteen: Publishing Student Writing   237

Ways to Publish in the Classroom, 237
Ways to Publish Outside the Classroom, 240
Publishing Outside the School, 243
Cautions About Publishing Student Writing, 246
Publishing Information for Your Kids
    (and Their Teacher), 247

Chapter Sixteen: Resources

I. The Musts, 250
   Stories from Classrooms, 253
   Writing About Literature, 254
   Revision, 255
   Grammar in Writing, 257
   Conferencing, 260
   What Writers Say About Writing, 260
   Writing Personal Narrative and Fiction, 262
   Writing Poetry, 264

II. Works Consulted, 266

INSIDE OUT
Developmental Strategies
for Teaching Writing

CHAPTER ONE

Where It All Comes From

As language flows ceaselessly within the self, helping to define and delimit the interior world of the self..., so it also flows ceaselessly...from the inside to the world around and beyond the self also helping to define and delimit and delineate *that* world.

—JAMES E. MILLER, JR. (1)

It all begins inside; inside the heads of our kids. There are ideas in there and language and lots of possibilities. Writing is a pulling together of that inside stuff. Writing is a rehearsal in meaning making. What we like to call "mind texts." The teacher's role in all this is to support those rehearsals, to help kids bring those mind texts to the page as powerful writings. It's the head-to-page trip that is so frightening and difficult for writers. Acting as coaches of writing, teachers can assist students by helping them understand the strategies they are using and suggesting others they might use, by raising questions and more questions as the text emerges, and by encouraging and supporting student decision-making throughout the growth of the piece. That role of coach is not an easy one to learn, and we're still working on our skills, but we feel we're beginning to understand how to help students say what they want to say on paper. That's where this book wants to take you.

Most of us have come through a long transition from those early idealistic days of trying to teach writing to high school kids the way we were taught in freshman composition classes. I remember assigning that first "theme" to my 150 eleventh graders and carrying home that awful stack of papers, and how I worked three weekends marking and correcting every error, and how I made a correction sheet with all the symbols—you know, like *Awk* and *Frag* and *P.* and *D.*—so that the kids could interpret my markings.

1

I remember that proud Monday when I took that stack of papers to class and announced I was returning their papers for them to read and heed my corrective advice and revise accordingly.

"What papers?" they said.

"Your themes; remember the ones on 'The Puritan Ethic in a Foreign Land?' Three weeks ago?" A few remembered the assignment. I handed back their papers and watched with anticipation. Most took a quick look at the letter grade and forgot it. One kid argued with me after class about a special use of the comma that I had circled; he was right. All of them seemed unimpressed with my hours of careful correcting. None of them seemed interested in dealing further with their writing. I was crushed. What an impossible task to teach writing to such apathetic, insensitive students. Beginning that day I affected a theory about the teaching of writing that served me well and left me without guilt for ten years. I discovered *Swartz's First Law of Composition:* "One cannot teach writing...one discovers *writers.*" Somewhere before the Foundation, God anointed a few (using a table of random numbers) to become good writers. My job as an English teacher was made suddenly clear with the new-found law. I had only to find those creative accidents of God, to dote on their writing, and to marvel at their creative genius. Students who were not of the chosen I could steadfastly ignore, hoping they would choose a vocational course of study or give up altogether.

Maybe that anecdote seems very foreign to you now in 1988. Maybe you've taken some courses in the teaching of writing, or maybe you've been in a writing project or read several hundred books on the teaching of writing. Maybe you've given your heart to the process and your classes are going much better now. Let's hope so, but I get around some in schools and I still see lots of teachers who remain frustrated about teaching writing, and much of that frustration comes from their own mistaken notions about how children learn to write, notions like the following:

Mistake 1

We simply have not provided kids with enough practice time. Writing is complex, high-level human behavior. It cannot be crowded into hurry-up quarter courses or left to one grade level or relegated to one day a week. Proficiency in writing requires daily practice, practice that is often sponsored by the teacher and is often initiated by the students themselves. Like developing oneself as a runner, becoming a writer requires a rigorous conditioning regimen. As the runner runs laps and jogs early in the morning, every day, so too the writer needs a consistent practice schedule.

Mistake 2

We have been far too preoccupied with the form and forms of writing. Too many teachers are preoccupied with the "we-don't-write-like-we-talk" syndrome, hammering away at the feeble attempts of their students to approximate the demands of this new, strange behavior called "writing." They expect too much too soon. They impose what Steve Judy calls "adult expectations" on beginners (2). We need a moratorium on concerns about rigidly defined forms of writing to give writers a chance to get their thinking onto the page. Miller and Judy say it better: "Form grows from experimenting with language" (3). Practice in languaging the tangled web of emotion and imagination is the only way a writer learns to control the complexities of fluency. Let them write and let the forms emerge.

Don't rely on finished pieces as the only evidence of students' ability to write. Trust that not every piece of writing must go through a process of prewriting, fluency, control, and precision. Provide writing experiences in the classroom that help them build a repertoire of strategies they can use "in progress." Students will discover their own strategies as they work. They'll find ways to get writing generated, drafted, revised and edited that we've not thought of before. The truth is that we'll borrow their ideas to help other writers if we are keen-eyed and responsive to what they show us.

Mistake 3

We have tried and failed miserably at teaching writing as a deductive process. We've done that part-to-whole, word-to-sentence business religiously, and most textbooks and curriculum guides are still based on such notions. It's such a seductive piece of logic: begin with the word, next the sentence, then the paragraph; then when they get *real good* they get to write the five-paragraph theme. Master the parts, get those labels straight. It all adds up. Unfortunately, in writing, the whole is far more than the sum of parts. By fragmenting instruction and drilling on one part at a time, we kill motivation and destroy the very process we're trying to develop.

Our thinking has changed a bit since 1981, when we proposed a developmental sequence. We are no longer certain that moving students from simple to complex, from personal to objective, from simple poems to extended analogy, or from simple short stories to highly involved stories is a way to measure their growth as writers. Much of what is happening in contemporary American writing convinces us otherwise. A simple short story of the type we see in *Sudden Fiction* (4) is as complex and artfully tuned as any longer story. Our growing interest in memoir, autobiography, diary, and journal convinces us that there is more to writing than our traditional emphasis on argumentation, form poems, or complex short stories. Even the simplest of poems requires control of language and vision. Intensity and vividness may be more difficult in a short piece than it will be in a fleshier piece of extended analogy. It's very individual. Each piece has its own challenges. We don't look at a student's one page story or two stanza poem with disdain. Length doesn't equate effort. Length doesn't impress us as it did when we first started teaching writing.

We have a sense that we know good writing when we see it. We cannot afford, as teachers of writing, to get hung up in our own ignorance of the complexity and individuality of this thing we call writing process. Writers fashion subjects in individual ways. We need to help student writers by designing occasions that help them rehearse through writing experiences. We need to coach them when they need a third eye or ear. Writing sequences or writing exercises for the sake of exercise or sequence will not help students develop their voices or their ability to control language. We need to judge when and how to interfere.

It is unrealistic to expect students to drill on the parts of the language or the parts of a composition for years in anticipation of some far-off future when they can begin to use the parts to explore the options of discourse.

My daughter bugged me for several years about taking guitar lessons. I, of course, preferred a less frivolous instrument like the piano or the cello. She took guitar lessons. I remember how excited she was after her first lesson. She couldn't wait to share "her song." She strummed those two monotonous chords and sang her song. She smiled. She was pleased with her song. That pride in producing a *whole* composition of her own was her motivation to continue and practice. Had her guitar teacher given her a quiz over the parts of the guitar? Had he told her to learn the names of the strings or to practice a chord until she got it right? No. One strums a guitar to produce a song. The song's the thing, no matter how simple. So must it be with writing. The piece is the thing— and we must learn to help young writers say their piece every time they write. There is technical knowledge to be learned, but writing is first to be read and communicated. No approach to writing that forgets the joy of writing your own song will work with novice writers.

Mistake 4

We have tried to teach writing without integrating theories of learning and theories of discourse. Curriculum guides and textbooks have changed as a result of our growing knowledge of writing processes, but there is still heavy emphasis on artificial sequences: the eighth grade report, the eleventh grade term paper. The topic sentence in the seventh grade. The descriptive paragraph in the eighth grade. None of these writing problems is tailored to the developmental ability of the student.

We know more about what's going on inside our heads, and we know that exercising the mental processes that lead young writers to solve problems of languaging and form is the best hope for real growth. Maybe schools aren't ready for curricula and textbooks that work from ideas rather than forms. In writing, ideas come first. Writers test the range of possibilities, learn something about adding or deleting ideas. They arrange and rearrange and add new ideas until sense evolves.

We simply must design a composition program that works with the natural development of the child, a program that nurtures writers in a supportive environment where the deep water of school prose is not the ultimate goal.

Mistake 5

We simply haven't stuck with it or followed through on anything we've done in the teaching of writing. The chronicle of a child's experience with writing in the schools is often a patchwork of stopping and starting, of quantum leaps and long silences. Writing is complex human behavior that provides for children what Nancy Martin has called "a range of writing purposes so that pupils are given more opportunity to express their thoughts on paper in a variety of ways" (5)

Beginning a book by talking about our mistakes may seem threatening to some. It's not our intention to point fingers at English teachers. We freely admit to being guilty of all these mistakes at one time or another. We point out the mistakes to dramatize the false assumptions and fruitless practices that underlie much of the teaching of writing in schools. The model for the teaching of writing that this book offers seeks to avoid these mistakes and is drawn from our experiences as writers and teachers of writing and the successes we've observed children experience—as they acquire their oral language.

"Hold it!" you say. "Talking and writing are very different behaviors." Partly true. Talking is primary human behavior. Children do not decide to talk. They begin making sounds as soon as they enter the world: they express basic needs of hunger or discomfort through oral language. Writing, on the other had, is an *unnatural* act. Even some very advanced cultures have developed no written forms of their language. But as Ann Berthoff points out, "The making of meaning is the work of the active mind...form-finding and form-creating [are] natural activit[ies]" (6). Children structure their world through their imaginations. The physical act of writing may be unnatural, but the synthesis process is inherently human, and it's a process children are already highly successful with long before they come into your class.

The most compelling reason to look at the language acquisition process as a model for teaching writing is its incredible success. A 100 percent effective, environmental-proof method is just what the teacher of writing needs.

If you have a young child around the house, you already know about the method. The child babbles, produces sounds (linguists say the child is practicing phonemes), quite uninterested in parental approval. The young child seems to delight in the sounds themselves, and fools around incessantly with language. Children learn quickly, however, that certain sounds produce results, and that they can actively involve their parents in their world by talking to them. When certain sounds are made, Dad listens attentively. When the first "da-da" comes out, Dad is delighted. He calls Grandma on the phone. He invites a neighbor over to hear it again. The language of the child becomes the center of the home environment. No father tells neighbors, "My child is so dumb he knows only one word!" The father is proud. He is supportive of his child's feeblest attempts to produce language. He is an active listener.

Children are thrilled by the attention they get from adults as they produce their oral language. It's so simple to manipulate those big people. "Wa-wa" produces a glass of water. No parent says, "I'm sorry, you may not have a glass of water until you learn to say 'water' correctly." The parents' behavior is supportive and positive; responses to children's requests are immediate and helpful. The language-learning experience is not painfully corrective or demeaning to the child. Approximations of the language are rewarded. Parents strain to puzzle out each new expression. They function as an active, supportive audience in much the same way we take the role of active, supportive audience for our student writers. We create an accepting, enthusiastic environment where writing is as habitual as talking or eating and equally nurturing to the student's well-being. We bring experience, as the best parents do, to support and nurture students through the challenges and frustrations. The principles operating in that process are worth using for teaching writing. Here are a few of them:

1. Incredible Motivation

Children enjoy producing oral language; they seem never to tire of it. Teachers of writing cannot expect their students to take pen in hand and thrill to the task of writing, or can they? Kenneth Koch and Barbara Esbensen tell exciting stories about working with children and poetry (7, 8). We, too, have collected reams of honest, powerful student writing. Many of the teachers we work with around the country display, proudly, similar examples of their extraordinary successes with young and novice writers. The joy of the first song on the guitar is not unlike the joy of the first story a child writes. Praise for producing written language and success in completing the task are closely tied to the child's desire to continue.

Support and recognition also extend children's interests and encourage them to take risks and invent new forms. Publishing children's writing, displaying it, calling attention to it, asking the children to share it: all build motivation.

2. Constant Support

Most of us have had at some time a mentor—someone who challenged us, excited us, and called forth our best efforts, encouraging us even when we failed. No one needs more support than the immature writer. The parent gives unqualified support to the young child's oral language efforts, and the child thrives on it. Why, then, do teachers of writing withhold support from novice writers? Have they forgotten how tough the writing process is? Did they ever know it firsthand? Teachers who write *with* their students won't forget.

I like to use the analogy of learning to ride a bike for the writing process. When a child first decides to accept the challenge of that two-wheeler, the parent is eager to help. The parent encourages, supports, and anticipates the fear of falling. "Don't worry; I won't let you go." And so while the kid sits on the seat, far above the ground, knuckles turning white on handle grips, the parent begins to run along beside.

"I'm going to fall, Mom."

"Don't worry; I've got you."

Supporting, running along beside, and occasionally picking up the pieces after a spill, the teacher of writing encourages wobbly writers:

"See, there, that's good."

"Don't worry, you'll get it."

3. Instant Response

What do you need most after you've written a piece of writing? Someone to read it to. Actually, Ruth and I didn't wait that long. We revised this chapter in a kind of frenetic duet: taking turns at the computer, rehearsing lines aloud, jotting notes on scratch paper, reading it aloud as we discovered new ideas. All writers long for a response. That's what it's all about—communicating with someone. Writers need immediate feedback. Teachers should walk around the room as the students write, reading over their shoulders: "Hey, I like that. Tell me more about this. You've got a good start, keep it going." Teachers should provide plenty of opportunities for student writers to share their work in progress with peers.

Have students share anything they've done. A word, a sentence, even an idea. They need to try it out now, to collaborate on writing projects, playing off another writer's ideas the way Ruth and I are doing with this chapter.

4. Wide Tolerance for Error

Have you ever been around children as they begin to extend their oral language? They make frequent mistakes. Some of it is unintelligible. The parent says "uh-huh" even when the utterance is only partially clear. The parent responds to approximations of the language. When children say "wa-wa," they get a drink. No one worries that they'll still be saying "wa-wa" at age sixteen. They'll get it right with some practice. Oral language learning is a pleasant experience for children.

Teachers of writing seem so tense about the process, so preoccupied with finding errors rather than meaning. Relax. Puzzle out your students' writings. Tolerate their inabilities to produce technically correct writing. Many of those idiosyncracies in their papers will straighten themselves out through practice. Writing practice has tremendous self-correcting potential. As Tom is fond of saying, "Getting it right comes from getting it down." Writers need an incubation period—time to get their ideas down and test them out. Time to develop confidence in a personal voice. Support these efforts and the controls will come along. Those controls that don't come along can be taught directly at more appropriate moments when the student is motivated to learn them because a piece in progress is important enough to get it right.

5. Frequent Practice Trials

Establish an experimental climate in your class from the very first day. Wean your students away from the "Are we going to get a grade for this?" syndrome. Use the analogy of the runner who jogs not for awards or recognition but to build stamina and endurance. Ask your students to write something each day. Encourage them to try different forms, different hooks, different angles. Establish writing practice as a fundamental routine in your class. Get a reputation as "the teacher who always makes us write."

6. Form-Finding Freedom

Most approaches to teaching composition remain oriented toward certain forms or modes. The problem with form-oriented approaches is that they force student writers to form subjects rather than encouraging them to produce written language and patiently help them find forms that fit their writings. In *English Journal,* William Irmscher differentiates between writing as skills and writing as behavior (9).

If writing is a collection of skills, then we should be able to invent some nice, neat technology of skills and a cumulative sequence to teach it. If, on the other hand, writing is behavior (and, therefore, complex, involving the whole person), then we have to approach writing instruction with holistic, growth-centered strategies. One thing is certain: kids have powerful language inside their heads, but most conventional writing instruction fails to help them tap these inner linguistic resources. Student writers can and will find their own forms if they are given the freedom and support to do so.

From the mistakes teachers make and from the observations we've made of the oral language behavior of children and from reading, our method for teaching writing to *all* students emerges. It is not a lock-step, drills-and-skills, part-to-whole method, but rather developmental strategies that build on the intuitive language resources common to all human beings. We believe that, simply stated, writers' processes move along a continuum from prewriting and fluency to control and precision. Or as Tom describes it to his students: getting started, getting it down, getting it right, checking it out. The book is organized around this model. We know that writing doesn't happen in such clear-cut categories. Words get messy and shuffled around on the page. What is partly fluency may be partly control or prewriting. We've pulled out parts of the process, confident that they will become blurred in classroom practice.

Fluency is the first consideration. It is the basis for all that follows. First, we show you how to get the kids writing and keep them writing. Without that daily practice in a humane and accepting atmosphere, writing is drudgery and grows very little. Second, we give you ways to work with kids once they have found a voice in their writing. We suggest a variety of exercises, things for you to try out with the kids that will help them control that voice and grow toward maturity in their writing. The process does not end here, however. We also show you some ways to push young writers toward fine-tuning their writing. We deal with expository writing here and give you some tips on how to do all this work and survive it. One of the important things a writing teacher needs to know is how to have kids do a lot of writing and somehow deal with the mountains of papers and keep one's sanity at the same time. In the final section we tie up some loose ends for you by describing an approach that encourages good writing and good revision and that we think has a lot of potential for your teaching. We also include a chapter on sources and resources that will aid you in your search for ways to nurture young writers.

We offer this book and these ideas to anyone who is serious about the teaching of writing. We do not believe this the *only* way to teach writing, but it is the approach we have found to be successful with a wide variety of students.

Notes

1. James E. Miller, Jr. *Words, Self, Reality: The Rhetoric of the Imagination.* Dodd, Mead, 1972.

2. Stephen Judy, *Explorations in the Teaching of Secondary English,* Harper & Row, 1972.

3. James E. Miller, Jr., & Stephen N. Judy. *Writing in Reality,* Harper & Row, 1978.

4. *Sudden Fiction: American Short Short Stories,* ed. by Robert Shapard, Peregrine, 1986.

5. Nancy Martin et al., *Writing and Learning Across the Curriculum 11-16.* Ward Lock, 1976.

6. Ann E. Berthoff, *Forming/Thinking/Writing: The Composing Imagination.* Boynton/Cook, 1978.

7. Kenneth Koch, *Wishes, Lies, and Dreams,* Vintage, 1970.

8. Barbara Esbensen, *A Celebration of Bees,* Winston, 1975.

9. William Irmscher, "Teaching Writing in Terms of Growth," *English Journal,* Vol. 66, No. 9 (Dec. 1977), pp. 33-36.

CHAPTER TWO

Notes on the Process

For writing *is* discovery. The language that never leaves our head is like colorful yarn, endlessly spun out multicolored threads dropping into a void, momentarily compacted, entangled, fascinating, elusive.... Indeed, writing is largely a process of choosing among alternatives from the images and thoughts of the endless flow, and this choosing is a matter of making up one's mind, and this making up one's mind becomes in effect the making up of one's self.

—JAMES E. MILLER, JR. (1)

Teachers are often afraid of teaching writing because they feel they don't know enough about how writing is done to teach it effectively. In this chapter we hope we can dispel some of your fears by sharing with you some of our observations about the writing process. We believe that the better we understand the process, the better we can teach writing. We've spent a lot of time watching kids write, concentrating not on what they were producing, but on *how* they went about doing it. What is the actual process that the writer follows when he or she writes? What are the stages of the process? What comes first? What second? What last? And how do writers move through the stages of the process? We've talked to students about how they write and asked them these questions; we've read a lot about writing and what it's supposed to be (the best of these readings you'll find in the Resources chapter); and we've thought a lot about writing and about what we do when we write.

I want to explore this most complicated of human activities with you for a moment by using two metaphors. The first is from a professional writer and theorist of writing, the second from a student writer. Together they help describe the actions we have observed in our own writing and in the writing of our students.

James Miller describes language as a ceaseless flow inside each of us (1). When we write, we dip into this flow and pull out things to put down on the page. We begin to impose order as we write one word after the other on the page, but there is that feeling of anxiousness, sometimes almost panic, as we try to capture meaning from this stream of language. We are afraid something will slip by, that we'll miss that special word or phrase we need to get it said right. Every writer knows that feeling.

Consider how I write this. I want you to understand and accept my feelings about what writing is. I write half of the first sentence of a pargraph, stop, scratch it out, write that half-sentence again, slightly different this time. The rest of that sentence was there a second ago, now it has evaporated. Something else occurs to me, and I finish the sentence. There are long "silences," one of the important parts of this business of writing, while I watch my interior flow of language and wait for just the right thing to surface. I back up to the paragraph before this one, and change or strike out. I jump ahead, anticipating where I want to go next. Other thoughts intrude, and I reread what I've written to get started again. And so it goes.

That is something of what writing is like even when it's going well, as this is. All these things, and more—usually happening so fast and so naturally that I'm long since used to it—all are part of the *feeling* of writing as it is going on.

Cary, a talented high school senior, describes the process this way.

I guess the best analogy to the way I write is that it's like a man beginning a maze. He tries his best to memorize every turn and path, and then runs ahead at full speed, running as hard as he can til he makes a mistake and runs into a wall. Then he gets up, checks his bearings, and starts again from this point (2).

That's a good image, and one with the feel of truth about it. Before you write, you're anxious, worried about getting it down. You try to plan things to say in your head. You worry—and you worry. You walk around the room. You stare out the window waiting for inspiration and that flash of insight that will take this onerous task out of your hands and put it in the hands of the gods where it belongs. You sharpen your pencils and line them up in a neat row on your desk. And you worry some more. You search your mind, gone suddenly blank, for a hook to get into it. A word or phrase or sentence to start it—anything to get it rolling. You sharpen the pencils again (3). (You don't even write with a pencil, do you?) And you finally catch a hook, take a deep breath, and begin. You rush as hard as you can through that first part until something doesn't work. You hit that blank wall that Cary talks about. But you'll begin again soon and drive through that first draft. And like the man in the maze, you really don't know exactly where you're going until it appears in front of you on the page. As Kurt Vonnegut says, "It's like watching a teletype machine in a newspaper office to see what comes out" (4).

One of the important aspects of these actions of writing that I'm describing is the chaos of that inner flow from which the writer draws things for the page and that all writers must struggle with. The immature writer needs to know that this feeling of chaos is natural, that even the best writers experience it, and that it's really one of the gifts of a human being writing. For in that chaos is variety, the kaleidoscopic flux of life itself from which the writer can capture things that are beautiful and good.

But the immature writer needs to know that there is also control operating in the writing process. Despite the chaos, the jumps and starts and silences, despite all the time spent sharpening pencils, when the writer writes there is purpose. Somehow the purpose is held apart from the chaos and kept relatively constant during the writing. Otherwise, writing would be impossible; maybe thinking itself could not happen.

Like speech, writing is close to the way we think. Language and thinking are, in a way, one and the same. Tampering with the way someone writes is tampering with the way he thinks. Teaching writing is a task to approach with humility and with sensitivity to the feelings of another person. You're bound to meet with resistance, and sometimes with resentment. And because it's so complex, there is not one sure technique that will teach all students to write well. Teaching writing takes patience and hard work and a good dose of tolerance and good humor. And that is especially true if you're dealing with older kids who have met with failure after failure in writing classes where they have been forced, grudgingly, to write for a teacher who had the red pen poised to "correct" the way they write. It just ain't that easy.

But why theorize? Why not just get on with the Helpful Hints for teaching this most human of human enterprises? And why talk about the Good Writer like Cary? You don't have to worry about him (he is usually a *she* in high school classes). She sits on the front row in your class and cheerfully cranks out those Grade A papers week after week— well organized, carefully worded, with a minimum of errors, and sometimes even good to read. It's those other kids who make you want to tear your hair and scream. Many of them are otherwise bright, articulate, and willing—except when it comes to writing. They put words on paper reluctantly, and badly. A class paper for them is an ordeal; they suffer when they write—and they make you suffer with them. And their papers! They read as though they had been composed by brain-damaged morons. Why not start with those kids? *That's* where the trouble is.

Well, first of all, it seems reasonable to know *where* we're trying to go before we decide *how* to get there. But more important is the fact that, in this complicated business of writing, knowing clearly *what* we're working for will give us some ideas about *how* this can be done. Teachers have had little success with most kids in working with the product of their writing, and it's time to work with the immature writers in our classes on the *process* of their writing. Janet Emig comments, "We have been concerned exclusively with the piece of writing, more particularly the simonized draft submitted for the devastation and the grade" (5). If you approach the teaching of writing from process as growth, you can ease the devastation and begin to really work on writing as the kids grow with it naturally. And Good Writers can grow just as much, if in different ways, as the immature writers in your classes.

Each time the experienced writer writes, she goes through the same stages with her paper as the stages in her *growth* as a writer. She becomes fluent; she controls her writing in sophisticated in-process ways; she strives for precision in her revision of the paper. The steps her paper goes through are the steps she has gone through as a writer over the years. And all writers go through the same process when they write. The student who struggles through a theme once a week and the professional who writes daily do the same things, only the pro does each step more in depth and takes the final steps further.

We hear you saying something at this point like, "My kids don't write that way. They just slop together anything and turn it in." But don't be too sure that most of your writers, good and not so good, don't follow these steps at least part of the way when they write. Take some time to watch them carefully as they write. We know that's when you do the attendance report and the lunch report and all those other clerical duties that plague you every day, but try to squeeze those in somewhere else, and just watch the students write. Ann Berthoff says that "Developing a method of composing means explaining explanations, writing about writing, thinking about thinking; sometimes that can make you dizzy" (6). That's true enough, but it's important in beginning with students in writing to remember this, also from Berthoff: "We aren't born knowing how to write, but we are born knowing how to know how."

When you first begin that writing class, talk to the kids about what they do when they write. Talk about where the hard parts of writing are. Ask them about the process of their writing. When you give them that first assignment, write with them on the same assignment and talk about the writing together, sharing with one another your feelings about the writing and about "what you do when you write this thing." Have them do some free writing (write for ten minutes without pausing and without thinking or worrying about it, just flowing the words on the page). When the students free-write, have them think about writing and write it out as though they were talking to you. Pass out a short questionnaire on writing (see Chapter 3), and go over the responses with the kids as a way to get them talking about writing. And watch them. Watch them writing every chance you get. We think you'll be surprised at how closely the stages of the process we've outlined match what they do.

This procedure has some far-reaching implications for teaching writing. For one thing, it may be that the immature writer has simply not gotten beyond the first steps in his growth as a writer. And this may be true no matter how long he has been in school or how many English classes he may have taken. The student who still has trouble *getting it down* (that is, who is not *fluent* as a writer) cannot be expected to leapfrog over *control* to the stage of *precision* where he will be able to do a good job of revising his papers. For that student, revision—either his own or yours in red ink—is a frustrating and wasted experience. It may also help explain why otherwise bright students keep making the same old mistakes over and over again when they write.

For the Good Writer, *getting it down* and *getting it right* happen at the same time. This is, in fact, that complicated thing that happens that most people think of as "writing," when the words are put on the paper, the First Draft. The experienced writer not only writes; he revises *in process* as he does so. Fluency and control occur simultaneously. But that's not all. As the growing writer becomes fluent, he begins to control his writing automatically. As James Miller and Steve Judy put it, "...people develop control over words as they use language for exploration of inner worlds and for making connections with others in dialogue and discussion. In making contact with others, human beings shape their language for particular purposes. We feel that organization, structure, style, and appropriateness evolve as people struggle to communicate with one another" (7). And we believe that what Miller and Judy are saying here about speech is true for written language in similar ways.

There seems to be something universal about this process, about how we think and how we create. Harold Shubert is an art teacher and a good one in a northeast Georgia high school. Students of very different abilities are drawn to his classes from all over the school. The first thing he does with them is to get them "fluent" in art, whether they are drawing or painting or working in clay. They do a lot of messing around, a lot of experimenting with their own expressions, a lot of checking out options. Harold encourages and praises the good things he sees—and there is always something good eventually. Then he and the kids get down to work on the forms that feel right for them. They practice a lot with those forms and begin to elaborate on them. By midwinter the halls of the school are crowded with paintings and drawings and beautiful things that the kids have created—fluency, control, and precision in the art class.

Fluency brings control in even the hardest and most frustrating cases, but you have to be patient. John is one of those LD kids. They tell me he's dyslexic. Reading and writing for him are epic struggles. He's been in my class for three years now. He and I work together on his journal. He writes very slowly, and all the laws of logic and education decree that John cannot become fluent. But this spring, while he was writing daily about skiing and motorcycles and sex and things that he really was interested in, and things that he really wanted to write about, something happened in John's journal. The words began to come. I watched them growing daily with wonder and excitement. John was as excited as I was. One thing an LD kid cannot do is spell. John is learning to spell and form sophisticated sentences and write paragraphs that hang together and have rhythm and movement. He is learning to write, and he is learning to write by writing a lot, and about things that he wants to talk about on paper. He and I still have a long way to go together, but he can write, if slowly and painfully, and he *knows* that he can write.

Some of the controls in written language come almost immediately when the writer learns to write. He writes from left to right across the page in most languages. The patterns of his sentences are already formed in the subject-verb-object order. His spelling may be rudimentary, his syntax may be inchoate, his capitalization may be scattered, his words may be simple and unsophisticated, his punctuation may simply not be there—but you can *understand* what he's saying because you share a common language with him. And that language works in predictable and patterned ways. A large part of this control comes from an intuitive carryover from oral language, but it goes beyond that in writing. When the student writer reaches the point at which she can put words down on paper easily, at which she has found her "voice" and uses it, she will be able to control her writing to a large degree. The amazing thing is that the control that comes in those modes of discourse in which the writer is fluent operates not only for such things as word choice and sentence structure but also in the large segments of writing, that is, organization. It works naturally and automatically at the word, sentence, and paragraph levels, and in the writer's sense of the whole work.

William Irmscher, in talking about growth and the process of writing, claims that:

> ...at an early age we are able to draw upon intuitive resources of language that allow us to compose from the very first time we try—without preliminary instruction. In that first effort—whether the composition is oral or written—we are concerned with all of the factors that the most sophisticated writer is also concerned with: ideas or substance, feelings or personal involvement, arrangement or structure, choice of appropriate words, the effect or style, and, if the composition is transcribed, certain mechanical marks that clarify the meanings and structures. From the beginning, we can integrate all of these components. After the first composition, no matter how rudimentary it is, all of the rest throughout school and throughout our lives is practice, growth, maturity, and refinement of the process: over and over again (8).

By the time the kid is in your class in high school, a lot of what he needs to do is to run laps. But it's more than running laps. The cognitive processes are there, and they're working, if we don't discourage him entirely with our red pen. Control will come when, and only when, he has time to find his voice in his writing.

We're not saying that all you have to do is get the student fluent in a particular mode and he'll suddenly begin to turn out perfect papers. Nor are we saying that you can't help him in many ways to control his writing-in-process so that it will be better. Nor are we saying that writing is easy. But we are saying that, just as in learning speech, control follows and is closely linked with fluency. *Getting it right* comes from *getting it down*.

Put another way, the inexperienced writer will be unable to *get it right* until he has learned to *get it down*.

There are a lot of other things to be said about the process of writing as we have observed it, but this discussion of theory is already too long and you still need to know what to do every day. The most important points in this book are made in the sections where they are of more practical good than here. But one more thing about all this needs to be said. Because we're convinced that writing is learned in a certain way with recognizable stages, and because we believe that writing proceeds in similar stages, then we believe that writing is understandable. Writing is wonderfully complex, beautifully intricate, sublimely and frustratingly human—but it's not a magic something that rises from dark depths within us, unknowable and unknown. We know what it is and how it works.

And that means we can *teach* it.

* * *

When this chapter was written ten years ago, the term *writing process* was being used in journal articles and in some college and graduate schools where composition instruction was offered, but rarely in high school English classrooms. And it was almost unheard of in elementary schools. That was despite the fact that Emig and Moffett and Murray had been talking about it a decade before that. The notion of *teaching* kids to write, instead of teaching grammar and demanding writing to demonstrate to them their errors in usage and mechanics so they could expunge them and become, therefore, "good" writers—well, that was a pretty new idea itself. Or so it seemed. Now it's hard to find an English composition or grammar textbook without the words *writing process* liberally sprinkled through it. That most of the books are bad is no real matter. While the few good ones are handy, a good writing teacher doesn't need them anyway. But this writing process business has become fashionable, even required in some schools and school systems.

That is all to the good, I think. (I have misgivings about *requiring* any approach to teaching in a whole school system.) Sadly, however, I believe that the first sentence of this chapter still stands. *Teachers are often afraid of teaching writing because they feel they don't know enough about how writing is done to teach it effectively.* There are a lot of misconceptions about the processes of writing and about teaching writing as a process. Dan and I go back to our experience as writers, first, and as teachers of writing, then to the experience of the better writing teachers we know. To teach writing in the most natural way possible in the necessarily artificial world of the school—that is our goal, and what all the talk of process in writing is about.

You will hear a lot of things about "teaching writing as a process," but keep in mind a few simple reminders as you teach it.

1) *All teaching writing as a process tries to do is to bring writing in the classroom closer to what "real" writers do when they write.* In other words, to teach writing in more natural and less artificial ways. Frankly, that often means to get out of their way and let them write.

My job as a writing teacher is not to put my students through academic exercises. It is to make writing a part of their lives, just as it is a part of mine.

2) *Be suspicious of any book that gives you "the process."* Process writing is not a prescription. We describe it in steps because it is easier to write about it clearly that way. We know the processes themselves are recursive, that any piece of writing I start does not follow neat, separate

steps. But it does start somewhere and end somewhere else, usually but not always with a finished product of some kind. The writing usually is better when talking, drafting, revising, reading aloud, and editing are part of the experience my students have.

All that books, including this one, can give you is the skeleton of the process. Your experience will have to supply the rest.

3) *Learning any process takes time.* There are no quick fixes here. Allow your students the time to learn what works for them.

4) *When you pay more attention to* how *your students write, instead of* what *they write, it will change the way you grade them.* For me it makes the job both harder and easier. Harder because grading what they are learning instead of a finished product is more difficult. Easier because I don't have to grade as many papers.

5) *What I am looking for in the process of writing with students are places where I can intervene to help them.* My experience tells me there are places where I need to encourage and stay out of the way, and there are a few places where I can help them make it better. I know, for example, it will not help to warn them sternly about various transgressions of punctuation and outrages of spelling *before* they start a draft. If anything, their writing will be worse for my efforts. But there are places where I can "nudge" them, to use Nancie Atwell's term, where I can prod and suggest and challenge. Sometimes this comes for me at the beginning when I help the student talk herself into the piece of writing. I make a place for it somewhere after the initial draft is done. It always works best for me when they ask for the help. But if they have not asked, I may insist on the teacher's prerogative before the final draft is turned in.

6) *The process doesn't work if the student is not fluent.* Actually, it does work. In part. I just need to be sure I concentrate on support and getting it going, saving heavy duty revision strategies and editing for later. If there is something wrong with the writing I'm getting from my students, I need to look closely at how I am teaching the process. Often, I will find I am too impatient. I need to slow down and teach them where they are, and where the specific piece of writing is growing.

7) *Writing process is taught by example.* To teach writing well, you become a writer *with* your students. A large part of what I do is to take the processes of a writer and make them visible to my students. I demonstrate how it's done the same way any other skilled person

demonstrates his skill to an apprentice. As far as I'm concerned, the job cannot get done any other way.

Teaching the Process: One Way to Begin

This assignment is a good starting place for writing process because it makes the "skeleton" more visible than some other kinds of writing. Dan taught it to me; and I think he got it from Donald Graves, a gentleman without whom our profession would be poorer in experience. It is one of those assignments, like free writing, that has become a classic. Usually just called "the Anatomy," although it goes by various names, you will find versions of it in classrooms all over the country, and especially among the National Writing Project folks. I use it a lot with my own writing, and I've taught it so far to students from third grade to retirement age. Like free writing, I have never known it to fail, a strong claim for any writing assignment. But you must do it with them.

Step 1: Remembering and sharing.

Talking is an important part of starting this writing, as it is with most good writings. Ask your students to jot down in a word or phrase three to five memories they want to learn more about by writing. Demonstrate this before they finish their lists by jotting three of your own on the board or the overhead. I ask them to pick memories they can locate in a particular place on a particular day. That seems to keep the writing away from vague and meaningless sentiments.

Talk about your memories with them briefly. Choose the one you want to write about, discussing your choice with them. I let my students help me choose the writing. Sometimes I take their advice; sometimes I have a strong writer's preference of my own. But it gives us a chance to talk about how writers decide what they will write.

Step 2: Selecting a memory.

Now it's their turn. Ask them to share their list with a partner, just as you have done with them. Warn them not to talk it to death or they won't want to write about it. Give them a ten minute time limit. Then fudge on it if you need to. Their job is to pick the one they want to work on. The talk has a lot of other benefits for the young writer as well.

Step 3: Jotting or other prewriting on paper.

At this point I either demonstrate jot listing for the writing I have chosen and then have them make their own jot list, or I demonstrate a technique Gabriele Rico calls "clustering" from her book *Writing the*

Natural Way (J.P. Tarcher, 1983). These two I know well. You may know other prewriting strategies like "turkey tracking" or "webbing," and prefer to use one of them. The point of all such techniques is to help students get details down on paper so that when they start writing, they won't run out of steam and their writing will be alive.

Jot listing is the easiest to start with. It is simply brainstorming words and phrases in no particular order to use in the writing. The first time we do this kind of writing together, I ask them to jot list in categories, "seeing," "hearing," "smell," "touch," to focus on sensory details.

Push your students to get down as many details as possible. Often the quantity of details on the jot list predicts the quality of the writing. I encourage them to stretch their lists as long as they can.

I try to get through this part before the end of the first class period.

Step 4: Getting it down.

This is the "zero" draft, the discovery draft. Encourage them to write fast, to free write. As Dan says, write around the hard parts. Push them to write through and finish it. If a student gets stuck, tell him to go back to his jot list. With this kind of writing you won't have many of them stuck.

Step 5: Sharing.

This reading to a partner or a response group is not for criticism. Mainly it is to let the writer "hear" her piece for the first time. It is a different kind of reading. I call it reading with a pencil, and I model it carefully. I don't read to perform. When it is finished I like to show it off by reading aloud, but my reading now may be halting and tentative. I stop often to add or strike out words and to make substitutions. I ask questions of my listeners as I read. "Does that part sound right?" "Did that sentence work?"

I require the reader to tell her listeners what help she wants with the piece before she reads it to them. That sets the tone for the listeners as well as the writer.

Step 6: Reworking.

There are papers that never go beyond the zero draft for one reason or another. But I push students to revise, and typically they resist. Word processing with a personal computer is a big help, when the magic machines are available to us. They make the job of fixing our writing so much easier, and the kids love them. I try to divide reworking between revision and editing, revision dealing with substantial things in the writing, what works and what doesn't, and editing dealing with fixing the errors. The actual experience defies neat divisions, but it helps me organize myself for teaching. I also work in a conference somewhere while all this is going on.

Step 7: *Publishing and celebrating.*

Some pieces will be reworked through several drafts, depending on the student's working style and the writing itself. And sometimes I ask for more work on a "finished" draft when I see problems in it. But there has to be a deadline for any kind of writing. That's just how it works. Then there is another conference for publishing. And we print it up.

I also like to have "read-arounds" so we can show off and enjoy our writings together.

Notes

1. James E. Miller, Jr. *Word, Self, Reality: The Rhetoric of the Imagination.* Dodd, Mead, 1972.
2. Cary Quinn was a student at Gainesville High School, Gainesville, GA.
3. The reference to pencil sharpening is from an interview with Ernest Hemingway by George Plimpton in *Writers at Work: The Paris Review Interviews* (2nd Series). Viking, 1963.
4. Kurt Vonnegut is quoted by Donald Murray. "Internal Revision: A Process of Discovery," in *Research on Composing: Points of Departure,* edited by Charles R. Cooper and Lee Odell. NCTE, 1978.
5. Janet Emig. "On Teaching Composition: Some Hypotheses as Definitions," *Research in the Teaching of English,* Vol. 1 (Fall 1967), pp. 127-135.
6. Ann E. Berthoff. *Forming/Thinking/Writing: The Composing Imagination.* Boynton/Cook, 1978.
7. James E. Miller, Jr., & Stephen N. Judy. *Writing in Reality.* Harper & Row, 1978.
8. William F. Irmscher. "The Teaching of Writing in Terms of Growth," *English Journal,* Vol. 66 (Dec. 1977), pp. 33-36.

CHAPTER THREE

The Classroom Environment

...Yet we always had a good time in class. Drawn together by a common interest and pursuit we enjoyed one another's company. Especially we enjoyed laughing together.

—ROBERT FRANCIS (1)

Let's face it. The thought of taking or teaching a "composition class" does not inspire many students or teachers. There are many negative feelings and nagging fears to overcome. The first few days and weeks are critical. Some attention to the physical setting—the way the room looks—and some attention to the psychological setting—the way the class feels—can change the composition class into a *writing class*—a place where kids feel like working and enter with expectations and a "what are we going to do today?" feeling.

The Way the Room Looks

I don't want to spend too much time talking about how to decorate your room. Interior decorating is, after all, a personal matter. Tables versus desks, carpets, workshop designs have all been described better by others elsewhere (2). The important point to make about decor is that there should be some obvious indications that you believe the physical environment is important. The fact that you've done something with your room is a signal to kids that you care about what you're doing. The opposite is also unfortunately true, so take the pledge. You will do *something* with that room to make it a warmer, less sterile place.

Remember one thing: the focal point of any good writing class is the display of student products. Elementary teachers do a good job of showing student work. Smiles and gold stars are everywhere. Teachers of young children don't go to this trouble because they're softheaded. They know that displaying student work builds pride and enthusiasm and dramatically enhances motivation.

Rule 1 for Writing Environment

MAKE A PLACE IN YOUR CLASS FOR STUDENT PRODUCTS.

- Let students know that writing is the primary business of your writing class by making written products the *center* of attention. Have a poets' corner, a graffiti board, a gallery of finished pieces. Display (framed, laminated, or glued on colored mats) some of your favorite pictures, and encourage students to post creative responses around them. Use three-dimensional displays and mobiles. Use the ceiling, the walls, the floors.
- Encourage students to display drafts and unfinished pieces of writing by designating a "Works in Progress" area.
- Have a "Quotable Quotes" display with typed excerpts from student journals (with author's permission, of course).
- Take pictures of your students while they're writing, and have your photographer friend enlarge them. Post them around the room.
- Post some of your own writing, as well as the writing of other teachers and adults in the school community. (Maybe the custodian is a secret poet...ask him).
- Post pictures and short biographical sketches of the authors of the displayed products.

Rule 2

ARRANGE THE ROOM IN A WAY THAT IS COMFORTABLE TO YOU.

The number-one priority in room arrangement is that it be a place where you feel comfortable. If you feel good about your room, chances are the students will too.

I prefer a workshop arrangement with a writing area, a responding area, a resource area, a revising area, and an escape area. I like the circle or semicircle for group reading and evaluation of student papers. This division of the classroom into specific work areas gives the student writer a functional place to be during the various businesses of writing. It allows me to move around providing help and counsel where I'm most needed. Students know what behaviors are appropriate in each area, and I can provide gentle reminders if I see students doing something inappropriate.

Many teachers and some students need quieter, more structured-looking environments. Don't apologize. Arrange the classroom your way.

Tom's classroon has desks in rows and looks surprisingly conventional—except for the mass of books, posters, and student products. He says he just feels better with rows. He frequently breaks up the rows, asking students to turn desks toward each other. In Ruth's room students sprawl out on the floor during reading, writing, and responding time. They use desks for large group discussions, art projects, and layouts for student publications; but many prefer the carpet for individual and small group experiences. Tom and I agree on one thing completely: we both need music in the writing class. We both keep a tape recorder in the room with a large library of different kinds of music. The music comes on at the drop of a hat: background music for workdays, foreground music as stimulus for a variety of creative responses. Students bring in the records; we tape them for class use. I've never been able to teach writing without music—it makes me feel better.

The Way the Room Feels

Far more important to the successful teaching of writing than the way your room looks is the psychological climate—the way it feels.

A good writing class must feel like a sage place. Writing is scary business; sweaty palms are the order of the day. Good writing teachers work hard at reducing fear in the writing class. If you expect students to experiment, to try things out, then you'll have to convince them that they won't be shot down in flames.

Offer support and plenty of pats on the back. Ask questions that show you are genuinely interested in what they have to say. Encourage students to externalize their feelings, and extend sympathy when the going gets rough. Tell them about times you've had difficulty getting ideas to work on paper. Show them examples of the way you struggle through drafts. To foster the reflective atmosphere essential to the writing classroom, offer extended periods of class time for students to find, draft, share and refine ideas. You'll foster a classroom community of writers if students know you care about each writer's progress.

A Writing Preserve

I teach my students to treat our classroom as a refuge, a haven for experimenting and trying out words. I don't tolerate cheap shots, and I tell them so. I post a large "No Hunting Allowed" sign on the door because writing occurs best in a supportive, protective environment. As you'll read later, this doesn't mean that we adopt a Pollyanna attitude toward writing or that everything everyone writes is praised or that we don't criticize one another's work. *No Hunting* simply means: "No cheap shots." The writing class must not become a hacksaw operation where people criticize each other's failures. If a piece of writing is bad, then it "didn't work." It either needs to be *reworked* or filed. If it needs reworking, then specific, constructive suggestions are helpful to the author: "How about throwing out that first paragraph and beginning here?" or "I want to know why this character felt he was a failure."

If the piece has no potential at all, then simply suggest that the writer file it and begin again. Beginning again is often the best remedy for an ineffective piece of writing. Note: "File it" does not mean fold, spindle, or mutilate. The piece that didn't work goes in the student's folder; it may be resurrected later.

It's so easy to get out the hacksaw. "That piece didn't do a thing for me," or "I won't read this piece until you learn how to spell." For most young writers, the hacksaw cuts deep. They find it difficult to separate your comments about their writings from your comments about them as people. Remind yourself often that students are most vulnerable when they submit a piece of genuine writing. Proceed with caution—put away the hacksaw.

Beginnings

Feelings of competition, grade-grubbing (the "Is this going to be graded?" syndrome), apathy, and even outright hostility are all factors that work against you in the writing class. I believe teachers must meet these attitudes head-on with some serious anxiety-reducing, group-building activities.

The first days in any writing class are critical. Because you want students to write often, because you want them to write honestly and openly, because you want them to share their work and respond to one another's work, and because you want them to accept criticism and work on revising their writing, you have many new attitudes and behaviors to develop in your students. If you want them to function as audience for one another's writing and to become careful critics of their own and others' writings, then you should attend to the psychological climate of the writing class. The following starter activities will help you get to know your students and help them get to know one another.

A few words of advice about these starter activities. Don't try to do all of them. You'll overwhelm the students and take the focus away from the purpose of such activities, which is to improve the climate for writing. In fact, I suggest strongly that you ask students to react to each activity *in writing* either in a journal or a short "feelings" paper. This reminds them that the central business of this class is getting words down on paper.

A good many composition teachers may scoff at these starter activities or label them as the games teachers play to entertain students. Many composition teachers take their work very seriously and think such games belong in drama classes or "creative writing" classes. In defense of these activities, I have found them well received by high school and middle school students. When used with follow-up writing activities, they cause the class to come together as a unit. These activities do not lessen the seriousness of the writing class or turn the teacher into an entertainer.

The First Writing

Right after I take the roll on the first day, I ask students to do a ten-minute free writing on their feelings about and experiences with writing. The free writing or shotgun writing or automatic writing that Ken Macrorie and others have used so successfully is an excellent way to begin a writing class. I ask students to write for ten minutes, without stopping, about themselves as writers. I suggest they give me a little past history of their experiences with writing. How do they feel when they write? Have they ever written anything they're proud of? Have they had any disasters with writing? Here are some typical student responses:

Writing. Actually writing is not that important to me—I prefer verbal expressions. All of my writing career I have received good grades on content and rather poor grades on grammar. This improved only somewhat last year after Trad. Gram. and Theme Writing. I get my ideas from my experiences and what I've read. I love to read. My major problem with writing is subject matter—how unoriginal. Anyway—in my journal, I just write down what I'm thinking about—very seldom do I get out and create something. I don't have time and like I said, I'd rather talk or read than write. Even now I've got writer's cramp.

—LAURA (3)

I have had bad experiences with writing since the first days of school. The main problem has been that I was assigned to write and *had* to write on the teacher's topic in the teacher's style. I love to write. I dream of someday writing a book that will be the most profound literary work ever; Nobel Prize in Literature and all that.

—TODD (3)

The worst time for me to write is now in a class with other people around. My favorite time to write is lying in bed on a cool night with a glass of hot rum tea. That's when I can really grind it out. I like writing abut pleasant memories like the beach, girls, drinking, summer vacations. I've always had the feeling that I've had to keep my writing secret, except for a couple of girls I have dated, because until now writing and music and art have been looked down upon by fellow "athletes." Until now I've been afraid of verbal sensitivity in my life but now I have more of a don't give a damn attitude about everything.

—TOMMY (3)

These excerpts are honest and full of information for the teacher of writing. Use them to talk openly with your students about some of the problems and frustrations of writing. Engage them in lively conversation about the whole process. Talking about writing should reduce some of the tension in the writing class.

Names

Names are important. Spend some time each day for the first week or so helping students learn one another's names. Don't leave this name-learning process to chance; writing classes go better with names. If you need some ideas for name games, see Gene Stanford's book, *Developing Effective Classroom Groups* (4).

I go around the room a time or two with the old name chain: say your name and the names of those before you and then use the "who are your neighbors" game in which you point to a student and ask her to name the person on either side of her. Nothing new here, but students tell me, "This is the first class in which I've known the names of everyone in the room." If you're not the name-game type, ask students to make themselves name cards to stand on their desks. Ask students to call one another by name. Writers' names are important. Work at it.

Lives

No less important than names are the students themselves. Who are they? Where do they come from? What do they do well? Motivating students to participate in your class will be easier if you can get them to invest something of themselves in the class at the beginning. Self-disclosure—sharing something about themselves—is a subtle and important way to do this.

One note of caution: move slowly with this self-disclosure business. Remember this is a writing class, not psychoanalysis. Your purpose in opening kids up a bit is to soften them so that they are less fearful of sharing their writings and more open to constructive criticism.

The least threatening of these activities is probably a simple questionnaire that asks students questions about how they spend their time, where they live, their favorite music, the last book they have read, the movies, TV shows, and so on that they have seen. Here's an example:

WRITER'S QUESTIONNAIRE

NAME _____

What do you like to be called? _____

How do you like to spend your weekends? _____

Do you have a job? _____ Where? _____

What kind of music do you like? _____

Who's your favorite singer or group? _____

What shows do you watch on TV? _____

Do you write poems or stories on your own? _____

Have you ever written anything you really liked? _____

Be sure to tell your students the purpose of such questionnaires: to know them and their interests better.

Sentence Completion Survey

Another low-threat activity is the sentence completion survey. This activity lets the students set the level of openness. If they feel safe in your class, they may be very honest. If they are still uncertain about the class, they can provide superficial answers.

SENTENCE COMPLETION

Instructions: Complete the following sentences. Write as much as you wish on each one. Your answers will be kept confidential unless you wish to share them.

1. I'm not happy _____ .
2. Sometimes I wish I were _____ .
3. I'm pretty good at _____ .
4. My friends think I'm _____ .
5. Writing assignments are _____ .
6. When I get home from school I _____ .
7. I'm afraid of _____ .
8. School is _____ .

9. The most important thing to me is ————————————— .
10. I have hopes ————————————————————— .

The follow-up on sentence completion activity is teacher response. Read the sentences carefully and write personal comments and observations on them. Select some of the most honest or humorous, or serious, and share them with the class. Be careful to protect the identity of the writer.

These three activities acquaint you with your students' attitudes toward writing, their interests, fears, and hopes. You can help them overcome writing problems, aid them in finding writing topics that interest them, and monitor their attitudes toward writing now that you know something about the way they feel.

*   *   *

We need to get to know our students in the writing class. They need to get to know each other. The next series of activities will open the dialogue among student writers.

Lie Game

My friend Ken Kantor says he invented the Lie Game. Ask each student in your class (if you have a large class, select 15 volunteers) to think of something that has or might have happened to them in the past—for example, "My father was an Olympic swimmer," or "I broke my nose in fourth grade," or "We have ten aquariums in our house and 100 guppies." Give them a minute or so to think about something.

Ask the students to take out a sheet of paper and number from 1 to whatever. There is one basic rule in this game: whatever they tell about themselves must be wholly true or wholly false. No half-truths are allowed.

Begin the game by telling something about your past. I usually tell a good lie: "I was on a high school basketball team that went to the state tournament," or "Right after college I spent a couple of years hanging out in Hollywood trying to make it as an actor." Whatever you tell them, make it a good one. Your lie or truth will be a model.

After you have made your statement, ask them to mark True or False beside number 1. Continue around the room. Keep it moving. Ham it up a bit. When all players have made their statements, get them to correct their papers by asking the person who made the statement to give the correct answer.

The purpose for the Lie Game is perhaps obvious, but let me sum it up. First, it's a talking activity. Second, it's a composing activity. Third, it's a self-disclosure activity and a good way to get the writing class moving.

Secret Telling

Use this activity early in the class. Pair students with someone they don't know well. The pair are to tell each other three secrets:

Secret 1—something you don't care if everyone knows.
Secret 2—something only your friends know.
Secret 3—something nobody knows.

To follow up this activity, ask the students to write a short piece about the other person without revealing any secrets.

Role-taking Interview

Another good way to get classes started is to pair students and ask them to interview each other for five minutes. They are to learn as many specific things about the other person as they can. At the end of the five minutes, ask each student in turn to introduce himself as though he were the person interviewed. He is to take the other person's name and speak in the first person.

Interview Poem

For the Interview Poem you need five good questions for students to ask one another. Brainstorm with your class or write the questions yourself. Brainstorming typically gets questions like: "What do you do on Saturday afternoons?" "What's your sign?" "What do you love most?" and an assortment of sex and drug questions. Use your own judgment. Students interview each other and then write a poem about the other person.

Discussions with students who have tried these activities reveal that most of them feel they talk more openly with class members because of the sharing:

> I told Sarah a couple of really important things about a certain person in my life and what I want in the future. I worked with Jeff on the interview poem. I found out his father died last year and he is still really bitter about that. I tried to write the poem about him to show that I was sensitive to his hurt and anger. I especially liked a couple of the lines he wrote about me. "Jennifer skitters her way through ideas, lining them up like lures for me to chew on." I feel comfortable with both Sarah and Jeff now. (5)

*   *   *

We try to plan at least one activity that involves students in creating
a visual portrait of themselves. This is an attempt to satisfy our natural
impulse toward image-making as well as promote the use of visuals and
visualization in the writing class. Here are four of our favorites.

Coat of Arms Game

You may have seen this before; it's been around awhile. It works in a
writing class for the same reasons the Lie Game works: it lets students
share some of themselves in a nonthreatening way. All you need for this
activity is a facsimile of a shield and some specific instructions.

Tell your students not to worry about artistic results. Do this
activity with them. As follow-up, students may share, in small groups, the
drawings on their coats of arms, explaining the significance of the
symbols; or you can post the coats of arms and hold a gallery walk.

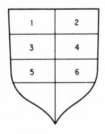

1. Draw two things you do well.
2. Draw the place where you feel most at home.
3. And so on.

As a *variation*, other value questions may be used. For example:
1. What is something about which you would never budge?
2. What is something you're striving to be or become?
3. What one thing would you want to accomplish by the time you're
   65?
4. Draw three things you're good at.
5. What is a personal motto you live by?

With younger students you can use silhouettes instead of shields.
Both of these activities work well in a composition class because
they involve the students in talking about themselves and their own
experiences. These personal experiences are the beginning writer's best
resources. Talking before writing is priming the pump. The disclosures

your students make during these activities also reveal information about them that a skillful teacher can use to motivate them further. You may learn that a student is an artist, loves motorcycles, reads widely, lives on a farm, is a musician in a band, works in a mortuary. The good composition teacher stores these nuggets and uses them at appropriate times to suggest topics, draw out students, cast them in the role of expert, or simply engage them in spirited conversation.

Remember, the purpose of those self-disclosure activities is not to pry into students' lives, to embarrass them, or to single them out. In general, the more you know about your students and the more they know about one another, the more a climate of openness and safety prevails. These are precisely the conditions that foster maximum growth in a writing class where students work closely with the teacher and with one another.

Secret Box

Make a hit on the shoe store for shoe boxes or ask students to bring them from home. Armed with scissors, glue, and 10,000 magazines, ask the students to decorate their boxes with pictures, words, or advertisements that tell something about themselves. "Ah, ha," you say, "a variation on the personal collage." Exactly. The outside of the box should illustrate the outside of the student: interests, hobbies, talents, and so forth. The secrets go *inside* the box. Ask each student to put three things in the box that reveal something about his inside self. Pair the students up and ask them to explain the outside to each other. They should reveal the secrets inside only if they feel comfortable with the partner.

Road of Life

For this activity all you need are paper and pens, or markers. Ask the students to make a map of their lives from birth to present. Tell them to illustrate the hills and valleys, the thrills and conflicts. Give them time to share the maps with at least three classmates. Collect the maps and decorate your walls.

Behind the Mask

Use butcher paper to cut out a huge mask, or give students construction paper to make their own masks. Supply them with a stack of newspapers and magazines and ask them to cut out and paste words and letters on the mask to form a message from behind the mask.

* * *

We have a natural inclination to compare one thing with another. In the final two activities students create metaphors of self in words or through a shape that represents them. In both activities students exchange ideas and information about themselves with their peers.

Impressions Word Game

Use this activity several weeks into the course after the students have become comfortable with one another. The activity brings students together. They talk among themselves, share humorous preceptions of one another, and learn something about themselves. In the process they practice creative uses of language and vivid detail. Prepare a ditto grid something like this:

Names of Group Members	Three Words	A Car (Be specific)	A TV Personality	A Food
1				
2				
3				
4				
5				

Divide the class into groups of five, give each student a copy of the grid, and ask them to write in the names of each person in the group. Now they're ready to go. Ask them to fill in the blanks. A few suggestions:

1. If your students have not worked in groups much, structure the activity carefully.
2. Make up the groups any way you wish, although random groups are probably best for this activity.
3. Tell students to be as *specific* as possible: If it's a car, what kind?...What color?...Any unusual things about it? (Dented fender, bumper sticker, etc.)
4. During the sharing phase, be sure that all students receive some feedback quickly.
5. Be sure the atmosphere is positive.

For follow-up, ask the students to respond to the activity by writing in their journals things they learned about themselves.

Wire Sculpture (Thanks to Hugh Agee)

All you need for this activity are pieces of floral wire about 18 inches long. Before you give each student a wire, spend some time talking about symbols and logos. We are all familiar with such logos as those of the Red Cross, the Olympic games, McDonald's golden arches, and others. Ask the students to begin thinking about a logo for themselves. Ask what symbol would best represent them. Pass out the wires and ask the students to shape the wire so that it becomes a logo for them. Sometimes I ask that:

1. The students shape the wire so that it makes a statement or represents an idea about something important to them.
2. The students shape the wire so that it becomes a "life line" that graphically depicts important events in their lives.
3. The students shape the wire so that it characterizes someone they have known for a long time.

As follow-up, have students pass the finished creations around the class and:

1. Discuss what the shape says about its creator.
2. Have the creator discuss his wire to explain its significance.
3. Have each creator explain his creation to at least three other class members. (Free movement around the class is required for this activity.)
4. Have each creator write a short paragraph discussing the significance of his creation. Mount the wires on construction paper and tape the written paragraph to the back of the paper. Set up a display of the sculptures and invite students to browse.

Variations of this activity can be done with straws, clay, paper, or paper clips. Manipulating a wire and then talking about the creation allows the student enough psychological distance to be more open and honest about himself. Because the task is multilayered, allowing for many levels of abstraction, it is appropriate for all levels of ability.

Students have exercised a wide variety of imaginative ways to generate the subject of self. They've written, talked, made visual representations and made metaphoric leaps—practiced many of the strategies they'll use to generate writing. Through these exercises your students have functioned as audience for another's writings and ramblings and visual representations as well. This is a classroom where you have already encouraged a community of sharing, listening, and advising.

Beyond the Classroom

After you've done everything to make your classroom a pleasant place in which to write, it will still be a classroom. Leaving that classroom—changing the environment completely—can produce dramatic and positive effects on student writings. Look around the school to see what interesting places are available. The cafeteria before and after lunch period, the gymnasium, the parking lot, the cemetery down the street, the shopping center around the corner—all may provide interesting environments for writing. Because any such deviations from standard operating procedures must be carefully defended to administrators, let me give this changing of the environment a name and make a few suggestions.

Walking Compositions

Defend leaving the classroom by saying that classrooms are often sterile places in which to teach writing. Students' powers of observation have been dulled. Good writers must see and hear and feel their environments directly. You are taking your writers outside the classroom to develop fluency, increase motivation, and sharpen their powers of observation.

Give students the opportunity to practice the Walking Composition on a regular basis (we think once a week is essential for establishing the routine). If students have occasional experience with the Walking Composition, the message they receive is: this is not important; it is fill-in, fun and games, an exercise when the teacher isn't prepared. You'll need routine and structure if you want the activity to be meaningful.

Give each student an instruction sheet something like this:

Grab your notebook and a pen or pencil. You are about to take a trip. As you walk, please observe the following guidelines.

1. Go alone (or be alone in yourself). Talk as little as possible.
2. You are a *sensory sponge.* Soak up and record sensations and observations.
3. Look for the small, important *details.*
4. Record your observations in four columns: things you see, hear, feel, and smell.
5. Be considerate of your neighbors.
6. Return in twenty minutes and select observations from your notes for a *place/feeling description* or a *sensory poem* or a *written meditation.*

Choose one of the following itineraries:

Tour A: Walk down the hall to the elevator. Ride to the sixth floor.

Get off, walk the perimeter hallway of that floor. Return by elevator.

Tour B: Take the elevator to the ground level; enter the snack bar area. Pretend to be studying and stay for five minutes. Return.

Tour C: Leave the building toward the parking lot. Turn right and proceed to the grassy knoll near East Campus Drive. Stand under a tree; wait five minutes and return.

Use the following list of procedures to be sure you have structured the activity carefully:

1. Make the necessary arrangements with administrators. They already think you're weird. This activity will not surprise them.
2. Have a preplanned, written itinerary for the tour. I usually have three such tours and ask students to choose their favorite. Give specific directions.
3. Ask students to go alone, and make them swear in blood they won't smoke in the parking lot.
4. Tell students to be a sensory sponge, a CIA agent, a careful observer. Have them make notes in four columns: what they hear, see, feel, and smell.
5. Set time limits for their return.
6. Follow up the activity with in-class sharing of observations and journal writings or short descriptive papers. The activity is excellent for short descriptive pieces because students must select from their list only those details that fit.
7. Use the short descriptive papers as the starting scene for a short piece of fiction. Ask students to imagine what might have taken place during their walk that didn't or what might happen there at ten o'clock tonight.

Remember, there are many ways of walking out of the classroom doors if you are not comfortable with the tour. "Go outside" with music, film, invited speakers, fine pieces of writing. Most of the subjects for student writing come from outside the classroom from their experiential, intellectual, and emotional lives. The classroom cannot provide the content to keep the writer enriched, but it can provide the stimuli. We can trigger memories and encourage student writers to sensitize themselves to the world around them.

Summary

Creating a unique environment for the teaching of writing is absolutely essential. A writing class should "feel" different from other classes. It must be perceived as a safe place, a place to experiment, and a place of encouragement, but it must also be perceived as a place where everyone may be prodded a bit and asked to rework and revise, and above all as a place where everyone writes and writes and writes.

Such an environment does not occur by chance or by the "I don't know what to do during the fifth period/ I think I'll have them write something" method. A writing class must be carefully and yet tentatively planned.

Notes

1. Robert Francis. *Collected Poems, 1936-1976*. University of Massachusetts Press, 1976.
2. Stephen N. Judy and Susan Judy. *English Teacher's Handbook*. Winthrop, 1979.
3. Laura Jacobs, Todd Williams, and Tommy D'Angelo were all students at Cedar Shoals High School in Athens, GA.
4. Gene Stanford, *Developing Effective Classroom Groups*. Hart, 1977.
5. Jennifer Kelly was a student at Boise High School, Boise, Idaho.

CHAPTER FOUR

Getting It Down

Everything worked. . . . It was one of those moments in your life where you've stretched yourself as far as you can, and it comes off right. It was fantastically exciting. . . . It was like painting a free-form picture. You're thinking with your subconscious. It's done by feel. And it came out right.

—KENNETH BROWER (1)

It doesn't feel like work. It's like saying to a skier, "Isn't it a lot of work to do downhill skiing?" He'd have to stop and say, "Well, you do use up a lot of energy. And it's work in the physical sense. But it's not done like work. It's done for appetite." That's the way I feel about writing.

—WILLIAM STAFFORD

Personal Writing

Personal writing, or what James Britton calls expressive writing, is the natural place for students to begin their experience with putting words on paper. The student writer's most important inner resources are words to use in talking about personal experience. Start with what they know and feel—and in their own words.

That does not mean that you walk into class the first day, glare your charges into silence, put the topic "How I Spent My Summer Vacation" on the board, and demand a five-paragraph theme *in ink* (blue, blue-black, or black, of course) with underlined thesis sentence, razor-precise margins, name-class-date in upper right corner, *neatly* written—and, an "Oh yes, don't write on the back." Well, you get the idea. Expressive writing is not merely writing about personal experience. Because a writing topic has "I" or "me" in it does not mean you will get personal writing. If writing in your class is governed by topics you pick, you will be disappointed in the results.

Academic writing too often is *Engfish,* Ken Macrorie's word for the lifeless, inhibited prose too often expected in English classes and read only by English teachers. It's pedantic and phoney—and it's bad. It's so bad that we have to use external motivation to get the kids to do it.

> The grade school student is told by his teacher that he must learn Engfish because the high school teacher will expect mastery of it. The high school student is told by his teacher that he must learn it because the college professor will expect mastery of it. The college undergraduate is told by his professor that he must learn it so he can go to graduate school and write his PhD thesis in it.
>
> Almost no one reads PhD theses. (3)

One reason Engfish is rampant is that writing in our schools has been essentially a neurotic exercise. We give the kids a writing assignment so we can tell them what's wrong with their writing. Writing in the English classroom too often is an excuse to use the trusty red pen. After all, it's our *duty.* Besides, we were taught that way. Remember when you were in the Eng. 101 class in college and you got that now-famous advice from an upperclassman about how to write that first theme—"Just keep the sentences short and simple. And don't try to say nothing!" or "Use some big words. But keep it short. They can't find as many things wrong that way." Well, we survived it, but it rarely did anything for our writing. And it does about the same for our students' writing.

Building confidence is your first job. As tender as the ego of the beginning writer is, there is little wonder that most of our students dislike and fear the experience of writing. Better said, they dislike writing—often intensely—because they are afraid of writing. To a large degree, our first job with most of our students is to teach them that they don't have to be afraid of writing—a task not really as difficult as it may first appear. For one thing, a little success goes a long way.

I remember two teachers of mine. Mrs. Crutchfield (yes, that's *Mrs. Crutchfield,* not Ms.—we called her *Missez Crutchfield* of course) was a stern eighth-grade English teacher at Fort Junior High School. She was a demanding lady who brooked no nonsense from the thirty of us who squirmed in our seats and assaulted paper with pencil more or less regularly. But I think I was a little in love with her for all that—all the boys in that overcrowded and restless room were. Otherwise, I remember her as a not particularly inspiring teacher, although she was thorough and precise. And I certainly was not an inspired student of the English language and thoroughly hated facing that blank sheet of paper each week—and I thought that was a perfectly natural way to be. We *all* hated writing, just the way God intended and our teachers expected.

Until one spring afternoon when I wrote a paper for her and, for some reason, got carried away with it and wrote far longer than the usual page called for. I remember that it was something about werewolves, a favorite subject of mine at that time. It must have been awfully juvenile drivel, but Mrs. Crutchfield praised it loudly and lavishly—I suspect more for the work I put in the piece than for its artistic merit. I blushed, I beamed, I basked in the glory of her approval. And I began to think that maybe writing this stuff wasn't so bad after all.

Her praise sustained me for the next two years until I met Mr. Cone, a young man who smiled owlishly behind his glasses at another over-crowded classroom, this time filled to the walls with high school sophomores. He was a demanding teacher also, and a writer of no small merit himself. When we pleased him, he sometimes would read to us from his writing. We liked that. It was a special treat.

"You're a good writer, Tom," he suddenly said to me one afternoon. It was in the early fall this time, and he was talking about some theme I had sweated over in class. I don't even remember what the paper was about, but I was hooked. I've been trying to please people with my writing ever since.

I know now that my experience is not unique, although it's all too rare in our English classrooms. I've seen students of mine who appear to have no real desire or talent for writing blossom into fairly competent, hard-working young writers. It's obvious that writing has become important to them because I've found good things in what they've written and told them so.

We offer you some alternatives in this chapter to the "How I Spent My Summer Vacation" kind of writing, and alternatives to the slightly more humane but rarely more successful "Tell Me About Yourself in an Essay" assignment. When you teach the new student-writer, the immature writer, you begin with only two real attainable objectives—to help the student find a voice in writing and to build a feeling of confidence in students that they *can* write.

Too often we demand that students write about things they care little about (and sometimes know less), and forbid them to use their own natural voices. And then we immediately search out every mistake, large and small, that they make writing within these narrow restrictions. And we worry that our students don't seem to have anything interesting to say, that they despise writing.

The human voice is the bearer of the human spirit. To still it would be, in effect, to still humanity....it is through language that the individual creates and knows his reality, and it is the human voice that projects that reality into the void. Perhaps our most precious possession and human legacy is the individual voice, but it is up to us to cultivate that voice and to make it heard in what we say and what we write. (4)

James Miller said that in *Word, Self, Reality,* one of the most important books about writing theory.

Your second task as a teacher of fledgling writers is to help them find their individual voices when they write. There is a lot of talk in rhetoric texts about *style,* but the writer's style *is* the writer's voice. It is the way they talk in writing. Donald Murray calls it the sense of a "strong recognizable individual" in the writing (5). The immature writers in your class need to write enough in an unthreatening situation to become comfortable with written language so that they can get a feeling for their own voice when they write. This means that they need to *practice* using their voice on the page, and they need to practice a lot. They need to do a lot of fooling around with written language; they need to *play* with writing. They need to write *every day,* and they need to try a lot of different things when they write. And in the early stages they need your almost unqualified support and encouragement of what they write.

Developing the expressive voice is an essential beginning for immature writers. The idea that only impersonal writing is serious and important, and therefore worth teaching, is nonsense. As Miller argues:

> So many people have been indoctrinated with the view that good writing is primarily "correct" writing, and that the best writing is "objective" and "impersonal" (and therefore devoid of the first-person singular), that there is abroad in the country an "ideal" prose that is so correct, objective, and impersonal that it is almost unreadable. This prose pours out of government offices, universities, businesses; has become a kind of establishment prose; and might be described as prose in the gray flannel suit. It is faceless and voiceless prose: the sound that arises from it is monotonous and boring. (4)

On the other hand, writing that is readable and interesting is expressive. As Miller and Judy point out in *Writing in Reality,* "The one constant that runs through all good writing is the writer's voice, the distinctive accent transferred from the depths of the self to the blank sheet of paper" (6).

And what does that voice sound like? There is no one answer. Each writer's voice on paper is as distinctive as a speaking voice. But there is always a moment of recognition when you hear that personal and genuine voice coming through someone's writing—as in this free writing by a student of mine who describes a friend of his from Pearidge, Georgia.

Phagan

Mike Phagen—Mikey, Meiguel, Pierre, he's got all kinds of nicknames. Everybody in Pearidge, Georgia, has a nickname or they aren't a real Pearidger. There isn't any set rules for becoming a select member of the Pearidge community—you just have to be accepted by the whole group and not break the Pearidge code. It wasn't written but it was understood. Now, Mikey is what I would call the Prince of Pearidge. People look up to him. People listen when he says anything about anything. In a way he is a legend. He was a dope addict—acid, THC, barbs, reefer—just one of the boys, more or less. Mikey took a liking to me because he saw I had a little common sense—back then a little was a lot cause every other Pearidger had none. Mikey—well—he's not too bright sometimes —like in the bars and discos. I'm talking about with the women. I still laugh when I remember some of his stupid funny lines he uses, especially when he didn't even need to talk at all to get what he was after.

—RICHARD (7)

Donald Graves has said that "with authorship comes authority" (8), and Donald Murray elaborates that "The student's experience is his area of authority. And all students have areas of authority because all students have experience" (5). Initially in the writing class our job is to help students write in their own voices about their own areas of authority— their own experiences, feelings, perceptions. We begin small with tasks easily finished, like a free writing about a person they know. We try a lot of different things. We encourage our students to experiment with written expression, tc play with written forms, to fool around with writing. Instead of demanding an impossible perfection, we encourage trial and error and an attitude of try-it-and-see-what-happens. As James Moffett says in fancier language, our job is "to help students expand their cognitive and verbal repertory as far as possible, starting with their initial limits" (9).

The Journal

One indispensable tool in helping the students expand their "cognitive and verbal repertory" is the journal. We talk more at length about the journal in the next chapter. I mention it here because, if for no other reason, the journal provides immature writers with some of the regular practice they need to become comfortable with writing.

In the journal and in the class, the student's experience with writing should be a *daily* affair. Quite simply, the student—especially the one just starting—*needs to write every day.* No matter how good the assignment and no matter how inspired the teaching, you cannot come into class once in a long while and dump a goodie on them and expect to get the kinds of results you're looking for.

Now before you panic at the idea of the mountain of papers to grade from those 150 or more kids in your classes who are writing a theme every day, take a look at the kinds of assignments we're suggesting for the beginning writer. These assignments are not designed to be—and should not be—red-penciled. They certainly need to be read and responded to by you or by other students in the class. Peer reading is one way to take the pressure off of you, and the reactions and comments of students her own age will often mean more to the new writer than yours will. You'll need to develop procedures for peer reading and peer evaluation in your classroom. *Sharing* writing is important for its own sake and is a powerful motivator for further writing. And if you work it right, peer reading will keep you from having to grade so many papers.

My student writers keep a journal, which is turned in weekly, and they write every day in class. And although I use a lot of sharing of writing with classmates in my classes, I also read every paper the students write and usually respond to them. I do not take papers home with me at night. I do not grade papers on the weekend. I am not a masochist, and I'm certainly not a superman. We will give you some tips later about how to survive the crush of English-papers-to-grade, but I think you'll find that once you switch from an approach of reading the student's paper to search out and mark errors to an approach that looks for things to praise and encourage—or just respond to as one writer-reader to another—that it has the additional advantage of making you able to read many more papers in the limited time you have each day. It's still very hard work, and there will be papers when the student has grown more sophisticated as a writer that you will spend more time on, we hope working with the student on revision. But the task is not impossible.

Personal Writing Exercises for the Beginning Writer

The exercises we suggest are to help the beginning student writer get it down on paper, perhaps for the first time. The emphasis is on the student herself, what she has to say in her own voice. They are intended as a catalyst to get you and your students started and to give you ideas to stimulate your own ideas.

Free Writing

Ken Macrorie is the proponent of free writing as one technique for teaching writing (3). His books *Telling Writing, Writing to Be Read* and *The I-Search Paper* use free writing as part of a complete writing program. Like Macrorie, I use it early with my students, and I go back to it often to loosen them up when they seem to be threatened by assignments or new material, or seem blocked by having "nothing to say."

Have your students write for ten minutes without stopping or thinking about what they'll say next. The important thing is to keep the words flowing across the paper. They are not to worry about spelling, punctuation, or usage. If they can think of nothing to say, tell them to write "I've got nothing to say" over and over until something occurs to them. This exercise should be repeated for several days.

High school students generally enjoy free writing, probably because it's a nonthreatening way to write, and it removes the restraints. And after a while with daily practice, patterns in their writing begin to emerge, and individual voices begin to grow distinct.

Free Writing Variations

Once the students are used to the idea of free writing, I like to have them play around with some possibilities as they write.

Ask the students to *listen* carefully as they free write, recording the sounds they hear around them, or ask them just to concentrate on listening while they keep the writing going without paying particular attention to what they're putting down until the ten minutes are up.

Have them free write to music, and use different kinds of music to set different moods as they write. My students particularly enjoy this, and free writing with Pink Floyd or Led Zeppelin changes radically with Tim Weisburg or John Coltrane, and even more radically with Beethoven and Tchaikovsky. At first I use only instrumental music so the lyrics will not distract the students. But later I have them free write to songs also, reacting to the lyrics as they write.

For students practiced at free writing, read them a poem or a brief prose passage and have them free write about it without planning or preparation of any kind. This exercise is a way to get those gut-level reactions to a piece down on paper. The purpose is to get feelings and ideas out that can then sometimes be ordered, with more thinking and talking, into a more complete paper.

Perhaps the best use of focused free writing I have seen is by Tom Dickinson, a social studies teacher. His students keep journals in the classroom, and he never lets them take them home. Tom is a challenging teacher who asks a lot of questions and never lectures. He likes to work with the whole class. I have seen him stop discussion abruptly in the middle of a heated debate with a well-chosen question and the instructions to "Give me five minutes." Out come the journals, the room is suddenly quiet, and Tom and his students write furiously for five minutes. Then he quickly calls on one student after another to read. They cannot comment; they must read what they have written. At some point he will read his, with no more nor less fanfare than he gives each kid in the room. And the questions and the argument continue. Dan starts a new class asking students to free write about *writing*. The results are sometimes surprising. Focused free writing has almost endless uses in the classroom. It's a learning tool you will want to explore.

Spontaneous Writing/Quickies

During the first days in class, get students into the daily habit of writing by having them write a Quickie—a half page of writing in ten minutes or less—at the beginning of each class. Personal subjects work well for these. Here are a few suggestions.

1. Given the choice of one, and only one, of these things, which one would you choose? Money, Fame, Friends, Love. Why?
2. Tell about one thing that makes you happy.
3. Tell something that makes you sad.
4. Talk about something you hate.
5. What *color* do you feel like today? Talk about why you picked that color.
6. Tell about your favorite song.
7. Plan the menu for the school cafeteria for a week. You may include anything you wish.
8. If you were a TV character, who would you be? Tell about what you would do in one episode of the program.
9. Imagine that you stayed out of school today. Where would you go? What would you do?
10. You are an artist painting your masterpiece, the painting that will make you famous for generations to come. What is the painting of? Describe it.

Movie Sound Track

Many short films are available to teachers that have particularly well-done or unusual sound tracks and no narration or dialogue. Three of my favorites for this exercise are *Which Is My World, The Ways of Water,* and *Homo Augens.*

Record the sound track of the film on cassette tape. Play the tape *before* showing the film and have students write an imaginary film script to match the sound track. Or they can free write using the sound track as the stimulus. Then show the film and have them turn their papers over and record their reactions on the back.

Memory Writing

The purpose of this exercise is to encourage student writers to use their best resource—themselves—as the material for narrative writing and to impose some controls on that material.

Tell the students that they are to concentrate on capturing the essence, the particular detail and feeling of each incident as they do the exercise, and not to be concerned with grammatically perfect or complete narratives.

The students are on a fishing expedition into the past, with the following instructions:

You are to go back in time to capture four incidents in your life. Each incident may be important or trivial, but it should be one that stands out in your mind. Record it as briefly as you can, but make it as real as you can.

1. Go back in time 24 hours. Remember one incident from yesterday. Record it.
2. Go back in time a week and remember something you were doing on this day seven days ago. Record it.
3. Go back a year for this one and record an incident you remember from about the same time of year. Concentrate on the particular details.
4. Now concentrate really hard and go back as far as you can. Record your first *clear* memory.

Then and Now

This is another memory exercise with a different twist. Have students look back into their memories and compare a person or place they remember *then* with their perceptions of the same person or place *now*. Here are a few suggestions of good then-and-now subjects.

1. Your backyard when you were six years old and now.
2. Church then and now.
3. School then and now.
4. The family car then and now.
5. A close relative then and now.

Remember to keep the writings short unless the student gets involved in a memory and wants to continue it. Your purpose at this point is to provide the stimulus to get students started as writers, not to demand long expositions.

*Here and Now (10)

You may want to pick a time for this exercise when your students are particularly stirred up about something or one of those days when the room seems to buzz with excitement or sinks into a gloomy silence for no particular reason. Ask the students to record the date and the time and write four words that say how they're feeling here and now. Tell them to think about the four words they have recorded and to expand on one or more of them. For example:

> March 15, 1981, 3:40 PM. Tired. Anxious. Hungry. Excited. I'm anxious today thinking about the book and whether I can do this right or not. Will people want to read it? This is the second time I've tried to rewrite this chapter. Maybe if I call Dan he can pull me out of it. A deadline coming soon. Besides, what am I going to do with that third period class tomorrow?

It's a good journal exercise, or you may want to do it as a Quickie. However it's used, the exercise helps students get in touch with themselves and gives them something real to say in their writing.

Try several, and choose the best one from each student to be expanded, or edited and published.

Fantasy Writing

Once your students have gotten used to the idea of writing every day or almost every day in the classroom, try having them stretch their imaginations with this exercise. You lead them on an exploration of their inner selves by having them imagine themselves in an unusual situation. Ask them to close their eyes and concentrate on what you tell them. When you finish the fantasy, have them free write their experiences.

Here are two examples you may want to use.

*The Cocoon

Get comfortable. You're in a lovely, soft cocoon. You're resting from the outside world for a while. You're comfortable and peaceful. Nothing is bothering you. There are no worries, no troubles in this cocoon. Feel the space and the softness around you for a moment. Now begin to build your own place inside your cocoon. It can be as big or as small as you choose. It can be any shape you like. Do you have music? What color are the walls of your cocoon? Is it decorated? Do you have pictures on the walls? You can be alone in your cocoon, or you can invite other people you like to be in there with you. You can have a window in your cocoon if you want to. What can you see out of that window? What kind of furniture do you have in your cocoon? What do you eat in there? What do you do for fun?

Now I want you to leave your cocoon and come back into this world. If you wish, you can bring something back with you. Touch it with your hand. And come back into this room. Open your eyes when you're ready.

The Street

You're in a town or a city you've never been in before. You're walking down an unfamiliar street. It can be any time of the year that you want it to be. It can be any day of the week that you choose. And it can be any time of the day that you want it to be—early morning, noon, afternoon rush hour, late at night—but make it a specific time and day and season of the year. As you walk down this street, look around you. You're seeing this place for the first time. Where in the city (or town) is it? What kind of neighborhood or district are you in? Is there traffic passing in the street? What kind of traffic, and how much? Are there other people on the street with you? Who are they? What are they doing there? Look at a few of them closely. Notice their dress, their faces. Look at the stores and shops, perhaps bars and night spots, perhaps houses and lawns, that you pass as you continue walking.

Listen to the sounds of the street around you. What separate sounds can you hear and identify? What are your feelings as you walk the street? Are you alone or is someone with you? Cross the street at the next corner and look at things from the other side.

Now come back from that street in that town or city. Come back to this room, but bring a feeling or impression from the street back with you.

Word Shaking

In Chapter 6 we talk about word shaking as a useful technique for teaching poetry. It's also a good way to teach the effective use of specific detail in description.

Select from a magazine a photograph that you find particularly evocative. Ask the students to study the picture. Brainstorm with them an overall single impression that the picture creates. Ask them to suggest as many details as possible to evoke that impression. Put these on the board as they are suggested. Talk about ways to word them, putting different possibilities on the board.

The students then select from the list of details on the board one on which to write a single paragraph that captures the feeling of the photo.

People Photos

A variation of the Verbal Snapshot idea, this assignment also is intended to involve quick, perceptive writings.

Have the students collect a number of word pictures of interesting people in interesting situations. These should be brief, accurate, and as precise as possible. You may want to collect these for several days, then select the best ones to share. But tell the students to concentrate on letting their eyes be the camera and their paper the picture.

C.I.A.

This eavesdropping exercise is one of my students' favorites, mainly because it takes them out of the classroom.

Send the students out to other classes and interesting places around the school—the front office, the auto repair shop, the gym. Threaten them with murder and mayhem if they're not nice and polite, but instruct them not to tell anyone why they're wandering around the campus.

They are to "collect" several conversations by eavesdropping on their neighbors around the school and recording what is said as accurately as they can. You can also extend the assignment to eavesdropping outside the school—in elevators, at bus stops, in stores. Phone conversations are excellent sources. Have your spies share their best conversations.

As a follow-up activity, you may have students take the raw material of their collected conversations and edit the best one into an effective dialogue or vignette.

Portrait

This exercise also encourages close observation and recording details. Have each student observe one of his classmates but without letting that person know he's the subject of the exercise. Tell students they are to concentrate on details that make their subject unique and interesting. Then they are to paint a verbal picture of their subject *without using his name.* Read these verbal pictures aloud and guess the identity of the subjects.

Walking Composition

Dan mentions this in Chapter 3, but I want to use this variation here. It's another favorite of my students. I like it because it involves them directly in their environment. Give them a choice of three itineraries with specific instructions on the route they are to take from your room to an interesting place on campus and back to the room. Remember to set specific time limits for the walks and when the students are to be back.

One of my walks, for example, takes the student down one hallway, around the third wing of the building where my classroom is located, up to the gym where the students are to stay for ten minutes, and back to my room by a different route. You naturally will want to enlist the cooperation of your fellow teachers and alert the principal before you turn the kids loose on an unexpecting school.

Ask students to take the walk alone, or at least not to talk to one another as they do the exercise. Tell them they are to soak up what they see, hear, feel (and take brief notes), especially watching for the interesting and the unusual.

When they return, have them share observations, and point out differences in individual perceptions. The exercise can be followed up with journal writings or short descriptive papers.

Sensory Tour

This exercise is a variation of the Walking Composition, but it is less structured.

Send your students out on campus with a definite time limit and the following instructions:

1. What mood are you in?
2. See something smaller than your hand.
3. See something bigger than you are.
4. Hear something far away.
5. Hear something very close.
6. Feel something soft.
7. Feel something rough.
8. Bring back several items that caught your eye.
9. What mood are you in now?

Listening to a Place

I've found that this simple variation of the Walking Composition can also give good results.

Ask students to follow these instructions in order:

1. Go to a place you like in or around the school.
2. Do not talk while you do this exercise.
3. Listen for ten minutes without writing.
4. Close your eyes for two minutes and concentrate on what you hear.
5. Rapidly write your impressions of the place.
6. Eavesdrop on the people around you and write down some of the things they're saying.
7. Bring your notes back here and we'll turn them into something.

Cemetery as Classroom

Somewhere in or near your town there's a cemetery, and cemeteries are interesting places for writers. When you take your students to the cemetery, have them try the following suggestions:

1. Explore, move, and meditate among the living and the dead.
2. Enter some observations and thoughts into your journal.
3. Try a ten minute free writing, using something you see or feel to get started.
4. Take a word picture. Photograph a tombstone with language.
5. Using a name you find here, write a first person narrative or a monologue in which you become that person.
6. Collect some sensory experiences—touch, see, listen to, and smell the environment. Capture these stimuli in short phrases.
7. Interview one of the permanent residents. Ask him or her questions and jot down your answers.
8. Look inside yourself, examine some of your feelings about being here.

A Note on Topic Finding and Getting Them Started

I feel that something more needs to be said about the business of authorship and authority. Once my students see that they can write—and that can be a big job itself—what I hear almost at once from some of them is "What do you want us to write about?" Years of conditioning have taught them to rely on the teacher. When I tell them they are the writers, they don't like it. "I don't have anything to write about!" the cry goes up. And the tug-of-war starts. They try to give the authority back to me for their writing, and I refuse to take it. This chapter gives you some of the "starters" Dan and I have used to make the job of finding something to write about less threatening. And starters like the Cocoon and Walking Compositions are meant to be catchy and interesting to adolescent writers. But I am aware that *how* you do it is more important than *what* is taught. The intent is to help students find things on their own to write about. Our exercises can become as artificial and arbitrary as those dreadful summer vacation essays. I have to remind myself over and over that *the writing belongs to the writer.* Imposing a topic, even through an exercise I like, doesn't help the growth of young writers. Still, your curriculum may demand certain kinds of writing, and you may have to compromise. In this area, like other aspects of teaching writing, I find writing with my students helps. If the writing works for me, if it is real writing for a real audience, then I feel OK about asking students to try it. Keep in mind your objectives with your young writers when you first meet them: first, to help each student find a voice in writing, and to build a feeling of confidence in your students that they *can* write. Avoid the trap of letting exercises like these become merely another way for the teacher to give kids The Topic. Sooner or later they are going to have to become writers on their own. All writing starters should build confidence and direct the young writer toward independence.

Donald Graves (*Writing: Teachers and Children at Work,* 1983) and Lucy Calkins (*Lessons from a Child,* 1983 and *The Art of Teaching Writing,* 1986) gave me the simple idea of encouraging students to keep a running list of topics for future writings in an individual folder. Graves and Calkins talk to elementary teachers, but I recommend their books to you. I keep a list of writing ideas in the front of my own journal. Like Graves and Calkins, Nancie Atwell (*In the Middle,* 1987) talks about those folders, but for eighth graders. She also talks about topic conferences and the part that reading plays in topic-finding in a healthy writing class. And her book is particularly strong on classroom management.

Another notion that may help you is not to be too concerned with originality. Writers steal from other writers. Consciously and unconsciously we copy ideas, techniques, novel twists, even vocabulary we like when we read others. It is natural and healthy for your students to borrow from each other. And from their reading. Good ideas are catching, and they should be.

I have taught an entire class using no other approach to stimulate writing other than daily free writing with my students and the journal, along with whatever reading we were interested in. Read Ken Macrorie carefully and try it sometime. You'll be amazed.

I try to grant my students the authority of the writer over their own writing. I maintain my authority in managing the classroom so it is a safe and friendly place in which to write and share and talk about writing. I also insist that they do write, and I set deadlines. But my only real authority in their writing comes as a writer with more experience who is willing to show them how. Their writing belongs to them.

Life Map

Becky Howard, a teacher at Westover High School in the city where I now work, has taken Dan's "Road of Life" exercise in Chapter 3 and elaborated it into one of the best starters for her ninth graders I have seen anywhere. Once I had the opportunity to teach a low level class with her. She began by showing us her Life Map, done on a large sheet of art paper, telling briefly the stories that went with each drawing. Then she passed out the construction paper and markers, and we did our own. Because hers was carefully done, we took some time making ours. (Mine is included here to illustrate the Life Map and the kind of detail that can be a part of it.) Then we talked about them, telling stories and laughing a lot. We shared each one with the whole class, and again took our time doing it. The talking was one of the highlights of the class. As usual, only those pictures on the map each of us wanted to talk about were shared. No, I will not explain mine to you. Come join the class with me, and we'll talk about *some* of it.

Becky modeled this kind of selective storytelling too. But she didn't stop there. When the Life Maps were displayed around the room, she used them as the basis first for an "Anatomy" writing and then as a kind of visual card file of memories we could use for several more writings. Any time I was out of good writing ideas, I could go to my Life Map. Some of those stories I haven't found the time to write yet.

Becky accomplished a lot in those first three weeks we worked with the Life Maps. She taught her kids, and they taught her and each other. She created a positive, working atmosphere in that room. She started each student with a major piece of writing that was successful and celebrated by the class. She modeled the working habits of a writer. She got us to laugh and talk to each other and feel good about ourselves. For some of our students that semester, it was the first time they had ever been applauded by their classmates and their teachers. Every kid needs that sometime.

Notes

1. Kenneth Brower. *The Starship and the Canoe.* Bantam, 1979.

2. William Stafford. *At the Field's End: Interviews with Twenty Pacific Northwest Writers.* Madrona, 1987.

3. Ken Macrorie. *Uptaught.* Hayden, 1970.

4. James F. Miller, Jr. *Word, Self, Reality: The Rhetoric of the Imagination.* Dodd, Mead, 1972.

5. Donald Murray. Workshop on Writing at Georgia State University, Atlanta, GA, Spring, 1979.

6. James E. Miller, Jr., & Stephen N. Judy. *Writing in Reality.* Harper & Row, 1978.

7. Richard Poston was a student at Gainesville High School, Gainesville, GA.

8. Donald Graves. Workshop on Writing at Georgia State University, Atlanta, GA, Winter, 1979.

9. James Moffett. *Teaching the Universe of Discourse.* Houghton Mifflin, 1968.

10. The exercises in this chapter marked with asterisks are adapted with significant changes from Sidney B. Simon, Robert C. Hawley, and David D. Britton. *Composition for Personal Growth: Values Clarification Through Writing.* Hart, 1973.

CHAPTER FIVE

The "J"

What provides you with subject matter is your own language—
and that's all. It sort of coils in your mind...and dictates
something to you. A writer is a tool of the language rather than
the other way around.

—JOSEPH BRODSKY

The journal is one of those phenomena of English teaching: an
instant hit with teachers everywhere. It zoomed like a skyrocket through
every cookbook and conference. Seven million teachers did it to their
kids on Monday. Like the collage and the "Write your own commercial"
activities, the "J," as my students affectionately refer to it, has been
used and abused at one time or another by most English teachers. Some
teachers swear by it; some swear at it. Some do both. As one veteran
confided in me late one afternoon, "I love journals, but it beats the hell
out of me to keep up with 'em." This chapter is dedicated to renewing
your interest in the journal and to giving you some ideas for using it
without slashing your wrists or filing for separate maintenance.

Simply stated, the journal is the most consistently effective tool for
establishing fluency I have found. True believers swear that the J works
on some mystical principle because nonfluent, nontalking, and apparent
nonthinking students have blossomed so dramatically through journal
writing. I'm a true believer; growth in fluency sometimes comes
dramatically for students who get hooked on the J.

It is possible that students become more and more engaged in
journaling because they write about subjects that are important to them.
The journal provides opportunities for students to write through their
questions, experiences, and imaginings. The writing may feel freer in
this place where spelling, punctuation, and usage will not be red-
penciled. This is the chance for students to think for themselves, and
their writing shows how enthusiastically they accept the challenge.

Look at this example of growth in a before-and-after comparison of a typical low-achieving sixth grader, Claude (2). Claude's first journal writing is halting and hostile:

I feel good just to be living but
I feel like killing someone
I want to kill someone who
boss me around

One of Claude's last journal entries was in response to a picture. Claude speaks as the character in the picture:

I just got my job being a lawyer. Every Friday we get our pay. This Friday I was happy. I got a raise on my check.

I used to get 150 dollars. Today I got 190 dollars. With my money I went to my car and got in. I was going home and a man stopped my car and pulled a gun in my face. He knew I had some money. I told him I only had two cents. He didn't believe me. He shot me in the wrist. I fell on the ground holding the two pennies. I was out cold. I woke in the hospital. My arm was hanging.

One week later I got out and began work as the same.

Claude's words come easily. He packs his writing with detail. He even includes an ironic twist, "holding the two pennies." The journal has drawn Claude out and changed more than his writing ability. Claude loved the journal and worked faithfully in it.

Why the Journal Works

Let me suggest several reasons why the journal works so well for many students. Let's go back to an earlier premise in Chapter 1: all kids have language inside their heads. That stream of feelings and remembrances and hurts and people and successful moments and colossal failures is all up there in their heads. The journal, because it's a private, protected place, becomes an invitation to open up, to explore, to dip into that stream of language. Good journal writing is fishing in the river of your mind.

Because the J is less structured and more subjective than most school writing assignments, many students find it instantly inviting, even seductive. This seductive quality means that many students will write more frequently and for longer periods of time. This practice effect certainly accounts for much of the journal's magic.

Second, because students use the journal to write about those things *they* are interested in, they often write with clearer, more powerful language. For all of our careful attempts to choose good topics for students, somehow student writing usually comes off better if the motivation for writing and the topic ideas well up from within the students themselves. The J is an idea market, a place where students explore ideas that interest them alone. They dance their own dance.

Another important feature of the journal is that it is intended for an audience of one. I tell my students, "The journal is for you; please yourself." Of course, they invite me to look over their shoulders to see if what pleases them also pleases me and has the potential to please many others. But basically, when students write in the J, they are talking to themselves. Because most school writings pose the teacher as sole audience, the journal represents an important shift. The J-writer becomes the most important critic. Some students who will slop any old thing together for me take pride and pains to make their journal attractive. Being allowed to write to please oneself is a rarity in school. Developing a distinctive, discernible voice in one's writing demands practice in careful listening. And as writers develop this voice, they also develop a heightened sense of audience. By writing and reading and reworking their writing in the J, student writers can make startling progress. When kids first read their journals, they act the way they did the first time they heard their voices on a tape recorder: "Is that me? I didn't know I sounded like *that!*" Becoming comfortable with your own voice in your writing and then working to make it more powerful and understandable is the beginning of important growth as a writer. Nancy Martin says it this way: "Expressive writing we think is the seed bed from which more specialised and differentiated kinds of writing can grow...." (3).

Of course, many students fail to find the journal an irresistible place to talk to themselves. Maybe they aren't introspective enough, or maybe they just feel silly doing it. For many of these students, the joy of the journal comes because it gives them a chance for a dialogue with the teacher. A sensitive adult who really listens and seeks to help the writer further explore and clarify thoughts and feelings may be a rarity in the lives of many of our students. I'm not suggesting that the teacher become a psychoanalyst or succumb to giving advice or preaching. The journal as a dialogue demands that the teacher be a good listener: nodding occasionally, encouraging, asking for clarification, smiling at attempts at humor, and even acknowledging ambivalence or confusion. Many of our students love to talk. They'll tell you more than you ever wanted to know about anything. The journal is a great place for conversations, and students warm to honest dialogue.

What's in It for You?

Let's face it; reading and responding to journals takes time. Even the most dedicated types get burned out on the J. "It's nice to see the students enjoying themselves talking my leg off in the J, but what do I get out of it?" For me the J is a great source of information about how I'm doing as a teacher. Even after fifteen years of teaching, I still need feedback on how the class is going and how the students are perceiving me. Students volunteer all kinds of evaluative comments about the English class, and they usually do it in ways I can accept and profit from. You won't need to pass out a class evaluation form if you use the journal. The students will keep you posted on the good, the bad, and the ugly.

Second, the journals keep me *with* my students. I'm one of those people who hate to be in the "out group." I want to know what's *in* with students. The journal is a potpourri of new sayings, new looks, new loves, and old feelings. I feel more in touch with my students and their culture (or lack of it) when I read their Js. One thing is sure: it beats reading *Teen* magazine or attending Ozzie Osbourne concerts.

Four Journals

I have been using the term *journal* as if the J appeared as a well-defined, readily agreed-on form. In fact, one of the joys of using the J as a teaching tool is its versatility. A journal is not just a journal, as an examination of the journals of William Byrd, H.D. Thoreau, Mary Hemingway, and Hugh Prather illustrate. More and more journals of writers, artists, naturalists, and housewives are published each year. Check out Ellen Gilchrist, Joan Didion, Anaïs Nin, John Barth, and Loren Eiseley for starters. Put a collection of excerpts together and read these with your students. This will help them find new ways to use journals, and it might give you ideas for classroom assignments as well. Let me suggest four different journals for four different purposes.

The Writer's Notebook

Most good professional writers keep a notebook, a place where they store ideas, observations, and insights for later use. A writer's notebook, as Macrorie suggests, "forces the writer to put something away in the sock everyday" (4). The notebook becomes the writer's workbench. The writer returns to the notebook periodically, reviews what's there, selects a project or two, and then works and reworks it. The notebook is a place to save things: a word, a phrase, an unrefined thought, the title of a poem or song. The title of this book and many of the ideas for chapters and activities first surfaced several years ago in our writers' notebooks. In fact, as Tom and I review our entries of the last few years, it's apparent that a book was growing somewhere in those journals even without our knowledge. The writer's notebook is a miniature greenhouse. If you keep planting seeds and nurturing the ideas stored there, good things happen and the results are sometimes surprising.

The writer's notebook does not look much like "school writing" a teacher could collect and grade. It is often marked by idiosyncratic systems of organization. Writers frequently use codes, shorthand, sketches, and bizarre notations. There's almost always some system of organization to it, but the writer alone may know the system. The key to a good writer's notebook is that, like Dannon Yogurt, it contains active cultures. Good writers throw nothing away. They put it all in the pot to let it work a little. Maybe only 1 percent of that stuff in the writer's notebook will ever be shared with anyone else, but the notes become a record, a chronicle of the winding journey of the writer's mind. The journal as writer's notebook has been used most frequently in the schools by creative writing teachers and their students. Because the thing is impossible to grade and because "creative" is often synonomous with the frivolous or chaotic, teachers have shied away from using it with their students. Actually the writer's notebook has good potential for even the slowest students, and we believe all students need to experience the joy of the writer's notebook somewhere in their schooling. The teacher will need to provide many of the stimuli and be much more active in getting students started and keeping them going, but all students can use the writer's notebook with profit.

Suggested Activities for a Writer's Notebook

1. people watching—Laundromat, bus stop, bowling alley, skating rink, elevator, cafeteria
2. CIA—eavesdropping
3. observing/describing
4. new words—vocabulary
5. themes—loneliness/kindness
6. poetry
7. dreams
8. tag lines
9. coinages
10. slogans/advertising's false claims
11. analogies
12. metaphors
13. minutiae

14. fabulous realities
15. ironies
16. newspaper stuff
17. contrasts: light and dark/old and young
18. dream journal
19. nature journal
20. work journal
21. first lines for stories or poems
22. reflections
23. ideas for other pieces

Let's face it. Practice improves performance. Journals provide a place for writers to rehearse and to experiment with subject matter, voice, and form. From these practices the seeds of essays, fiction, or poetry may sprout. To encourage students to recognize the journal as a source for topics, give some in-class time each week for reworking journal material. Comment on style *and* content. Look for potential. Publish good stuff.

The Class Journal (CJ)

If you subscribe to the "Write Three or More Times a Week Club," as we do, the class journal is a teacher-saver. At the beginning of each quarter, we instruct each of our students to buy a notebook. The notebooks are kept in the classroom, and the students do most of their writing during the regular class period. This journal forms the basis of a daily work grade and simplifies evaluation. I usually start the week off with a fifteen-minute writing on Monday, called Weekend Update. In this assignment the students look back over the weekend, commenting on any significant events, or talking about anything they feel like. In the last part of the entry, students may say something about the week ahead. For the remainder of the week, the CJ comes out at the drop of a hat. If I show a film, the students respond in the CJ. If we have a particularly vigorous class discussion, I ask them to do a wrap-up in the CJ. If the principal announces a new policy or if the students feel a recent test was too difficult, out come the CJs so that they can explain their position fully.

The CJ works particularly well for responding to literature. Class discussions are much more enlightening if students have first logged a response to the selection in their CJs. Reading, writing about reading, and then discussing become habits in my class.

The Dialogue Journal (DJ)

Ruth and I have found good success lately with dialogue journals. Students write their questions and reflections on a particular work of literature to a partner. Partners read and respond to each other's journals, often engaging in lively exchanges. We find that they get past teacher questions to the heart of the issues that are important to them. Here's a sample of dialogue journals from Heidi and Darin. Darin writes first of his reading of Barry Lopez's *River Notes*.

D. This Lopez guy is definitely strange. Is he on something or what? He lies down by the river for two years to get to "know" it. I love that passage where he says, "I place my hands like frogs beneath the water...." Wow! Great metaphor! Do you think he is a naturalist? I mean did he really go out and carefully note how the river comes around the bend? Or is he a poet? He uses so many metaphors. Or is he trying to create myth here with all of his allusions about the heron?

H. I can't quite figure out why we're reading this. Lopez isn't strange, Darin, he's downright WEIRD. I couldn't make any sense of why he was lying around with his ear to the ground until I started thinking about how he was probably trying to hear the pulse of the earth. In metaphor it would be something like listening to the heartbeat of the river. Or is he listening for something more general? I was just wondering if he wanted to hear the heartbeat of nature. I think he is a naturalist. His metaphors all come from nature like the one on hands as frogs that you pointed out. What is the difference in a simile and a metaphor? I thought "like frogs" was a simile? Is the heron a metaphor to something that becomes mythical? I thought it was interesting that you thought it might be mythic. I hadn't thought of that.

D. I've read a little more of this stuff and I'm kind of getting into it. I was really interested in his Log Jam chapter and how he linked all those little stories together. More on that later. O.K., Heidi always the purist. Yes, technically a simile is a comparison using like or as, and a metaphor is an implied comparison, but that's English major stuff. I think of metaphor as any connection you make. mmmmm ... O.K. heartbeats of the earth. I am impressed with how carefully Lopez listens to the earth. ..."the sound of birds' breath rolls oceanic..." Wow! (5)

The Project Journal (PJ)

One of the frustrating responsibilities that inevitably accompanies the assignment of a project, novel, or research paper is all of the elaborate checking the teacher must do to see that students are doing the work. That old human instinct to leave everything until the night before it's due is particularly strong in adolescents. Most good teachers reluctantly assume the responsibilities of setting deadlines for note cards, rough drafts, and progress reports. We have found the project journal to be an efficient way to keep students on track during a project that stretches over several weeks.

Group Projects

Asking students to work together in a group to prepare a presentation is still a worthy idea. The problems for the teacher are obvious, however. Are they really getting anything done? Who is responsible for what? Is everyone carrying a fair share of the load? The project journal can answer most of these questions. Ask each member of the group to keep a PJ throughout the project. Ask students to log their participation in the project, their responsibilities, and their evaluation of the group's effectiveness and progress. Collect these each week, and you have a quick check on how the group is doing. The final entry in the PJ can be a summary essay commenting on how well the project was done and what things the group might do differently.

Novels and Plays

Teaching a class novel or play offers another good opportunity to use the PJ. Students enter responses to their reading *as* they read. The responses may be personal observations, questions, feelings, and even digressions. Reading student responses gives the teacher some idea of the thoroughness and the level of comprehension of the reader. The PJ substitutes for frequent threats and pop quizzes and sermons. Collected once a week during an extended reading assignment, the PJ gives you a written record of the student's effort and understanding of the work.

More important than its efficiency as a check on student performance, the PJ gets students to *respond in writing as they read*. You can structure the responses any way you wish. Here are some entries we ask for:

- Record new words for vocabulary study.
- Jot down memorable quotes.
- Speak directly to the character and/or author.

- Make guesses about what will happen or what might have happened.
- Speak as one of the characters.
- Digress into personal experiences similar to those of the character.
- Questions, questions, questions.

In other words, encourage interesting and varied responses to the work. Don't let it become a drag. One final incentive: tell the students you will let them use their PJs to answer your essay questions on the end of the unit exam.

Research Paper

I hear a groan or two out there at the mention of the research paper. Yes, it's alive and as problematic as ever in schools everywhere. Most veteran teachers who must teach the RP every year have worked out an elaborate survival scheme with deadlines and checks and handouts. Beginning teachers frequently stumble through the process, vowing to do it differently next year. If you're still looking for a manageable system to teach the research paper, try using the PJ. Because every assignment in the classroom must have a name, we call this a *research log*. We ask students to get a looseleaf notebook and divide it into six sections:

1. *A working bibliography.* Each potential source is entered in complete bibliographic form.
2. *Notes and quotes.* This section takes the place of the old note cards and is keyed to section one.
3. *Working outline.* Because it is virtually impossible to outline anything until you know what you want to say, this is a tentative outline that may change weekly as new ideas and materials surface.
4. *Flashes of brilliance.* This is an ideas section. If a student gets a good idea for a beginning or an ending or wants to be sure to remember something, this is the section for such entries. We encourage students to have their own thoughts about the research topic. Cutting and pasting encyclopedia and *National Geographic* quotations is not serious research.
5. *Weekly summary.* Each week the student logs time spent on reading, writing, looking, and thinking. The student and the teacher have the opportunity to observe how research time is spent.
6. *The rough draft.* Ideally a rough draft grows over time. This section encourages students to write parts of the rough draft whenever they are ready. Sometimes the ending comes first; sometimes a student is ready to write one section before another. Encourage reading and writing *during* the research period.

Encourage students to share their insights, questions, and discoveries with a classmate as the research paper forms. A live audience helps the writer search through and explain information. This valuable practice gives the researcher a preliminary rehearsal before drafting sections of the paper. We think using the research log to write the research paper encourages students to do more thinking and writing before the final draft. It also gives the teacher a clearer idea of the students' progress and problems during the research process.

Reflections on the "J"

Students anticipate the opportunity to respond to classroom activities and exercises in the J. If I forget or decide not to have them respond, they frequently remind me with a "Hey! Don't we get to write about this in the J?" The J is particularly effective for getting students comfortable with writing as a way of responding. They frequently like to share excerpts from their Js, so writing facilitates talk and vice versa.

Provide some time each week for revision. For me, Fridays are rework time. I ask students to select some entry from the week and work on it. We focus on different strengths and weaknesses of their writing each week. Sometimes the focus is on proofreading—working to eliminate surface errors in spelling, capitalization, and punctuation. Sometimes it's on beginnings or endings. Sometimes it's on a particular function of writing: telling, arguing, describing. Sometimes it's on rewriting for a different audience—the principal, your best friend, a parent. Sometimes there is no focus; we pick something from this week and rewrite it.

The J is a weekly record of a student's responses to the class. Most of the entries are short and can be read quickly each week. The piece the student selects to rework is read more carefully and evaluated, based on a particular focus. The student writes often; the teacher reads all of it, but spends grading time on only one short selection each week.

The J has taken me away from book reports and pop quizzes and other frustrating devices. If I want to know whether students have done the assigned reading or if they are prepared for class, I ask for a response in the J.

Suggestions for Using the Journal

As we said earlier, using the journal effectively requires some patience, persistence, and expertise on the part of the teacher. The collected wisdom of teachers who use the journal consistently tells us:

- Journal reading and writing are time consuming.

- Begin using the journal on a small scale; set a time limit (two or three weeks is a good start).
- Use the journal in only a couple of classes at any one time.
- Stagger the collection date so that you receive only one class set at a time.
- Use "journal starters" to get your more reluctant students going.

The journal is a good way to begin the school year or a new class. Or use the journal during a particular unit: the short story, a Shakespeare play. Find a context for the journal; work it into the normal class routine.

If you are using the journal for the first time, you may find these suggestions by Alice Stalker helpful. Alice's success with the journal, even with low-achieving students, qualifies her as a journal expert. Plan to write a journal *with* the students so that you'll get a better feel for just what it takes to keep a journal. Some tireless veterans always write a journal with their students, sharing entries right along with them.

- Explain the journal assignment in detail. Use student examples if you have them.
- Set aside regular class time for journal writing. The first ten minutes of class are frequently wasted. Establish a routine. As the students enter the room, they pick up their journals and start writing.
- Stimulate journal writing—put quotes on the board, posters on the wall, read poems to them, discuss a recent happening, tell a personal story, play a song you like, ask their opinion about a class activity.
- Encourage "extra" entries and digressions in the journal.
- Enclose things in student's journals. Look for cartoons, newspaper clippings, pictures, and other trivia that may connect with that student. (6)

Responding to and Evaluating the Journal

"But how do you grade the thing?" Somewhere during most of the workshops I do with teachers on the journal, somebody raises this question. Grading and the journal are two apparently mutually exclusive processes. My best advice is to work out a point system (5, 4, 3, 2, 1) or a check system (+, ✓, –), which gives students credit for their thoroughness, or simply assign a certain number of pages per week. Above all, use a system that de-emphasizes evaluation and is quick and easy for you.

My own experience tells me you need some systemized way of evaluating journals to simplify your life and to give students a clear idea of what you expect in the journal. My system is a simple, three-point check. The three criteria for journals in my class are *Truthful, Thoughtful,* and *Thorough.* That may sound like the Boy Scout oath to you, but it works well for me. I use excerpts from the student's own writings to illustrate the criteria. I collect the journals weekly and give each journal a 1, 2, or 3 rating. Unusually good journals get five-star ratings, "journal of the week" awards, or copious verbal praise in class. I believe such a system is positive and encouraging to journal writers and not overly burdensome to the teacher.

Tom works with pages. He requires three a week. He offers extra credit for motivation to do more: 2 to 5 points per page. He says, "It's entirely possible for a student in my class to make up a major test score by being involved enthusiastically in the journal. I do pages because it's a quick way. Even if I can't get it all read, I read beginnings and ends and spot-check throughout."

Ruth has given up on grading and responding to journals altogether. The alternative is: students pair and exchange journals, then hold conferences with their partners. Each writer marks two or three entries that they would like their partner to notice particularly. Ruth gives the pair time to discuss the entries and share reactions. She's found that keeping a journal partner for a nine-week period establishes intimacy that pays off in the quality of responses given. The partner conferences wean the students from "I only want the teacher to comment" syndrome. Ruth says, "Some students will want teacher comments, though they are satisfied with their partner's comments. They mostly want to say, 'Hey, look how great this question is,' or 'I finally figured out how to describe that boathouse.' It's their way of letting us know our reactions are important."

How you respond to student journals is much more important than how you grade them. The whole idea of journal writing is to stimulate internal motivation for writing. Our students care much more about the comments a reader makes in their journals than numbers or letters because they are writing to communicate thoughts and feelings.

Suggestions for Responding

- Be an *active* reader.
- Encourage the student to share excerpts from the journal with classmates.
- Suggest future topics. Notice profitable digressions.
- Ask for permission to publish good stuff to share with other students.
- Above all, be truthful yourself.

- Write an extended response, a short poem, or ask questions.
- Avoid empty comments like "interesting," "nice," or "good idea."
- Make me laugh; make me cry.

Problems with the Journal

Veteran users of the journal have no doubt encountered all the following problems. One good piece of advice is to talk with an experienced journal user before you begin. If you've never tried the journal before, however, you may appreciate a short digression about potential pitfalls.

Protect the Privacy of the Journals

Don't ever read them aloud to other teachers or students without the author's permission. The surest way to lose the honesty and openness of journal writers is for them to find out their trust has been violated.

Be Honest with Students

Sometimes students tell you more than you want to know. Detailed accounts of sexual adventures, drinking in the parking lot, and smoking dope in the johns may be honest writing, but when a parent finds his child's journal with such entries and sees your nonjudgmental comments in the margin, you may get called on the carpet for failing to uphold conventional morality. Whenever students tell me things I don't want to hear or use unacceptable language or make obscene offers, I tell them to "cut it out."

Look for Something Good

Sometimes you get journals froms students you don't like. These kids' values are quite different from yours. Their writings rub you the wrong way. Try to find something positive to say. Don't give up on the kids. If they are writing, there is hope. If they lean back against the wall in sullen isolation, you don't have much of a chance to help them.

Avoid Sarcasm

It's easy to get discouraged with students when you know they're doing only the bare minimum. You know they have ability, but they slop any old thing in the journal and you see very little happening. Don't make nasty comments in the journals. Be patient; stay with it. They may have more ego involvement in their journals than you think.

Take a Break

If the journals start getting stale or if you find yourself running out of enthusiasm, stop them for a while. Don't burn yourself or your students out on the journal. It's too valuable in the writing class to kill through overexposure.

A Success Story

Teachers are a strange lot. They are masters of delayed gratification, and the happy ones have found ways to let a few dramatic successes cover the sadness of their failures. My favorite journal success story comes from a former student, Charles. As a first-year teacher, Charles found himself in a very difficult teaching situation. His students were openly hostile and the administration ineffective. He decided quite idealistically to win his students over with the journal. Charles tells the story in a letter:

I wanted to start the quarter off with something really different and catchy, but I quickly found out that so many things I considered fun and exciting were considered a bore by the kids. Luckily, I decided to use the journal. The results those first days were fantastic. I encouraged complete honesty and emphasized that I would not hold any cuts about me personally against the student. The kids were really puzzled about this journal bit. Obviously, they had never heard of a journal. But I could not believe the response I got. After they found their work was strictly confidential and that I honestly would not hold anything against them and that I did not grade them as such and even resisted the strong temptation to correct their spelling and grammar—a temptation you will probably feel in reading this letter—they began to really get into the journal. I honestly believe that I know more about many of my students and their feelings than other teachers who may have known them for years. Also, the journal gave me much feedback on the impression I was making and the teaching job I was doing. In addition, I think I may have discovered a "basic kid" who is a gifted writer—though I will admit my inexperience in making such judgments.

After my first week I took all the journals home. I was exhausted spiritually, physically, emotionally, and mentally. I had been through a living hell. I picked up a journal. It said "Our new teacher is so dumb! He gave a stupid vocabulary test, and everyone cheated like crazy, but he has such a big nose and is such a midget that he could not see. This class is such a bore." I wanted to cry. Instead I wrote back. "Thanks for sharing your thoughts with me. I appreciate your honesty. I wish I could get in the circus with my giant nose, but I have been unsuccessful. Anyway I enjoy teaching and enjoy having you in my class." I put a smiling face at the end. The next week this girl wrote on Friday in her journal, "Good-bye! I am really going to miss you this weekend." Later the next week her parents came to Open House and said, "Margaret said 'Mother, you will *really* like Mr. Walker!'" (7)

Notes

1. Joseph Brodsky. From an article by Francis X. Clines. *New York Times,* October 23, 1987.
2. Claude Patton was a student at Clarke Middle School, Athens, GA.
3. Nancy Martin et al. *Writing and Learning Across the Curriculum 11-16.* Ward Lock, 1976.
4. Ken Macrorie. *Writing to Be Read.* Boynton/Cook, 1984.
5. Heidi Anderson and Darin Weyrich were students at Boise High School, Boise, ID.
6. Alice Stalker. "Using the Journal," presentation given at Language Arts Conference, Athens, GA, 1976.
7. Charles Walker. Personal letter, Sept. 1975.

CHAPTER SIX

Writing Poetry

To me [a poem] is a clarification, or a new way of seeing something. I don't know whether that quality of novelty is the one that I'd stress, but I do feel that novelty is important. I want to be shocked into seeing, or startled, or brought to see things in a way I haven't seen them on my own. . . .

I also like music in a poem, which is something that's gone by the boards pretty much these days. Or maybe it's a different sort of music now; maybe my ears are not yet accustomed to it.

—CONSTANCE CARRIER

I say, "Well, forget that intention. Listen to the poem you are writing; don't listen to that conscious voice, that obligatory 'daddy' that says, 'No, thou must not do this.' Listen to what your imagination is really doing."

—PHILIP LEVINE

"Can I write a poem instead?"

I looked up at him from my carefully made plans for that Monday morning class. Plans I had sweated over the night before. What I was really thinking about before Johnny broke into my assignment-giving routine was how badly I wanted another cup of coffee right then.

"Do you think you can handle it?" I asked with only a slight edge of sarcasm in my voice. I was looking for something to get these kids going. It was a large Basic English class for juniors, loud and often defiant—I had lost some sleep over them already. Besides, it was too early in the course to be fooling around with poetry.

Johnny's big hands fumbled with the anthology of too-hard and too-dull stories, and worse poems—but cheap and on the state's approved list.

I stalled him. "Look, what about one of those other writings? How about an interview with one of the characters in the story?" Was he trying to duck the assignment? He hadn't done much so far with his writing.

"Naw," he said, "I got an idea, but it's a *poem*. I don't feel like doing none of that other stuff." So much for planning. But he did look as if he was interested.

"Do it," I said. He smiled and went back to his seat in the back of the room. At the end of the period he turned in this:

A Kiss

A kiss is short and sweet, but
after that it is gone forever just
a soft quiet touch in your memory.
Showing your love and
care for her and letting her know
she's yours. Just a touch of the lips
is now forever gone, but soon
another one will be coming on. (3)

I was disappointed. That was *all* he had written in response to a story we had spent so much time on? I suspect that your reaction now is similar to my thoughts then. The poem is inchoate and rather silly. Nothing very profound *is said* in those fifty-five words. Besides, it doesn't *look* like a poem. By any adult standard, it's just not very good stuff.

But Johnny's eager and proud expression when he turned in the piece kept me from saying anything right then. It seemed to be important to him somehow, so I reserved judgment and took it home with the other papers. I put it aside until I read the others. I really didn't know what to do with it.

When I reread the poem, I was thinking about *Johnny* and not about the *assignment*. It was the first thing he had written in which he was personally involved. It was *real* writing, not just writing for the teacher. Of course, it was adolescent. He was using his own experience to respond to a reading assignment in which he saw some of his own feelings reflected. And although the piece may not be profound, it does work as a poem. It has movement and rhythm, alliteration and rhyme, figurative language, and a gentle sort of irony. And it has a striking image in the third line—"a soft quiet touch in your memory." Johnny used the techniques of the poet, not because we had labored over rhyme and meter and metaphor in class, but because he had something to say and intuitively used those language resources, automatically fitting the form to what he was saying.

In poetry, as in all writing, the technical aspects of the poem are really of secondary importance; good writing is *honest* writing. The writer risks feelings with us, and we respond to the words because they touch our feelings through shared human experiences. The subtleties of form, the intricacies of vocabulary, the erudition of allusion may contribute to the experience and to our pleasure in the work, but without that risk-taking and sharing of feeling, they are an empty shell. For an adolescent boy in a large and rowdy high school class to write about kissing a girl this way, he has to take quite a chance with his reader.

Which raises an important point about Johnny's poem. Steve Judy talks about the danger of imposing adult standards on students' work in the classroom (4). One of the best ways to encourage immature writers and help them control their writing, without crushing them with the weight of unreasonable adult expectations, is to use the natural audience in the classroom. Johnny's adolescent poem was written for adolescents; it was read and responded to by adolescents. And they liked it so much that they put it in the school literary magazine. That did more for his writing than anything I could have done.

In this chapter, Dan and I talk about writing poetry as it is done by three kinds of kids—slow kids, young kids, and gifted kids. (Johnny was a slow kid in a slow class.) We try to give you some techniques for teaching poetry writing for each of these groups, although the approaches overlap so much that, with a little modification, any of the techniques should work with any of the kids. Before that, however, there are several points that need to be made about teaching poetry writing. We'll use Johnny's poem as a reference point.

1. *The growth process in writing poetry is the same growth process operating in all forms of writing.* Most writing teachers are intimidated by poetry, although they teach it effectively in their literature classes. Usually kids are given no opportunity to write poetry or, worse, are expected to start generating Petrarchan sonnets or haiku (the more difficult of the two forms to write!) the first time poetry writing is assigned. The results are predictably dismal, and teachers are further convinced that students cannot, and should not, write poetry.

Poetry grows the same way prose does. It's not a mysterious process. When Johnny wrote "A Kiss," he was just becoming fluent as a writer. He needed a lot of practice. Strong criticism would have been of little help, and would have done considerable damage, until he reached a point where he was more comfortable with the forms. And you can already see at this early stage in his writing that form was beginning to come.

Especially in poetry, content controls form. The natural spoken rhythms of the language help form lines and even stanzas as the student writes more. You may want to suggest alternate forms for a particular verse, but that should come later in the process. The best thing you can do at the beginning is to *let* form be controlled by content.

2. *If there had not been a plan for writing in the classroom, with many options and with personal writing encouraged and supported, then the poem would never have been written.* Writing must be planned, but there must also be freedom for the students to explore their own forms of expression. And when it does happen, especially those first few times, it must be supported.

In other words, students must have the freedom to start some place. Whenever possible, remove the restrictions, give them their heads, and be receptive to their efforts. Class environment is crucial, and you set the tone.

3. *The important thing is that Johnny wrote what he wanted to.* That's the whole point of a writing class. As long as he's writing about what's important to him, then his writing is real, it's motivated, and it's likely to improve.

When poetry is first written, it is almost always personal. But so is all real writing. As immature writers grow, their writing will natually become less egocentric, but, as Nancy Martin says, "at the heart of any writing which is poetic in function will be *a felt response* that is expressed" (5). They will strive to reach their peers, and perhaps eventually a wider audience, and that growth will move them gradually away from what is sometimes painfully personal writing. The intimate nature of these early efforts, however, puts a heavy burden on the teacher. Tact and sensitivity are required when a student writes about that first kiss.

4. *At this point in the writing, quality is not really important.* Expectations of Wordsworthian or even Brautiganesque prosody will only stop the kid from writing. Lower your standards a little. At first the emphasis should be on honest writing and honest responding. Understanding and recognition are what students are seeking. Save the criticism for when they are more accomplished.

And encourage them to practice. Take a risk yourself. Respond with a poem of your own. Give them lots of opportunities to write and share their poetry.

5. But it doesn't stop there. *Gently push students to widen their audience.* Display poetry in your room. Publishing student poetry in the classroom is easily done and is the best possible way to encourage more poetry

writing. When others are regularly reading and responding to their
writing, students work hard at shaping and fine-tuning their poems.
Student readers are always the best audience for student poets.

6. *Kids like poetry.* There's a kind of freedom in writing poetry that
appeals to many kids. They feel less threatened by poetry than by prose
writing. Johnny is a good case in point.

Because poetry is usually an intense and brief writing experience,
students are often able to write and rewrite a complete draft in a class
period and get immediate satisfaction from the finished job. They also
can receive an immediate response to what they have written. This is
especially important for slow kids for whom writing is an ordeal,
threatening failure.

7. *But when poetry writing is taught, prose should also be an option.* Just as
Johnny had the choice of writing poetry when the assignment was prose,
the student should have the choice of *not* writing poetry in any given
situation. Understandably enough, some students are afraid of poetry.
Johnny may be an exception, but there is evidence that most writers
must write prose before they can write poetry. It's not unusual even for
an accomplished poet to begin a poem with a prose sketch.

The writing teacher can be alert for prose pieces from the students
that are rich in images and wordplay that might easily be turned into
poetry (the reverse is also true, of course—poetry can become prose
sometimes). And students can learn a great deal about their language by
switching forms with a piece of writing. There's also the option of
prose-poetry, a form of writing popular with modern writers and one
that has many possibilities for the classroom. The best way to encourage
reluctant poets, however, is sharing with them and the class the writing
of their peers. They see that it's not so hard after all and will often try it
themselves on the next assignment.

8. *Understanding poetry follows most naturally from fooling around with
poetry.* To teach poetry by parsing lines, unstringing iambs, and
calculating rhyme schemes is a barren exercise unless students have
done a lot of writing, sharing, and talking about poetry previously.
Reading is important, of course, to the poet. But put off Wordsworth
and Milton and the classic poets until later. Instead, get out poets like
Brautigan, McKuen, Lifshin, Gunther, Wise, and the songwriters your
students listen to all the time. I believe it's time we declared a
moratorium on the Great Symbol Hunt in poetry teaching and, instead,
allow students to create their own symbols. Even if students never write
very good poetry in your class, they will learn about poetry by playing
with it. And they will enjoy reading poetry more.

9. *Writing poetry is one of the best ways to study language.* As students

write and share, and write again, they begin with their knowledge of
words from spoken language. But they expand on that knowledge very
quickly. Every time they grapple with a different image, a subtle
emotion, an elusive rhyme or line ending and have to hunt for a word
that fits, their language grows. Every time they ask you, "What's the
word for this?" or say, "This word doesn't sound right here," they're
growing as users and writers of language.

10. *Grade poetry very carefully and very gently,* just like all writing in
your class. Many teachers don't give students the opportunity to write
poetry because they don't feel they know enough about writing poetry
to grade it. However, the approaches to writing we are suggesting will
revise your grading strategies and make the question really unimportant.
All I will try to suggest here are some alternative methods to red-pencil
grading that I have found particularly useful when kids in my classes
write poetry.

Early poetry from the student is *not graded at all.* It is read and
responded to; it is shared and published in some form. It may be
displayed in the room, or dittoed and passed around, or read aloud. The
student is given credit for doing the assignment. I use a point-grading
system for this. A portfolio or folder may be used in which the writing
can be kept to be examined in a private conference to decide on a grade
later. Or selected pieces can be revised, with the student, for careful
grading after practice with writing poetry.

Once a student is a practiced poet and begins to demonstrate control
of poetic form, my grading usually consists of insisting on revisions of
pieces of writing in certain ways to encourage him or her to attempt new
things with poetry. There are choices, and the student picks the specific
works to be revised. I haggle, I make deals, I bribe with grades to get the
writing done. At times I even call over a couple of other kids from the
class to read a piece in question and arbitrate a dispute over revision. I
respond as a *reader* to the student as a *writer.* The grade is negotiable,
depending on the extent and kind of revision done—and it is not given
until it is done.

Every once in a while I find myself with a class in which most of the
students write poetry with ease. They control form and content, are
sensitive to audience, and seem to be able to write poetry at will—and
revise it effectively. That takes time, and kids will have to write a lot of
poetry and struggle with a lot of revisions, getting it right, before they
reach this stage. Most high school students never get there and should
not be expected to. But when I sense poetry control in a class, it's time
to push them out of the nest. I encourage them to publish outside of
class and outside of school.

Do not try this too soon. Even the best student poets react at first with fear. It's a big step to move from the safe approval of their friends to the harsh scrutiny of the marketplace. *And they must be well prepared for it and know what to expect.* A rejection slip is hard to take for any writer, much less one inexperienced in the ways of publishers. Once they are prepared, we get down to work. In conference and in groups and as a class, we pick their very best stuff. We fine-tune those poems, reading them again and again for flaws. We prepare them for publication, working together as editors. And we search for places to send them. I usually recommend the little magazines (*The International Directory of Little Magazines and Small Presses* is listed in the Resources chapter) as being more receptive and more humane to unknown writers. And I always send some of my stuff off when they do. Then we watch the mails together, together going through that anxious time of a writer.

These days of feverish activity are the best possible in a writing class, and they don't come very often. But that look in a kid's eye when he bursts into your room waving an acceptance letter from a little magazine in Podunk will keep you working hard at teaching poetry for years!

11. *If the poem is just plain* bad, *look hard for something* good *in it—* especially if it is an early one from the student. Search for an interesting image, a well-done metaphor or simile, a phrase, a *word!* If there is nothing in that poem you can *honestly* applaud (but there almost always is), then you are reduced to Ken Macrorie's suggestion that you tell the immature writer to "keep writing" (6).

If the poem is from a student you know is practiced enough to exercise some control, and if you are asked for a response, be gentle but *be honest.* And perhaps have the young poet try again. Your judgment as an informed reader is important. Don't be afraid to exercise it when the time is right.

Teaching Slow Kids to Write Poetry

We are indebted to Kenneth Weber, teacher and poet, for reinforcing our biases in this section and for suggesting strategies he has found successful in working with slow kids and poetry (7). The main thing to keep in mind is that they do like and can write poetry if it is approached positively. Patience is important. These kids have been frustrated by failure after failure in their writing. They need encouragement and support. Control will come only gradually and should be imposed very gently.

Weber makes the point that poetry reading and poetry writing are more naturally taught together. And poetry is a "community trip." You go through it with the students, exploring and enjoying together. It's a tradition as old as the wandering scops and Homer. And following the tradition, poems in the classroom need to be read aloud and shared often. Poetry, more than any other kind of writing, is something you share together.

In the basic writing class, that means you may have to do a lot of the reading aloud yourself, at least at first. Many of these students cannot read well, and you will need to help them through the poems you bring into class. They are self-conscious about reading what they have written. One approach you can take early in the class is to read the students' poems to the class, with their permission, of course. But there are other ways to share their poetry.

The important thing is that these kids need immediate response to their writing. Because poetry is a short, intense experience, it lends itself to the kinds of things that can be done in a single class period to give the kids fast results. And *publishing* in the basic writing class, as in all writing classes, is very important.

Name Poetry

This simple kind of poetry—name poetry—works with the poetic line from the most natural of starting places—the student. You will need a supply of butcher paper or newsprint, felt-tipped pens, masking tape.

Students write their names down the page, one letter per line. Each letter becomes the first letter in the line. I suggest they begin with one-word descriptions, asking them to be honest about themselves, and I put mine on the board first, making it up on the spot.

Sometimes the kids get in on the act and yell out suggestions as I write it, as they did with this one.

*T*eacher
*O*dd
*M*oustache

*L*aughing
*I*ntense
*N*utty
*E*asy going
*R*iter [sic]

(You may want to cheat and write yours the night before class.)

The second poem is written with lines, and I ask the students to tell a mini-story about themselves or simply write about themselves. Teresa had school on her mind.

> *T*oward the
> *E*nd of the day
> *R*estless in class
> *E*ncouraging my
> *S*illy self to go on
> *A*lone (3).

Winford is more religious than most, and he rhymed his name in this way:

> *W*e walk along the dim shore
> *I*n the light that shows the way
> *N*ot the light that brings the day
> *F*or He is the Way
> *O*ne man that leads the way
> *R*eads the words that he had to say
> *D*eath carry me away (3)

But Gene just likes to be strange:

> *G*o to the moon
> *E*liminate the sunshine
> *N*orth of the south star
> *E*ast of the western hemisphere
>
> *S*it on all the cheese
> *M*irage of purple creatures
> *I*n and out of the shadowing light
> *T*o the far side where it's dark
> *H*oles and mountains disappear (3)

After several tries, we work together choosing the best poem, cleaning up spelling, thinking of better words to use in places. The finished poem is copied on the butcher paper and hung up in the room.

If your students are interested, name poetry has other possibilities. Writing a name poem about another person in the class is a way to share personalities. And if you want to push the students to be a little more sophisticated, you can try having them rhyme the lines, or you can have them write lines with a specific number of words or syllables per line. (Five words or ten syllables usually work well enough.) Or you can branch out into more abstract subjects for name poems—love, hate, beauty, death, life, friendship—the list is endless.

Prose into Poetry

Have your students free write several times while listening to different kinds of music, or have them free write on such topics as rain, snow, wind, a cat walking, fear. Help them pick the piece that is most "poetic." Encourage them to throw away everything in it they possibly can. Then chop what is left into lines, making it a poem.

Happy's poem started as a journal entry about day dreaming. We cut it into lines first.

Daydream (original prose draft)

Where have you gone, so many times I wonder/And I turn around, there you are/but it's only a dream./Thinking of old times when you walked down the hall/You're on my mind all the time,/on the road, and everywhere/Where did you go when it ended?/Somewhere far off./When I think of you, it's a sad expression in my mind./It was talking with you all those crazy lines./I dream of a dream with you in it and I am lonely./It was only a daydream with you/as only a vision in my head./It was only crazy to dream that daydream everyday./Yes, you were the one in my life./Trying to get you back into this world of mine is only a dream I once had./The nights are dark/and filled of many things I wish I had said./I let you go into the clouds/and now you're nothing but a dream/and I'm the dreamer/ wanting to see/this dream of you come true, someday. (3)

Then we marked off stanzas where the natural breaks in ideas seem to fall, and I suggested what might be cut out to tighten the poem a little. And Happy had made a poem.

Daydream

Where have you gone, so many times I wonder,
And when I turn around, there you are,
But it's only a dream.

Thinking of old times when you walked down the hall.
You're on my mind all the time.
On the road,
Where did you go when it ended?

When I think of you, it's a sad feeling in my mind.
It was talking with you all those crazy lines.
I dream of a dream with you in it.

And I am lonely.

It was only a daydream with you.
As only a vision of the past in my head.
Trying to get you back into this world of mine,
Only a daydream I once had.
The nights are dark
And filled with many things I wish I had said. (3)

It is also interesting to have students turn poems into prose.

Don't Forget the Good Old Paraphrase

Paraphrasing a poem is a good exercise in dealing with language. With slow kids you'll need to pick the poems carefully, however. Keep them short. Narrative poetry works well. So do song lyrics. Remember, the purpose is to play with language and meaning, not study classic poetry.

Sometimes an assignment to paraphrase a song can turn into considerably more than that, as in this response to the Jefferson Airplane's "White Rabbit" by Cindy.

The drumsticks, gently tapping
    Are vibrating my eardrums.
The music, gradually louder
    waves crashing against my brain.
    Slick's voice; uncaring, evil/telling the truth
The pills slowly falling
    thousands from the sky
The trip is really freaky
    with white rabbits and all
Grace singing in the corner/telling them all
    Go ask Alice/She thinks I'll know . . .(3)

And this fine but disturbing poem by Jimmy began as a paraphrase of Leo Kottke's song "Morning Is the Long Way Home." But it soon became its own work, far removed from the original song/poem.

Bleed Silver

The streets unfold.
a town. It throws.
a straight. It hits.
But warm, wet blood/burns cold, wrenched steel.

And light bathes
A cool green glow moves
Softness is the real dream
Real dream.
How can you ask why?

Wet glows fade to
Glowing realities
So bright as to seem vision.
But beyond the point is the only/Living Silver.

Your silver spoon bleeds
a fatal wound
From my steel
That always unfolds the street. (3)

Personal Poetry Anthology

An anthology of personal poetry takes time, and I suggest that you allow at least a week for it. Bring in several poetry anthologies with themes that will appeal to your students. Favorites of mine are *On City Streets, The Poetry of Rock, The Poetry of the Blues, Reflections on a Gift of Watermelon Pickle, Some Haystacks Don't Even Have Any Needle, Two Ways of Seeing.* Talk about the titles of the collections and the way each one is organized, using the table of contents. Talk about the kinds of poems in the collections and why they were chosen for each book. Talk about the illustrations. Read some of the things the editors say in the prefaces and introductions.

Have students work in pairs to make their own anthologies. I suggest that each anthology should contain about twenty short poems picked because the students like them and because they go together. It should have a brief preface or introduction, telling why the poems were chosen and how they are related and organized, and a table of contents. I encourage my students to illustrate their anthologies with magazine photos or their own drawings and to make fancy covers for them with original titles. I also encourage them to include some of their own poetry or the poetry of their classmates in their collections, but I don't require it.

The personal poetry anthology is a good exercise for involving students with poetry, but it should not be attempted before your students have had a good bit of experience with poetry, both reading and talking about it and writing it. It's also an exercise that requires a lot of work. Slow kids will need help finding and choosing the poems to go in their anthologies. You will have to make material available to them and help them with each step in their editing jobs.

Found Poetry, Dada Poetry

Have the students search for quotations they like from any source and on any subject. Suggest they look for quotations in songs, posters, advertisements, signs on the street, movies, favorite TV programs, news broadcasts. However, for slow kids, you'll have to make available in class as many sources as you can find—newspapers, magazines (the ads are good for this), copies of album inserts, favorite short books, posters.

Have the students share with the class particular favorites they have found, and put the best ones on the board. Talk about the *words* and *phrases* that are most effective, that hit the hardest, that sound the best.

The students may work individually or with a partner or in groups of three (I suggest no more than three for this exercise). Brainstorm with them subjects for their found poems. Subjects should be fairly general— school, things I like, things I hate, favorite sports, life in my neighborhood, love, children, working, my friends, happy things, bad things, weather, seasons. With a general topic the students are less likely to become frustrated in looking for fitting quotations. Emphasize that they are to look for quotations that get at the feeling of the topic chosen, and not necessarily ones that describe it exactly.

After a subject is chosen, have students find and copy quotations, in no particular order, that they like for it. At this point it is helpful to show them examples of found poems on topics similar to the one they have chosen, preferably poems made by other students. If no student examples are handy, you may want to share found poems of your own. This one is from the local newspaper on a normal day.

Classified

APARTMENT FURNISHED
Bachelor
unique duplex
carpet, icemaker, micro oven
bar and fireplace
TV and AC
lakefront.
883-1401

FIREWOOD
all oak
cut, split, delivered
after 7 pm

MAID WANTED
no ref. light work
nights

MONEY TO LEND

Then you work with the students choosing the best order of parts for their found poems, deleting things not needed, cleaning up the final copy.

A refinement of this kind of assignment for more advanced students, or for slow kids who have become involved with poetry, is the modified Dada poem (nonsense poem). I use the term to refer to a poem fabricated from pieces of other writing, and not for the literary and artistic movement attributed to Tristan Tzara. To make a Dada poem, the student takes words, phrases, sentences, or lines from other writings (from a daily newspaper, for example) and combines them like a puzzle to make a poem, usually absurdly funny. This Dada poem was pieced together from popular songs.

Mamas don't let your babies
grow up to be cowboys with
four hungry children and a
crop in the field.
My mama's got a squeeze box
she wears on her chest and
my daddy don't rock-n-roll.
Love me tender or do you
just want to fool around?

• • •

Baby, come back! Any kind
of fool can see—you're sixteen,
you're beautiful, and you're mine.
I see a bad moon rising,
so take it on home.

—TERESA AND HEIDI (3)

As a further refinement, have the students make Dada poems by combining lines, parts of lines, and single words from other poems, either poems dealing with a single subject or well-known poems from one poet.

The Good Old Reliable Cinquain

We suggest a little later in this chapter that you use the cinquain to teach yonger children to write poetry, and we'll show you how Kate Kirby has used it effectively with her sixth graders. I also include it here because this five-line formula poem is one that slow kids like to write. It's short and can easily be written in a single class period. It uses step-by-step rules that are easy to follow, but it makes the student concentrate on word choice. And it's a poetic form adaptable to almost any subject.

I suggest that you teach the cinquain in three stages, moving from a loose word cinquain form to the rigidly structured formal cinquain based on syllable count.

The Simple Word Cinquain

The first time your students write cinquains, have them write a simple five-line poem following this pattern:

1. The first line contains one word, usually but not necessarily the subject of the poem.
2. The second line contains two words.
3. The third line contains three words.
4. The fourth line contains four words.
5. The last line again is only one word, which may be repeated from line one.

> Frog
> Funky warts
> Making foggy sounds
> Lovely, Madly, Slimy, Green
> Frog
>
> —TERRILL (3)

> Rain
> Damp grass
> Lonely, Misty Trees.
> Lost in thoughts of you.
> Empty.
>
> —DAN

The Regulated Word Cinquain

This poem is like the first, except the content of each line is prescribed. It's harder to write.

1. The first line contains one word that names a thing.
2. The second line contains two words that describe the thing in line one.
3. The third line contains three words that describe an action related to the thing.
4. The fourth line contains four words that express a feeling about the thing.
5. The fifth line contains one word that sums up the entire poem.

> bass
> dark silver
> ambush from silence
> shattering the pond's stillness
> predator

The Formal Cinquain

This is the form invented by Adelaide Crapsey and is based on the syllable count of two, four, six, eight, and two syllables per line. *I do not recommend* that you begin with this more difficult form with slow kids. But if they have written word cinquains and seem able to move on to something more difficult, then they probably will enjoy this form. Students who are already experienced with poetry should have no trouble with the formal cinquain.

> moon up
> over the trees
> shadows dance in cold light
> something moving down the darkness
> silence

> —TOM

The cinquain is a *friendly* kind of writing to do. Slow kids, younger kids, even those students who are accomplished poets already—all of them like the cinquain. And like all poetry written in your class, it should be shared, copied, and passed around or, better, put up for display.

Teaching the Exceptional Student Poet

I want to share an experience with you (8). It was late in an afternoon in early autumn, and I was still in my classroom reading student journals, trying to finish that final stack to return to a class of juniors the next day. No one was around but me and the custodian working down the hall. A good, quiet time to work and think. I was reading Jimmy's journal.

Jimmy was a tall, lonely kid, a quiet and sometimes intense student who sat in the back of the room. He was a competitive swimmer and a good student. We had talked a little about canoeing, a shared interest. He liked to write, and I always looked forward to reading his journal each week. I knew he wrote poetry sometimes, but I had seen little of it. In a large class with a lot of work to do, the good and quiet student is lost in the daily uproar. But the writing in his journal this week seemed particularly sensitive to the details of his surroundings and to the subtle changes in them at this time of the year.

I can't remember exactly what it was that struck my attention. I think it was the fragment of a poem he had started but abandoned for other things. It was only five or six lines long and stopped in midline. But it was good. Outside the classroom windows, the wind played with sunlight in the trees. In Jimmy's journal I wrote a note praising the fragment, and quickly I wrote this:

Perspective

maple leaves:
each one holds
a piece of sky
and the earth
in its place—

from this window.

The next morning I returned the journals in the usual buzz of excitement I've come to expect when a class gets involved in the journal—some laughter and smiles at what I'd written responding to them, some groans at my bad jokes, some arguments over points for credit, some "Hey, look at this" to neighbors across the aisle. I gave Jimmy his journal.

"You going to finish that poem? It's real good."

"No, sir, that one doesn't feel right."

He smiled when he read my poem but said nothing. I was disappointed. "Well, so much for that," I thought.

But two days later he came into the room beaming and thrust his journal into my hands.

"I wrote a good one this time. Want to read it?"

Peep Show

creakcreak   slam
  as the door opens m swallows
Howdy Pete so Pete ducks under the senile no-pest strip
  m pulls up a cokecase
Whazat Pete cause Pete's bin stackin wheat but still says he
  feels *good* as he spies the flask stickin outta Pete's
  overhauls
he smiles standin neath n old Marlboro sign thatzall faded
  face dirty m hard as Pete's calloused palms

I knew that, at sixteen years, Jimmy had the fine touch for detail of a full-fledged poet. But he refused to share his poetry with the class. For all his skill, he was always shy about his poetry and never willing to read it aloud in the classroom. Only much later was he even willing to share it in print. But I had to decide how to respond to this poem. I believe that modeling is important in the writing class. The only response, as a writer, I could properly make to Jimmy's poem was to write a poem.

Cross Roads

holding the white line off my left foot
topping the rise easy
about 5 miles out of Braselton
TEXACO BILL GROGAN'S Gen. Merchandise
the signs, where the roads cross
amid the Kudzu and cornfields, pines
I've stopped here for gas before
nobody says much
a halfdozen men beside the gas-pumps
astraddle coke crates and nail kegs
one leans against the smooth gray store-front planks
and cuts even curling slivers
from a stick with a Kabar held in a thick hand
his eyes under the John Deere cap are steady
suspicious of the motorcycle
he spits amber tobacco juice into the dust
"ain't that thang kinda dangerous, boy?"

I free my head from the helmet
and nod at him and smile

but he is satisfied
the eyes are silent

he flicks them away across the hot fields
dismissing me from his concern
with the warning

and I leave
my head imprisoned again in the helmet
leaning smoothly to the road
the white line running fast at my foot

they recede quickly in the twin mirrors
shrinking backwards
but I know the cross roads very well
and I know I'll stop there
next time through

It wasn't as tight as Jimmy's poem, but I liked it. And what it began
was a dialogue in poetry that continued for the entire year. A week or so
later Jimmy was doing a little deer hunting, which was the subject of his
second poem.

Burlesque

rehearsing the sight, the squeeze, the kick and fall
oceans beating my brains to dust inside my stand   alone but
surrounded
by years-old images of other hunters here before me
    my gun illuminated by a single shaft of filtered light
rests against a tree bole
and also rests   inside the cavity in my shoulder
    worn away by years of constant contact with the stock
(the firm steady wooden support)
it is a part of me   but remains a useless amputated limb
because it is separated   separated and dead
in my mind it also tracks the deer
    tracks the deer and kicks and kicks and kicks and conquers
and time   the ever-present harlequin   knows this and more

the deer so cautious   sniffing the breeze
fool   he does not know his danger

now now the sight rehearsed
my gun raised from the dust and given life by me
hard, steel-grey   still, silent   waiting
long-rehearsed the sight
oceans beating my brains to dust
the squeeze   the kick   the fall and
and   and dust

And I responded with one about backpacking and a favorite place in the Georgia mountains.

Jacks River
Cohutta Wilderness

the fire-watcher

my boots hanging over my head
wet from the river
that gives and takes
pulling the life from your legs
cold as night and death
and beautiful and strong
my bare feet warm at the fire
but the river talks to me
over the rocks
with laughing promises of another life
and rest
the trees are changing in layers
up the hollow
and high there is sun
very high over the ridge
just touching the tree crown
red and yellow, bright
and the river laughs beside me
over the rocks
the trees are changing
and I warm my feet
and stare at my boots hanging over my head

and listen

To which Jimmy, in turn, responded with this magnificently complex poem from his experience canoeing the Chattahoochee River.

The Nexus

the river/here/below the bridge
  it never changes—
  new faces and water and habits/but
  /always the same river
the fighter/the fulcrum
that cannot/give without/taking
or take without giving
it is/its own slave/and/it
pulls us in
onto the treadmill/the sluice/the canoe as it settles
breaks/through the leaves—
  a pasquinade of success
  /reflected from the water/again—sliding forward
and hearing a roar
the bend in the river can't quite contain/develop
  into a frothing fist/looking quickly—
  then in—

a drawstroke to/the right
we miss one/rock but hit another/and another
sending to safety/us in our canoe—
  made by/so many different/hands . . .
  /molded into a shell/an animal/a spirit
  vengeful/and/treacherous—
"Goddamnit" from the stern
when we/swirl back/into the current
to be taken away
/and see trees flash by like saviors/
we pull and pull/and pull
but are taken on
down into the rapids/that build into a
white/forest of hands/grasping hands

  and/
the river/soaks our/safety in contempt
  /sprays it back/in our/faces
  at the entrance to its soul/and fire spurts out

  then rushes us/further
  and/
capsizes our canoe/swamps
us and/leeches/into our clothes
/hair and skin and/boots
and closes over us like night

/and contaminating/germs
we're coughed up on the bank
and left to dry/while/the river keeps/changing
but we've taken back part of the river
and when it dries out of our clothes
it
will be dead to us forever

I think that was the best thing he wrote that year. He wrote several very fine pieces, and he pushed me to write. But perhaps the most important result from the experience of sharing poetry was his growing confidence in himself as a writer. He was always too shy to read his poetry aloud in class, but he and a few other talented student writers started a literary magazine later in the year (they let some of us teachers help). And they actively sought out and published other writers in the school. That magazine, student-generated and student-supported, remains a going concern in the school. Jimmy has since gone on to be a published poet and a serious writer. I feel good about that.

Like Jimmy, your talented student poets may be shy and reluctant at first to share their poetry. Gently push them to publish—first in class, then in school if you have a literary magazine, and finally in the harsh and frustrating world of the writer's marketplace. The good student poets need to become aware of their audience and to expand that audience. Your job is to show them how.

Whenever possible, write, share, and revise your own poetry with your student poets. If you are sensitive about someone else seeing what you write, think how vulnerable they must feel. There's no substitute for it. Grow a tougher hide if you have to, but *write and share your poetry with them.*

Good student poets can and should be encouraged to use models from the best poetry in their literary heritage. They need to read widely, especially in the modern poets, and they need to try those forms that appeal to them. Give them room to experiment. The journal, of course, is invaluable. Encourage them to play with the intricacies of meter and rhyme scheme, the complexities of free verse forms, the subtleties of metaphor and imagery. Originality is often not as important as exploration, and an interesting failure is more valuable than a dull, polished draft. But also insist that student poets regularly choose their best, revise it, and publish it.

Teaching Younger Kids to Write Poetry

I also want to tell you about Kate Kirby's writing program (9). Her students were sixth graders (that most difficult age!), mostly black, mostly poor, and all with serious problems with school and learning. Not a promising group of student writers. Yet these students went from being able to write only one or two halting sentences to writing pages by the end of the year. And they were excited about writing. They enjoyed writing, poetry especially. And they enjoyed sharing their writing with one another, and with the school. They were *proud* of what they wrote.

Something else happened to these kids who had been failures in school and who now saw that they could write poetry that was good and that other students liked. In most cases their attitudes semed to change. Their feelings, not only about writing, but about school and, most important, about themselves, changed dramatically because they were in a busy and exciting class where the teacher encouraged, supported, and accepted what they wrote. As Dan pointed out in Chapter 5, Claude, a student in the class who, like several of them, was sullen and withdrawn, wrote this early in the year. "I feel like killing someone. I want to kill someone who boss me around." By the end of the year he was writing, "I feel good to be in the world and to be alive. . . . I happy to go to a good School to Be in a good class. I feel nice every day. I feel nice all the time."

Kate's work with these kids (the class was a Title I reading class) is particularly appropriate here because the kinds of things she did work well with all students. Her approach is primarily a combination of Kenneth Koch's ideas about devising for kids poetry assignments that relate to their experience and with which they can be immediately successful and Barbara Esbensen's method of "word-shaking" that gets the words out of the kids' heads and on the board where they can use them, a ready-made vocabulary for the writing assignment (10). Esbensen, however, insists that the specific assignments in her program are not as important as an accepting, encouraging approach to writing and a well-planned, sequenced strategy for teaching writing.

Kate says six things made her program work:

1. *Frequent writing with well-thought-out stimuli.* Her class's writing day was every Thursday. Once the routine was established, her students looked forward to that special day when they got to write. There were none of the "Aw, do we have to do *this?*" kinds of comments. Planning is also important, however. Kids should write at least once a week in any class (it's not unreasonable to expect many students to write *every* day), but assignments need to be carefully sequenced, each one following the one before it and building on what is already learned and anticipating what is to follow. And the assignments need to be as interesting to the *students* as possible.

2. *Constant teacher feedback.* Kate says that in her class it was

important that she read everybody's writing as they wrote it. You'll need to do this, particularly with kids who have trouble with spelling, punctuation, vocabulary, or simply the physical act of writing the words on the page. Have the kids read portions to you aloud, ask them questions, praise the good, help correct the unclear. "Oh, that's really *good!*"was the expression most often heard in Kate's class. In talking to kids about their writing as they are doing it and getting them to reread parts of it, a lot of self-correcting will happen. It's best to work with them while the writing is fresh, while it's still happening.

3. *Immediate publication.* "Publishing in the class had a lot to do with their liking to write, with their wanting to write," Kate says. One of the reasons she was so careful to read everybody's stuff as they wrote it was so that *she* would understand what was on the page when she went home that night and typed the best of the class's work up on a ditto. The class got Thursday's poetry back on Friday in printed form. From that immediate and weekly publishing, the kids and Kate picked the best things to go into their book *Dy-No-Mite Writing* (the kids named it), printed at the end of the year.

4. *Editing student writing.* The use of the word *editing* here, instead of *correcting,* is important. Kate points out that "language usage was *modified* for the purpose of *readership* if it was to be published." The first and most important thing was that the student writer got his words on paper. Then she sat down with individuals or with small groups and "talked it through" if the piece was good enough to print for the class. The point was not hunting for errors, but getting it straight for publication.

Early, most of the editing suggestions came from Kate. Later in the year, students were confident enough to work on *revision,* helping one another work on second and third drafts of pieces they especially liked pulled from folders where they kept the year's writing. Again, the stimulus was seeing their works in print.

5. *Using student examples.* Both Koch and Esbensen talk about the importance of reading aloud kids' poetry to kids, instead of using adult models. You should build a collection of the best of your students' poetry of various kinds to read and to help get an assignment started. The advantages of this approach are obvious. It gives students a reasonable and understandable model for their own writing. It shows them that they can do it too.

6. *Word-shaking.* Kate says that "word-shaking is a necessity and a super stimulus to get kids into *thinking, imagining, feeling,* being *confident* in handling words, and *writing* the stuff you'll want to read." Actually, she came up with her own method of word-shaking—filling the board

with words from the kids for a poetry assignment before they start writing—before she read Esbensen's *A Celebration of Bees,* which is the most complete treatment of this technique. Especially with younger kids, it gets the words already in their oral vocabulary in front of them in visible written form. As you and the students brainstorm words to describe the wind or rain or snow or whatever, they see that they do have the words to write good stuff. It warms them up to the assignment, and it gives them the spelling of words that might be difficult for them. Often students will not use words they can't spell for fear of being embarrassed. Word-shaking is a solution to this problem. It also helps students get started with a piece of writing.

We can't give all the writing assignments Kate used with her kids each Thursday for an entire year. What we can give is some idea of a *sequence* of beginning exercises and a few of her favorites.

Class Poetry

The class poetry or collaborative poem is a good place to start. Each student contributes one line of the poem anonymously. You collect the lines and put the poem on the board. A student can claim ownership if the other kids in the class like the line.

The form and something of the content of the line should be given in your instructions. Kate asked her fourth-period class to begin their lines with the word "I wish..." and to include in the line a cartoon character, a color, and the name of a place. The kids, of course, often broke the rules, but that's not important. What is important is imaginative combinations and the repetition that holds the poem together.

I wish that I was Superman so that I could fly to Florida,
    spend the night at the Palms Hotel and go to the blue beach.
I wish I could see Donald Duck standing on his hands eating an
    orange and drinking water.
I wish that I lived in the country so that I could have some
    horses and a red and black house with a bulldog.
I wish I was Bugs Bunny so the kids will think I am funny.
I wish I was Shazam because when I hit the ground everything will
    say, "Bam!"
I wish I was in a spaceship going to the moon.
I wish I was like Spiderman and could spray people with my web.
I wish I was in Florida where I could kill Mr. Jaws.
I wish I had a go-cart so I could jump the Grand Canyon with
    Evel Knievel.

I wish I was in the city to meet Flip Wilson.
I wish I was superman and could fly all over New York City.
I wish I was Ultraman for I could fight all the monsters.
I wish I was in the country where I could have beautiful flowers
    all around and grass growing everywhere.
I wish I was Fat Albert because I want to be fat and have a lot
    of friends to play with everyday.
I wish I was a blue jay so I could play in the sky and live in
    a tree in my own little nest.
I wish I was a red car and could drive away to Atlanta forever.
I wish I was Popeye eating spinach so I could beat you up.
I wish I lived in Atlanta so I could be close to Six Flags.
I wish I had a dog that had his tail on his face and his name
    was Pluto.
I wish I had a farm that had horses, cows, chickens, and Porky,
    Pluto, Daffy, and Mickey Mouse working on it.
I wish I had a date with Mickey Mouse, and everything went goofy
    because Minny Mouse showed up.
I wish I would turn bright red so you could go to bed.
I wish I could turn my back and count to thirty and see Grapeape
    dirty.
I wish I saw Superman in color on TV on Halloween and then I
    would grab him out of the TV.

—FOURTH-PERIOD CLASS

Koch suggests several other ideas for collaborative poems in *Wishes, Lies, and Dreams*. And the same form can be used later for individual poems.

Small Group Collaborations

Three or four students work together or with the teacher to write a formula poem. This way, ownership is shared. Kate uses a modified cinquain form for this assignment. Students suggest topics. The emphasis is on word choice.

Movies
Exciting, action
Killing, cussing, kissing
Buttered popcorn and Coke
Movies

—ZACHARY, SHIRLEY,
    BRENDA, JOHNNY,
    AND CLAUDE

Motorcycles
Powerful, dangerous
Roaring, speeding, crashing
Body flying through air
Casualty

—JULIUS, CHARLES,
AND ANGELA

From here it's a natural step for kids to write their own cinquains. These can be dittoed anonymously at first (or with only initials), or they can be printed and displayed in the room, or out in the hall.

Poetic Picture Contest

Soon after the groups write cinquains, Kate brings an armload of magazine photos to class. The kids may write a poem (cinquain, wish poem, or other form), prose poem, or a prose story about the picture they choose. These are typed up anonymously and displayed with the chosen pictures in the room. The class picks first- and second-place winners. The contest always generates a lot of excitement about writing.

Being the Thing

Kate says, "We never talked about personification or any of that stuff," but one of the assignments her kids liked best was writing prose-poems beginning "If I were..." *wind* or *rain* or *sun,* or whatever the weather outside the room might suggest. Children enjoy being the thing, and metaphors come naturally from their active imaginations.

If I was wind, I would make people's hair go up and down.

—EMMA

I get up and get in my orange chariot and drive across the sky. After a while I stop and change to a yellow chariot and I drive on. When I come to my last stop, I change to a red chariot and go to a valley...and I rest. But before the next morning I go to the east and start again.

—JANET

If I was the rain I could hear the children splash me.

—PATRICIA

If I was snow when the sun comes out, I would hide in a very little corner.

—MARY

Sometimes a student will come up with something more sophisticated, and you have to be sensitive to possibilities. When Kate first gave the assignment to "be the wind," Gary turned in this.

The wind blows freely across the sky and I just sit and look at the clouds go by and I think of a way to be part of the wind.

She was excited by the natural feeling of his writing and the clear image of clouds in the wind. She asked Gary to try writing more on the wind. He added this part.

The wind blows across the sky making birds free and high.
The wind cools the sun blows the trees and gives me a breeze.

But they weren't through yet. They looked through some books of modern poetry for models and edited the appearance of his poem. They worked together breaking the first part into lines and using the spacing technique that is particularly appropriate to this poem about wind and freedom.

The wind blows freely across the sky   and I
    just sit   and look at the clouds go by,
And I think of a way to be part of the   wind.

The wind blows across the sky   making birds
    free   and   high.
The wind cools the sun, blows the trees   and gives me
    a breeze.

—GARY

With the Being the Thing poems, like all of her assignments, Kate always did word-shaking to get things started.

She agrees with Esbensen and Koch that young children should be discouraged from using rhyme in their poems because the results are often nursery-rhymish, and they spend more time trying to rhyme than on the writing itself. However, there's always that one student who *has* to rhyme his poems.

Wind is as fast as
    a jet,
But when a windstorm comes up
You haven't seen nothin yet.
It blows like a whistle, pushes you
    on the ground.
It keeps on blowin and makes you
    lay down.
It sneaks up on you and makes you raise
    your hand.
It puts you on its back and takes you to
    another land.
It takes you through the woods, up
    over the trees
Then to the ground and makes
    you sneeze.
It pops you on the back and then
    on the head.
It takes you to your house and puts you
    in your bed.
That is what the wind will do
    it's true.

—JOE

And that's fine too.

Color Prose Poems, Writing About Feelings

Throughout the year Kate had her students write about their feeings. The first time she tried it the results were disappointing. She got such things as "I feel fine" or "I feel good" or "I feel bad today." After that, she always did word-shaking with them before they wrote, and the fluency of their writing gradually improved.

Often she had her students write about colors and include their feelings about the color. The results were imaginative prose-poems.

Blue is like the ocean. It makes you think of the Blue sky
and pretty Blue mountain streams. Blue is like Blue birds
flying in the breeze. Blue is like a mountain flower that
blooms once every five years. Blue is like granite rock all
smooth and warm by the rain.

—STACY

Green is like a meadow with flowers and children running in the grass. Green is like the wind sweeping over a meadow on a sticky green day with all the green flowers and people. Green is like children walking down a aisle with beautiful green flowers. Green is the best color in the world.

—PATRICIA

White reminds me of sadness because I think of the salty tears running down my face. White's the color of a cold, cold day when you're looking out of the window. White is the color of a broken heart...

—CHAD

And then, of course, there was Joe, who rhymed his poem.

red makes me happy

red is for Apples. if you don't like Apples
don't shake my tree. don't throw them away—
give them to me.

—JOE

Immediate and long-range publication of student writing, working with students as they write, acting as editor rather than grader of student writing, word-shaking to encourage fluency and to stimulate writing—these are the things that helped make Kate Kirby's writing program an overwhelming success. But there are other things harder to describe about how she teaches writing to young children: her enthusiasm and her positive approach as she works with kids and their writing; her sensitivity to what the student is trying to say and to those flashes of brilliance she finds and encourages. Without that, the exercises are empty and the techniques barren.

Three Prose Exercises

This chapter is about teaching poetry, although you have no doubt already been thinking about how some of the assignments could easily be used for prose. And I want to share quickly with you three prose exercises Kate used with her sixth graders that were particularly successful. I also chose these because they seem easily adaptable to older kids.

Strange Questions and Strange Answers

Kate adapted this exercise from *Making It Strange* (11). You simply ask a series of questions, making them as strange as possible, and encouraging the kids to write strange answers in response. Then you share the answers. It's a good way to work on personification and metaphor. It's also a good early exercise to get the kids writing.

These are some of the questions Kate used. You can add your own.

- Which is sweeter—rain or July?
- Which is louder—a smile or a frown?
- Which is quicker—yellow or black?
- What is crisper—winter or celery?

The Pencil

As a variation of the Being the Thing exercise, Kate gave the students these simple instructions: "You *are* a pencil. Tell me a story." This is what Claude wrote:

> Someone picks you up and puts you on his ear. My gosh—he's got dandruff! I just hate it when he bites on me and when he turns me upside down and eats my head off...

Later she asked the students to write how it felt to be *sharpened*.

The Bullet

Also a Being the Thing exercise, this was one of the favorites of Kate's students. It's a *sequenced* writing. Give the students each set of instructions in order and let them write about that part before going on to the next step.

1. Imagine that you are a bullet in the gun of a trigger-happy outlaw. You are lying in the chamber of the outlaw's gun. You are about to be fired. Remember, you are the bullet. What thoughts rush through your mind as the outlaw takes aim?
2. The gun is fired! You shoot out! What are your reactions? How does your body feel as you hurtle through the air with the wind rushing by you?
3. You are now just a few feet from your target—the heart of a stage coach driver. What are you thinking about as you get closer and closer to your target?
4. How would you feel if you hit the driver and he died?

This is a good beginning exercise for narrative writing because it does not overwhelm the student with a whole story to write at one time. And it helps teach organization. There are many possible variations of the exercise.

More About Poetry

There really is a magic to poetry. It will capture some students if you give it a chance. We either make it harder than it is, or ought to be; or we teach it with gimmicks. Don't get me wrong. I'll use a gimmick in a heartbeat if it will interest a student and get him writing; I become concerned when the writing doesn't grow beyond the gimmicks. I've found, however, that students become poets if they're around poetry a lot. It's catching.

And I cannot say it enough. *If you write poetry, your students will write poetry.* I do not presume to teach what I do not practice.

Reviewing the chapter again after some years, I'm concerned about how you might read categories like "slow kids" and "exceptional student poet." I don't like ability grouping. I believe it is bad for kids and we ought to quit doing it. And my experience tells me it just plain does not work in the writing class. The fact remains, in every school where I have worked, with one exception in Richmond, Kentucky, the kids came to me categorized as either "high," "average," or "low" by the school. And the defeatist attitude and poor self-esteem of the young writer in the low level class is what you and I have to deal with, whether we agree with the system or not.

Every poet seems to teach poetry differently from everybody else, and I may have been asleep at the switch ten years ago, but there seems to be a lot more help teaching it than there was then. *Writing!* magazine (General Learning Corp., 60 Revere Dr., Northbrook, IL 60062) is a good source for poetry ideas and all kinds of writing. Don't overlook Florence Grossman's high school text, *Getting from Here to There: Writing and Reading Poetry* (Boynton/Cook, 1982), and the fine books by Stephen Dunning and his colleagues for Scholastic. And if you don't know them, the Teachers and Writers Collaborative (5 Union Square West, New York, NY 10003) is a good place to start. Their *Whole Word Catalogue* is still in print, along with its thicker sequel and a lot of other resources you will want to get your young poets started.

Here are a few more suggestions for beginning poetry in your classroom.

1. *Read poetry* aloud *a lot.* Somebody in the room will get the idea and write some of their own. Pretty soon everybody will be writing poetry. This works better if the poetry you read to them is your own.

2. *A simple starter is what I call the Spontaneous Word Poem.* The idea is from a sensitive article by Lamont Leon (*NEA Today,* May 1984). Bring a shoebox to class. Call it your "imagination" box and ask each student to take a word from it, but keep the word a secret until you call on them. Then put on the board each student's word, one under the other in columns, skipping around the room from student to student. Or list the words any other way that looks good to you.

Now the poem is written. Yes, it's just that simple. Except your next job is to *perform* it. Read it aloud and beat out the rhythm of the words with a pencil. Sing it. Read it like a death march. Cry it. Read it fast and breathlessly. Read it with sombre significance. Play with it. Have fun with it.

Don't erase it. Leave it up as a reminder that poetry is in the hearing, and in the surprises.

3. *In the same article, Leon suggests starting kids with haiku because the Japanese form is short.* The point is not to stress the 5 syllable/7 syllable/5 syllable formula, but to get them to look for and record vivid images in three short lines. Get them to look for surprises, not just shoehorn words into a 5-7-5 pattern. Haiku is as much a way of seeing as it is of writing. One way to encourage them to look for surprises is to take your favorite haiku and put them up on the overhead without the last line. Ask your young writers to supply a third line of their own and to stretch for the unique image.

Go outside. Brilliant autumn days, sharp winter ones, and those magic days in spring require haiku writers to touch them.

4. *Don't overlook the simple List Poem.* A favorite formula lists the senses about any subject you pick.

A frog, for example.

> It looks like—*a baggy suitcase.*
> It sounds like—*sandpaper.*
> It feels like—*a wiggle.*
> It smells like—*green.*
> It tastes like—*yuck!*

Or you can use colors for a quick and enjoyable poem.

> Red sounds like—
> Dark blue tastes like—
> Black feels like—
> Purple smells like—

And there are many, many other kinds of List Poems. Musical Metaphors, Lies, Wish Lists, 10 Interesting Things, 10 Boring Things, Ugly Things, Lovely Things. And don't forget Catalogues of flowers, birds, animals, cities, countries, friends and the pleasure of playing with the names of things. Remember what you are looking for are unusual combinations, unique twists, surprises.

5. *You can even cluster a poem, as Gabriele Rico demonstrates in* Writing the Natural Way. The object is to write a poem to someone you know well, beginning with a bold statement like "This is a poem about..." or "This is my poem for..." Perhaps a jot list would work just as well about the subject of your poem, although I like Rico's clustering technique.

In this poem to my daughter, what I tried to do was put it all into one long sentence. You can see that it really is a kind of formula poem with the opening and then *who* and *whose* clauses followed by a series of *ands*. It's also a nice way to end this chapter.

Anna

This is my poem to Anna, whom I hear talking and playing somewhere in my happy house

whose gap-toothed laughing is pure body-joy and sunlight to her daddy, dancing dark eyes and third grade jokes, and open mouthed singing

who is sitting in the green yard with a cat nobody can touch or even get close to curled purringly in her lap in the sun

and who is running across the afternoon, knees and elbows and boyish strength and little girl skinniness and the fun of just running for no reason

whose watching can be heron-still but never quiet, looking at woodpeckers, frogs, shiners, lizards, baby squirrels, bugs, and looking a long time at turtles and at the living day growing around her

and who does her homework on the floor, books open and scattered like fallen birds around her, intent on the hard mysteries of math, the jokes of spelling, the games of social studies and stringing questions across my evening

and because I listen in this house for your talking and I dance inside at your laughing and because you're almost NINE and this spring is greening toward summer

and to tell you a daddy's love is one thing but I really like you, too,
Daughter

Notes

1. From "An Interview with the Poet, Constance Carrier," by David
Bernetich. *Pembroke Magazine,* No. 14, 1982.

2. Philip Levine. From an interview in *Reading and Writing Poetry: Successful
Approaches for the Student and Teacher,* Oryx, 1983.

3. Johnny Sheridan, Teresa Lott, Winford Butler, Gene Smith, Happy Smith,
Cindy Strickland, Jimmy French, Terrill Brawner, Teresa Lyle, and Heidi Falls,
all of whose poetry appears in the first section of this chapter, were students at
Gainesville High School, Gainesville, GA.

4. Stephen N. Judy. *Explorations in the Teaching of Secondary English.* Harper &
Row, 1972.

5. Nancy Martin, et al. *Writing and Learning Across the Curriculum 11-16.* Ward
Lock, 1976.

6. Ken Macrorie, *Uptaught.* Hayden, 1970.

7. Kenneth Weber. *Yes, They Can.* McDougal Littell, 1974.

8. This section of the chapter is reprinted, with some changes, from
Connecticut English Journal, Vol. 10, No. 2 (Spring, 1979). Jimmy Barfield is from
Gainesville, GA.

9. The following student writings are from Kate Kirby's students, Clarke
Middle School, Athens, GA.

10. Kenneth Koch. *Wishes, Lies, and Dreams.* Vintage, 1970; Barbara Esbensen.
A Celebration of Bees. Winston, 1975.

11. *Making It Strange.* Prepared by Synectics, Inc. Harper & Row, 1968.

CHAPTER SEVEN

What Is Good Writing?

Quality...you know what it is, yet you don't know what it is. But that's self-contradictory. But some things *are* better than others, that is, they have more quality. But when you try to say what quality is, apart from the things that have it, it all goes *poof!* There's nothing to talk about. But if you can't say what Quality is, how do you know what it is, or how do you know that it even exists? If no one knows what it is, then for all practical purposes it doesn't exist at all. But for all practical purposes it really *does* exist. What else are the grades based on? Why else would people pay fortunes for some things and throw others in the trash pile? Obviously some things are better than others...but what's the "betterness"?...So round and round you go, spinning mental wheels and nowhere finding anyplace to get traction. What the hell is Quality? What *is* it? ...

A person who sees Quality and feels it as he works is a person who cares.

—ROBERT M. PIRSIG (1)

I know good writing when I read it. So do you. But what Robert Pirsig says about quality, and our perception of quality in our lives, is also true of writing. Knowing that writing is good is one thing. Determining exactly what *makes* writing good is more difficult. Perhaps it's a sense that the writer took care with what he wrote, as Pirsig suggests. *Good writers* care about their writing and take care in writing it. Or perhaps a feeling for good writing has more to do with what James Dickey said he looked for when he read a new poet. "I wish merely to be able to feel and see and respond to what the poet is saying, and with as much strength and depth as possible" (2). Considered in this way, good writing is writing that touches me on a personal level. It's writing I can respond to. And the stronger the response, the better the writer?

Well, that's part of it. Still, that's not much help when you're faced with a stack of student papers. You know what you've done before has made no difference you can see. And you're probably thinking with Gene Olson that "Writing is like falling in love in that we know it happens but no one is quite sure how it happens" (3).

One reason we have not been as successful with student writers as we could have been is that our only criterion for quality in student writing has been correctness. It's a tenuous thread when the "goodness" of young writers hangs by whether they can avoid a narrow range of errors in spelling, punctuation, diction, and formal usage. Teaching writing with correctness as the only criterion is deadly. And except for a very few students, who manage to write well in spite of our intimidation, the error-avoidance approach to teaching writing produces uniformly bad writing.

Dan and I maintain that you can find and nourish quality in the writing of your students without scouring their papers for surface errors. Donald Murray uses a phrase we like when he talks about the "listening eye" of the writing teacher (4). This listening eye is the sensitivity the teacher must develop to see the good things in the writing of even the most immature student writer. One of our first jobs—and maybe the most important—is to look for potential in the often-stumbling attempts our students make. Murray points out that some sign of skill in any area in a paper is hopeful. Perhaps it's only a few words in the whole paper, but we can begin to build from that strength.

Listen carefully with your eyes when you read those first attempts of your students, and train yourself through practice to be sensitive to the good things that are there. Peter Elbow reminds us that "a person's best writing is often all mixed up together with his worst. It all feels lousy to him as he's writing, but if he will let himself write it and come back later he will find some parts of it are excellent. It is as though one's best words come wrapped in one's worst" (5). What our students need first is for us to help them see their best words that are usually hidden by their worst. Skip the detailed criticism and offer, instead, encouragement in those areas where it will do the most good.

Sometimes improvement comes almost spontaneously from practice. Peter Elbow again: "The mind is magic. It can cook things instantaneously and perfectly when it gets going" (5). Your open, receptive attitude will probably bring out more potentially good writing and cause more real growth in your student writers than anything else you do, but you still have to have a clear idea of what you're looking for when you pick up a student's paper. Otherwise, even your best intentions and most positive reactions are random, perhaps confusing, and finally ineffectual.

After you have gotten your students started writing and after they're used to writing daily, then you'll need to approach their writing systematically, looking for the best things they are doing and helping them see the good and how to grow with it. First you get them writing—you can't do anything until they're no longer afraid to put words on paper. Then the work of growing good writers begins by growing the good in their writing.

So what is good writing? What are the criteria we can use in the classroom?

Ken Macrorie says: "Most good writing is clear, vigorous, honest, alive, sensuous, appropriate, unsentimental, rhythmic, without pretension, fresh, metaphorical, evocative in sound, economical, authoritative, surprising, memorable and light" (6). Whew! That kind of list almost takes your breath away. What we propose is working criteria for good writing in the English classroom, touchstones that will give you a systematic review of the most important qualities of good writing that you can identify and encourage and build on in student writing.

There's nothing really new about the ten categories we give you here, and the influence of Macrorie, Murray, Miller, Judy, and others will be immediately apparent. We've kept the list as simple and as short as possible, knowing that long and tediously complex catalogs are of little use to anyone, especially teachers grappling with the immediate problems of student writers, and all those papers. The criteria are listed more or less in order from the most basic to the most sophisticated. But that does not necessarily mean that your students will demonstrate that they can write in a recognizable human voice before they begin consciously to use words rich in sound effects and imagery. Nor are the categories mutually exclusive. In the act of writing, many things happen at once, and the mental processes are incredibly complex—especially when the writing is going well. Listen to Peter Elbow again about the magic that can happen at such times: "You should expect yourself at times to write straight onto the paper words and thoughts far better than you knew were in you. You should look for it and want it. To expect anything less is to consider yourself brain-damaged" (5).

Most of the examples used with these criteria came from a mixed sophomore and junior class of mine. The papers are revisions of Verbal Snapshots (see Chapter 4), collected for two weeks in journals, with the most interesting picked for more careful work in class. I used one ordinary set of papers to demonstrate that you can expect to find these qualities to some degree in the writing of *all* your students in *every* set of papers you read. It's not only the exceptional paper written by the rare and brilliant student that has good writing in it.

The Kirby-Liner Working Criteria
for Good Student Writing

Good Writing Is Interesting

1. Voice   One human being talking to another
                  Makes the reader believe
                  Strong, recognizable imprint of the writer

2. Movement   Words building/pull the reader along
                  It goes somewhere with variety
                  A sense of order

3. Light touch   Writer doesn't take himself/herself too
                      seriously
                  Even-tempered

4. Informative   Important
                  Has substance/says something
                  Adds to our experience

5. Inventive   Unique experience
                  Something new/or something old in a new way

Good Writing Is Technically Skillful

6. Sense of   Makes contact with the reader
   audience   Anticipates reader's needs
                  Compliments the reader with meaning

7. Detail   Concrete
                  Photographic
                  Selective
                  Words that put the reader there

8. Rhythm   Words that sing
                  Sounds effortless

9. Form   How it looks on the page
                  What it looks like in print

10. Mechanics   Observes conventions of spelling, punctuation,
                      usage
                  Enlightened control

There are two main attributes of good writing, to which all other qualities are related. Good writing is interesting to read, and good writing is written with technical skill. Good writing is fun. The first and most basic requirement we make of anything we read is that it interest and/or entertain us. Without that, it becomes drudgery. Good writers create and keep the interest of their readers. And this is where we need to begin in teaching quality in writing to our students.

A reader's interest cannot be sustained for long, however, unless the writer demonstrates some skill with the techniques of writing. The craftmanship with which words, sentences, paragraphs are manipulated in an essay—or such things as dialogue in a short story or imagery in a poem—these affect our judgment of a work and either frustrate us or add to our pleasure as we read. Therefore, the two important questions for us to ask when faced with a stack of student papers are: What are the qualities that make writing interesting? and What are the attributes of technically skillful writing?

What Makes Good Writing Interesting?

1. *Good writing has a voice.* Good writing talks to you with a real voice; it has the recognizable imprint of the author on it. Ken Macrorie calls this quality the "record of the authentic voice of another person," and Donald Murray says that "The writer's voice may be the most significant element in distinguishing memorable writing" (6, 4).

A lot of rhetoric and composition texts talk about *style.* A writer's voice on the page *is* his style. And that human sound is what makes a piece of writing real for us. That's the reason bad translations are so frustrating to read, and that's why best sellers are not written like doctoral dissertations.

> I looked down at the terribly small piece of chicken on my plate—somehow there just didn't seem to be any justice—I always received the smallest piece possible.
>
> The girl sitting next to me looked at me for a slight moment as though I was a creature from another world and then turned back into her own small world—herself. She laughed a high inhuman laugh that seemed to pierce the whole room with sound.
>
> First I thought she was laughing at me and my measly portion of chicken—but only of news of how her ex-boyfriend had received a blow in the eye which now wore the colors black, blue, green, and a tinge of red.
>
> I thought how she would look that same way but then another devilish though entered my mind.
>
> "I hope she gets fat!"
>
> —TRACY (7)

Tracy is beginning to find her voice as a writer, and in places in this paper I hear a very human voice talking about an irritating neighbor in a crowded school cafeteria. There is a hey-I've-done-that-too kind of feeling about the piece that gives it its humor. We share experiences and feelings with the writer because she speaks in her own voice.

To have a real voice, a piece does not necessarily have to be written in first person singular.

> Waiting eagerly behind the dark stage wings for her music cue to enter into brightly colored spot lights. Lights with cool and warm colors. Nervous, tense muscles, and pounding heart. Thinking over her part before darting on stage to do her dream ballet.

—LYNN (7)

Good writing is *honest* writing. Lynn takes a chance with her reader, sharing something very important to her. There's no mistaking that the "nervous, tense muscles, and pounding heart" are hers. And if my only remark about her paper is to put "FRAG/—30%" in the margin beside that phrase, then I will have proven myself an insensitive pedagogue (and a poor rhetorician). She risks herself a little with me. My responsibility is to be receptive, to *listen* to her voice. And encourage her to use her voice when she writes.

If you want your students' writing to have a real voice, then you will have to accept their individual voices and be accepting of what they have to say. If they turn in papers that are stilted and dead, ask them to "tell me about it" when they next write. Structure ways for them to *talk* about it before they write it. And help them find their voices by free writing often. In fact, the only way the students will find and refine their voices in their writing is to practice using that voice on the page regularly—and I recommend *daily*.

2. *Good writing moves.* Good writing starts here and goes to there, and it pulls the reader along with it. Whether it's a narrative or an elegant argument or a poem, there is movement and order to it. Macrorie says of good writings simply that "they build" (6). Good writing also gives us enough variety, enough changes and twists and turns and sometimes surprises, to keep us interested and reading.

A sense of order appears in student writing first as the straight chronological this-happened-first-and-then-this-and-finally-this order of the narrative. Lynn's piece has less than fifty words, yet it shows this kind of order—a ballerina waiting, her nervousness growing, and the beginning of the dance anticipated.

You will also find that students will begin to place special emphasis on the first and last sentences of their writing. They feel the movement and order of the piece and are looking for ways to strengthen it.

> She was in a bad mood anyway. He kept on bugging her, so finally right before the curtains opened she agreed to go and buy him popcorn. Secretly she had a crush on him, but he was sitting next to another girl. It was a very scary movie, when she came back the theater was silent. She walked down the aisle with a big bucket of buttered popcorn. He was sitting directly behind her, when she started to hand it to him, both of their hands slipped. In the silence of the movie, all there is to hear is—"DUMBASS!"
>
> —KATHY (7)

Kathy's opening sentence is particularly effective. With a casual and natural sounding ill-will, it starts moving us toward the climactic ending of a too-loud and embarrassing vulgarity uttered in the silence of a dark movie house. Tracy's writing about the frustrations of the cafeteria has a similar movement, but there the action is all in the flow of thoughts and feelings of the writers.

Fairly early you can expect your students to begin playing around with more complicated movement.

> Holding his hand, I was anticipating the shock. Slowly and smoothly the music flowed. Mouth agape, Henry stared blankly at the screen. As the girl opened the closet door, Henry's grip tightened. Suddenly the dead man's body rocked back and forth through the doorway. With a shriek of terror Henry's hold on my hand was like a tourniquet.
>
> —BETH (7)

Macrorie talks about creating oppositions that bring surprise, and Beth does something like that in this piece. It's a narrative, of course, and therefore chronological. Beginning and ending are stressed as in the other examples. But the movement zigzags back and forth from the boy holding her hand to the action on the screen, building tension in a short space that is released in the last sentence with Henry's shriek.

Some of the writings in that set of papers seem to begin anywhere and end nowhere, with no sense of order at all. But a close reading shows that most have some kind of movement somewhere in the paper. And as these young writers grow, some of their writings will become very complex. But the place to start is with simple narrative order and the encouragment to "tell me about it."

3. *Good writing has a sense of humor.* Good writing often laughs. I like a statement by Victor Frankl that humor is one of "the soul's weapons in the fight for self-preservation" (8).

Three of the four examples we have already read from the set of papers treat their subjects with humor. Sustaining humor is as difficult as sustaining high seriousness.

Babysitting

Babysitting...Cleaning up the toys and papers and clothes and baseball cards and the bubble gum stuck to the rug, the half burnt pots of spaghettios and the dried grape juice on the white counter. The boys you thought were God's sweet angels turned out to be the dirty dozen instead. One thinks he is the six million dollar man, but is the fifty dollar hyperactive midget, who is working for the CIA on figuring out if babysitters are the backbone of the U.S.'s economy crisis. *Everyone* needs babysitters, at least I think everyone needs them.

Babysitting...Fighting over Hogan's Heroes and Gomer Pyle, compromising on Sesame Street (Well, I guess Stalag 13 deserved a rest). A moral came from an animated fable called "The crow and the pitcher." This show can be found to be very stimulating, but don't you dare tell anyone I said that. They all think I'm spastic already, and I really don't want to visit my friends in Milledgeville on anything but a social visit. One of my friend's daddy is the Chief of Security for the *State Hospital,* and he told me I can have a room at half-rate. Laugh. It was a joke. I *think* it was a joke.

Babysitting...Mr. Rogers blaring on the screen, the phone ringing, the door bell buzzing, and the already burnt spaghettios burning again, only all at once this time, and just when you are on the verge on taking that room at the State Hospital, the dirty dozen comes in and says, "Hey, you're not such a bad sitter." I've won the first half—score Dirty Dozen 14, Tired Tyrant 20. Yet, the second half is coming, and I don't think my reinforcements can take bathtime *and* 8:30 bed check. I thought I enjoyed kids. But Jekyll and Hyde here seem to want to change my mind, and I have to admit the offer is tempting.

Babysitting...The tired tyrant was just accused of uncalled for brutality since no extra time is scheduled past the routine 8:30 bed time. She will be sentenced to die at 3:30 Wednesday afternoon (the next time I sit for the Rat Patrol). I would prefer daisies and forget-me-nots to carnations. You can't afford roses or baby's breath, because life is cruel to English Teachers who should be guru prophets or Yamaha dealers.

Babysitting...Life is ending so it doesn't matter what a few generous words that "Spazz" may have left, except I would like to get a kiss from the whole muppet gang, especially the Cookie Monster. I will also sue them for all they are worth (which is quite a lot) if I get that incurable disease "Manikin of the Mouth."

The End

Well, I think I would like George Burns to write my monologue from now on—Johnny Carson's writers stink. Moral: You can figure out many things to do when you have to do something.

—ALICE (7)

Alice's rambling essay about the perils and joys of babysitting is successful, in part, because she laughs at herself, and because of the real voice we hear talking to us.

Good writers don't take themselves too seriously even when they're writing about a serious subject.

As I gain the crest of the mountain I see in the fading light the solitary figure of my father as he loads his muscular arms full of firewood. I walk up silently expecting not to be heard but his keen ears catch the noise of what I thought were silent footsteps. He turns and with a quick dodging motion I barely escape a flying piece of wood. He laughs and I open the door for him.

No words are spoken until he notices that my hands are empty of game.

"Where's the meat?" he says as he throws another piece of wood on the fire.

"Still in its skin, I guess." I laugh at my remark and he looks at me sternly and I get the message that he'd rather I keep my remarks to myself. A silent period takes place as we sit down to eat supper.

—BILLY (7)

I like this excerpt. It shows a relationship between a boy and his father handled with a light touch. As Macrorie points out, "You'll be surprised to find how many writers you admire are humorous or light" (6). By the way, Billy is one of the best woodsmen for his age I know.

The excerpt comes from a narrative of his about bear hunting, which he will tell you is very serious business indeed.

Laugh with your students when they are funny, keep your silence when their humor falls flat or misses the mark. Encourage them to write in their own voices and not to take themselves or any subject too seriously.

4. *Good writing is informative.* Good writing *says* something. It adds to our experience. Murray says, "There must be content in an effective piece of writing. It must add up to something. This is the most important element in good writing, but...it is often discovered last through the process of writing" (4). He also says that each writer has his own area of authority.

> He's a large one I thought as I saw the track in the soft mass that ran beside the creek. I unslung the battered 30-30 Marlin from my back and even as I did it I could see the moss rising back from the track. I clicked the safety off, this track was fresh, very fresh. I had no intention of running into a big brownie at this time of the evening. The sun was setting and the woodland around me was taking on the murky shapes of coming night. I turned silently and started away slowly and carefully with my rifle still cradled in my arms.
>
> —BILLY (7)

Billy's area of authority is hunting. He writes about it well because he *knows* it well.

All writers, even the most inexperienced student writers, have their own area of authority. We need to tell our students that they have unique experiences to talk about. We need to teach them to reach into their memories for those experiences that will say something to their readers.

> Backstage at a ballet performance is one of the most hectic places imaginable. Costumes are hanging everywhere. The smell of hair spray, sweat, and ballet bags fills the room. The make-up lights are hot and very bright which practically causes your make-up to run before getting it on. People are nervous, fidgety, scared. I noticed that some were very quiet, going over steps in their minds, and others were nervously chit-chatting, trying to take their minds off being scared. The excitement in the air is thick. Curtain is in 5 minutes.
>
> —SUSAN (7)

Susan, like Lynn, is an aspiring ballerina. She gives us a glimpse into that world and shares feelings about it that only someone with her experience and perspective can. To use Murray's phrase again, she "satisfies the reader's hunger for information."

Billy and Susan also ask something of us. They challenge us to move into their worlds, however briefly, and take part in their experiences. As Macrorie says, good writing asks something of us as readers, but it also rewards us with meaning.

5. *Good writing is inventive.* Good writing says something new. Or it says something old in a new way. Writing is infinite in its possibilities: the perception, emphasis, voice, concerns, and—perhaps most important—the *imagination* of each writer is different from those of every other writer.

Alice's writing is certainly inventive, and Billy's way of presenting the relationship between his father and himself is not what I would have expected. But even quieter writings, sometimes with almost no overt action involved, may suddenly flash with the writer's inventive way of saying things.

Photoscript Final

An older man, about fifty years old, sits at a roundtop table. A cup of de-caffeinated coffee, sipped noisily at one minute intervals, is in front of him to the right. A pack of cigarettes rests, at an angle, on the plate-sized, half-full, ceramic ashtray to his left. His rugged, aged semi-line-creased face is covered from the cheekbone down with a salt and pepper beard. His upper lip is invisible in the multi-earth-colored mustache. He sits with his right elbow resting on the table with his forehead planted in his palm. The smoke stained fingers are visible in his dark brown fine hair. On the table in front of him he reads the words off of the paper that he has written. He destroys the still image, in what seems only a split second, to light a cigarette, sip the coffee, clear his throat, then he resumes the position. His smoking cigarette strategically and instinctively finds its place in the right hand, between the yellow fingers.

—RICHARD (7)

Richard's description is static, until there is a brief flurry of activity that returns to stillness, and that emphasizes the statue-like quiet of his subject. It's finely done with a subtle touch that makes the piece memorable. I particularly like the cigarette that returns, as though by itself, to the smoke-yellowed fingers of the man reading at the table—

and ends the piece with quiet emphasis. This is pretty sophisticated writing for a student writer.

What Makes Good Writing Technically Skillful?

6. *Good writing has a sense of audience.* Good writing anticipates its audience. The writers are aware of their readers and their needs as the writing progresses, sometimes directly by answering questions readers might ask or talking to the *"you"* who is reading the piece, at other times in ways as complex as the elaborate compliment paid the reader when allusions are used in a poem or in the subtle intricacies of a well-formed argument. But always there is the feeling of *contact* between a real person writing and another real person reading.

Sometimes the writer plays with the reader. Alice writes for an audience of one—"I would prefer daisies and forget-me-nots to carnations. You can't afford roses or baby's breath, because life is cruel to English teachers who should be guru prophets or Yamaha dealers"— but the joke is really for the entire class who know my reputation and the fact that I enjoy motorcycles. Even in a private piece, the feeling for a reader out there sharing the experience of the writer adds to the enjoyment of the work. This next paper by Richard was intended as a personal writing, perhaps one that I would not even read (see Chapter 4, cocoon exercise).

Cocoon

I float in peace in my cocoon—fluffy cotton walls, not visible to sight but soft to the touch. Air sweet. Sweeter than honey to the taste. Being suspended as I am in total weightlessness my mind is free, free as the wind is free to blow and take residence any place it pleases. Having this freedom I travel to the limit of boundless thoughts—Here I can be sad but not cry, happy but not smile, wonder but not be confused, find answers to questions not asked, war with the real, be at peace with fantasy. I have been shaken and torn away from my cocoon—I want to return—I never want to leave. If you see me but cannot find me—*that* is where I shall be...I was really there—

—RICHARD (7)

Although it's private, Richard cannot resist a playful nudge to his reader as he ends his fantasy. And one of the most important steps in the growth of the immature writer is when he becomes aware that there is an audience out there. Richard seems to have reached that awareness.

7. *Good writing uses detail but not too much detail.* Good writing is selective. It selects just the right details from the chaos of sensation that threatens to overwhelm the writer, and it particularizes the experience for the reader as it does so. This is the quality Murray calls clarity—"a simplicity which is appropriate to the subject. The writer has searched for and found the right word, the effective verb, the clarifying phrase" (4). Along with the writer's voice, perhaps it's the selection of detail that makes what is said more *real* to us.

As I was sitting in the library, I noticed an old man at the table beside me. He looked like a retired soldier. His face was old, dark, and wrinkled as if from the worries of war. He was rather fat and very tall. He was dressed in a khaki shirt and pants, and the pants were tucked into a pair of old boots. The boots were faded green and looked like they'd been through hell. He was reading *Douglas Reenan.* It looked like a rather boring book. His briefcase before him was stacked full of books and old papers which were yellow at the edges. His glasses were lying on top of the briefcase. There were more books lying on the table—*American Espionage* and war books. His eyes began to droop. He put down the book, rubbed his eyes and leaned on his knees with his elbows. Then he picked up another book and began reading in the middle of it.

—SUSAN (7)

I like the way Susan particularizes the old man with his khaki shirt and pants tucked into boottops, and I like the way she includes the titles of a couple of books he is reading, and the glasses lying on the briefcase. Her description has a photographic reality because she chooses to include little things that help us see the man.

Look at these telling details from the examples of student writing used in this chapter:

"...the colors black, blue, green, and a tinge of red."

—TRACY (7)

"Mouth agape..."

—BETH (7)

"...the toys and papers and clothes and baseball cards and the bubble gum stuck to the rug, the half-burnt pots of spaghettios and the dried grape juice on the white counter."

—ALICE (7)

"His rugged, aged semi-line-creased face...the mutli-earth-colored mustache...His smoking cigarette...finds its place in the right hand, between the yellow fingers."

—RICHARD (7)

I have found that the student writer who is beginning to find a voice and who has a sense of audience will be able to use details effectively with little trouble. I try to show my students many models, pointing out effective uses of the little things, and I encourage as much close observation for writing as possible. And if they are ready, most of them seem to improve in picking up and using details that make their writing feel more real.

I find it much harder to teach students to cut their writings. Economy with words seems to be an ability that comes very late in the growth process of a writer, and my students are reluctant to throw away any of the words they've worked so hard to put on the page. With only one exception, all the student writings in this chapter could improve with a little careful cutting. The economy in Lynn's piece about the ballerina about to go on stage probably comes as much from her subject as from anything else.

Young writers seem to need to be comfortable in using detail before they are able to learn what they need to throw away. A Hemingway's ruthlessness doesn't come along very often. Any real success I've had teaching students to tighten their writing has been done individually and almost word by word. That kind of revision is complex and subtle and demands careful work done in conference. But come to think of it, I don't like to throw any of my stuff away either.

8. *Good writing uses words that sing.* Good writing is rich in imagery and associations, strong in rhythm and repetition, filled with word-play. The skillful prose writer uses the language resources of the poet, choosing words that are effective in sound and in metaphor. This is sophisticated stuff for most student writers, but you'll find that some of your students show signs of skill with word-play.

Look at these words that sing from the examples of student writing in this chapter:

Rhythm, repetition, and variation
Laugh. It was a joke. I *think* it was a joke...Mr. Rogers blaring on the screen, the phone ringing, the door bell buzzing, and the already burnt spaghettios burning again....

—ALICE (7)

Paradox, words that play with each other
Here I can be sad but not cry, happy but not smile, wonder but not be confused, and find answers to questions not asked, war with the real, be at peace with fantasy.

—RICHARD (7)

Imagery, the dramatic scene
As I gain the crest of the mountain I see in the fading light the solitary figure of my father...

—BILLY (7)

The smell of hair spray, sweat, and ballet bags fills the room.

—SUSAN (7)

Association, metaphor and simile
His upper lip invisible in the multi-earth-colored mustache...He destroys the still image...His smoking cigarette strategically and instinctively finds its place in the right hand...

—RICHARD (7)

Emphasis, the right verbs and nouns and adjectives
Mouth agape, Henry stared...

—BETH (7)

...the fifty dollar hyperactive midget...clothes that build into mountains...

—ALICE (7)

Sounds of speech, real dialogue
"Where's the meat?..."
"Still in its skin, I guess."

—BILLY (7)

Good writing seems to flow. There's nothing halting or awkward about it—it *sounds* easy. Like a good gymnast or archer or guitar player, the good writer makes a very difficult task seem effortless to the audience, and like them, achieves this apparent ease through practice, through caring about what is done, and through careful attention to detail. As James Dickey puts it, "I work it over to get that *worked-on* quality out of it" (2).

Working it over—and over, and over again—and listening with a practiced, sensitive ear each time is the only way I know for your student writers to make their words really sing.

9. *Good writing has form.* Good writing is graphically well designed. As Murray says, "A good piece of writing is elegant in the mathematical sense. It has form, structure, order, focus, coherence. It gives the reader a sense of completeness" (4). What we are ultimately concerned with is the ability of the writer to visualize the work *in print.*

A feel for form in writing is most obvious in a student writer's poetry.

> So came the night;
> It dropped down upon me
> I was blanketed by purple blackness
>   and everything was dry
>   and everything was wet
>   and everything was cold
> And my head fell forward in sorrow
>   But it was useless.
> I saw it in the shadows, in the
>   corners, behind every tree, every
> opaque object; but I still saw it.
> It creeped behind me and my
>   spine melted in the heat
>   of Death's passion.
> It grabbed me and held me
>   squeezing my last breaths
> into the fog.
>   and everything was dry
>   and everything was wet
>   and everything was cold.
>
>   —LYNNE (7)

Lynne has learned to use the line in her poetry—line endings and beginnings for emphasis, and line indentations to build her refrain. She *sees* the poem as it would appear printed and manipulates its form accordingly (and rather surprisingly in a few lines). She wants the poem read straight through, for example; there is no stanza break to create a pause.

Concern with form is properly the last, or one of the last, things you'll take up with student writers. To insist on too rigid a concern for form alone will only teach students to create a hollow shell. Some seem never to have a feel for it, although most have at least some sense of form. They know to write in paragraphs, for example—unless, like Alice, they create new forms to suit their treatment of a subject.

Bob Boynton comments on form in student writing: "There's no reason why people can't write good stuff in non-paragraph form (and not just poetry)" (9). Form finding is legitimate writing behavior even for young writers. Encourage your students to experiment with form.

10. *Good writing observes the conventions of mechanics and usage.* Finally, good writing observes those social conventions of written discourse that are expected by literate readers. Punctuation, spelling, and consistent usage are the most obvious. Notice that we list these conventions of *correctness* last in the criteria because we believe that eliminating surface errors is one of the last things a student writer needs to deal with. Once they are accomplished to some degree, they need to know that their readers will judge what they have to say by their ability to spell, put commas in the right place, and select the right endings for verbs. There's nothing wrong with insisting that competent writers also become competent proofreaders.

Oh, yes, there's one more category. I think it's the most important one.

Good writing is what you like (and what the writer likes). Dan and I believe that our working criteria can be of practical value in your classroom, but we realize that you're the expert in that room. You're the final authority for your student writers, and you have the responsibility for teaching them to write as well as possible in the time you have with them. Don't be afraid to trust your own judgment about what is good and bad in their writing. Make your own list of criteria to use with them, think about that list, and talk about it with your students; revise it frequently, but use it systematically.

Gene Olson says something that I try to keep in mind as I teach writing. "You can read all the books that have ever been written about writing and listen to lectures about writing until your ears twang but when you finally face the blank, accusing sheet of paper, you must realize that your writing is *YOU*...and you're stuck with you" (3). Finally, what we're trying to teach student writers is to recognize and pursue the good in their own writing, to make sound judgments about what is effective human expression and what is better changed or discarded. What we're trying to do is to make them the judge of quality in their own writing—to help them become people who see and feel quality, and who care.

Making Up Jokes About Bicycle Spokes and Red Balloons

I recently saw the qualities of writing in this chapter put on a kind of rating sheet for a state writing contest. At first I was pleased. It's always nice when you see someone has read what you have to say and thinks enough of your ideas to use them. I'm grateful for that. But we don't need another rubric for writing contests or writing assessments. We don't seem to be able to do much with writing in any official way other than grade it, score it, assess it, or make a contest out of it. That bothers me, a lot.

I can think of a lot more wonderful things to do with writing, and so can Dan, beginning with sharing it, celebrating it, talking about it, crying over it, maybe even cussing it when necessary. Mainly *enjoying* it and *struggling* with it together. Together. That to me is what teaching writing is.

We'll stand by the criteria in this chapter. We still like them just fine, thank you. Mainly because they are the criteria of a writer. You may have different words for how you look at your writing, and that's fine too. Share them with your kids. Don't use them to grade with. We grade too many papers anyway. Use the words you have to help your kids look at their writing as writers, and see the quality that is there.

Yes, it is there. Our job is to give them a name for it.

When I look at my own writing—and I put off judging it critically for as long as I can—I ask myself three questions before I ask somebody else "What do you think?" I look at it hard and ask, first, Does it tell the truth? In other words, is the piece as honest as I can make it. And I'm not concerned with realism here. Once past that test, the other two are usually asked and answered quickly. Does it say enough? And then, does it say more than it needs to?

What I expect from all of my students is that sooner or later they will read something to me and the class that will knock us off our feet, almost always because it's so honest and revealing—and surprising. I wait for that moment when they write something better than they know or expect. Then we begin to talk about voice and movement and a light touch and all of these other things writers need to talk about together.

Oh, yes, in case you didn't know, the title of this section is from one of John Prine's songs. The lines are "I drove an English teacher half insane/Making up jokes about bicycle spokes and red balloons."

Notes

1. Robert M. Pirsig. *Zen and the Art of Motorcycle Maintenance.* Morrow, 1974.
2. James Dickey. *Babel to Byzantium.* Grosset and Dunlap, 1968.
3. Gene Olson. *Sweet Agony: A Writing Manual of Sorts.* Windyridge, 1972.
4. Donald Murray. Workshop on Writing at Georgia State University, Atlanta, GA, Spring, 1979.
5. Peter Elbow. *Writing Without Teachers.* Oxford, 1973.
6. Ken Macrorie. *Writing to Be Read.* Boynton/Cook, 1984.
7. Tracy Tate, Lynn Aaron, Kathy Owen, Beth Murray, Alice Murray, Billy Sailors, Susan Carpenter, Richard Poston, Susan Hayes, and Lynne Moore were students at Gainesville High School, Gainesville, GA.
8. Victor Frankl. *Man's Search for Meaning.* Simon and Schuster, 1972.
9. Bob Boynton. Quoted from our editor's notes on the first draft of this chapter, 1979.

CHAPTER EIGHT

Responding to Student Writing

If any one word can stand for the essence of creating a climate...that allows creative impulse to grow and flourish, I think it would be the word *accepting*....This does not imply dishonest praise for something that is not as good as it can be. [Rather,] it means that you can look for and find in their work something of real or potential value, something that can be talked about seriously with a view toward strengthening it....

—BARBARA ESBENSEN (1)

Writing in isolation without lively response is like other solitary activities: singing in the shower or dancing in a coal mine. They may be pleasurable diversions, but without some response from an audience, they do not get much better. Most writers, and particularly your students, need the reactions of other human beings both during and after they write.

More to the point, they will demand to know what *you* think about their writing. Thus, the critical moment in any writing class is when beginning writers put their words in your hands. "Well, what do you think?" "You don't like it." "It isn't very good, is it?" They watch your eyes. You can't fool them with facile praise.

Over the years kids have developed a kind of self-preservation instinct in writing classes. They try to figure out what teachers want and give it to them. They have also learned to insulate themselves against the criticism of the writing teacher. If you're successful in drawing them out, in getting them to take a chance with language, then you must also accept the burden of bringing them along with sincere and measured response.

The secret of building good writer-responder relationships lies in the "touch" of the responder. Overly harsh, picky, and niggling criticism will spook any writer. The *only* way to help writers improve is to draw them out slowly with honest encouragement and support. I hear a little murmuring out there from those who label this kind of responding as soft-headed because it "doesn't discriminate enough between good and bad writing." The successful writing teachers I have observed are an idiosyncratic bunch, but they have one strong similarity. They draw out writers by searching for the good in their writings and by looking for potential with the same vigor some composition teachers waste on the great fragment hunt. Successful writing teachers never sit around in smoke-filled rooms ranting about how badly their students write or reading the latest collection of fault-ridden papers to horrified onlookers.

Good writing teachers have a positive mind set. Good writing teachers, because they have a backlog of miracles, know that student writings are full of clues to hidden potential. Good responding technique is at least fifty percent mental. Get your mind right, put your hand on this page, and resolve: "I will look for the good. I will go with anticipation to my students' writings."

Responding as a Person

You may need to spend some time practicing this responding business. Teachers are frequently unaware of the extent to which they respond as correction machines rather than people. Your response should be essentially a shared reaction. Participate with the writer by sharing your own thoughts and feelings as you read the writing. Look at these student papers and my responses to them.

My horse was painted red. The eyes and the bridle and saddle were painted on with black paint. I could ride that horse for hours. When I was mad or excited—I'd hop on that horse and ride it so hard that it would leave the floor and bang back down with a wonderfully loud wood-on-wood, spring-breaking ka-plam! One thing that really pleased me then was that the horse was always in the same mood I was. If I wanted to ride her hard—she seemed to want to fly and crash on the floor—if I was tired and rocked very slightly back and forth—she sometimes went to sleep before I could rest my head on her neck and "rest my eyes." She died one day in a fire at my aunt's house—but then I was "too old" for my horse and too young to be told about the fire.

—RITA (2)

Response

Your horse story brought back memories of an old, yellow horse who used to stay on our screen porch. He too was always ready for a rough ride. He was especially good at getting me over a serious pout. I particularly like the way you captured the sound of the horse hitting the floor: "wonderfully loud, wood-on-wood, spring-breaking ka-plam!" The irony of your last line "too old" and "too young" is also well done. Maybe you could do something with that in another paper.

My teacher was Irish—long black hair and icy blue eyes—the same color as the ocean in the Spring when it's glassy and I can see my toes. She always wore sexy clothes, tight skirts and sweaters that showed her breasts at the top. She always sat on the steps during recess watching us play, a sailor cap with the rim pulled down over her eyes, her skirt pulled up to her thighs revealing long perfect sun-tanned legs. The boys were crazy about her. They fought over that cherished place next to her on the steps daily.

—SHIRLEY (2)

Response

Ah those Irish teachers...I remember falling heavily for Ms. O'Rourke in the third grade. She still has a part of my heart. Nice job with the details: "icy blue eyes, sailor cap with the rim pulled down." You have a nice touch with people descriptions. Any more memorable characters in your past you could remember for us?

We moved from Lincolnton to Louisville the summer before I was in the fifth grade. I didn't know anybody. My mom had told me that the girls across the street from us had a "Man From Uncle Club." She said that they wore sweatshirts with "The Man From Uncle" written on them. This seemed strange to me. I had been used to Barbie dolls and an occasional exploration of the woods behind our house. "The Man From Uncle?" The first day that we were in Louisville, I cried all day. Why did we have to come to this stupid "Man From Uncle Place"?

—SHERI (2)

Response

Your piece brought back vividly the traumas of moving during elementary school. How I hated that first day in a new school! Your piece is good because you remembered specifics. The "Man From Uncle Place" is perfect. You've got a good ear for conversation. Try using dialogue in your writing. Let your mother speak.

My responses are personal and specific. I'm not suggesting that you should use every student paper to tell a story of your own, but you do need to find a way to let the writer know the story has touched you personally. Recounting a personal memory, arguing that you felt differently, or simply saying, "I can really tell you feel strongly about this," are all ways of letting the writer feel the impact of a personal reader.

Looking for the Good

The most significant role any teacher/reader can play is that of skilled responder: offering concrete, helpful suggestions about specific stuff in the writing. To respond means simply to react—orally or in writing—first as reader rather than as teacher. If we've got to look for the real reason kids don't learn to write, it's right here. Most teachers are not practiced as responders to student writing: editors, proofreaders, critics, raving lunatics, error counters, yes. But responders? No. Most kids never hear any specific, human, teacher-as-responder comments about what they write. First, teachers must discover the power of responding. Forget grading and evaluating for the moment. That kind of responding is less than helpful with beginning writers. Real responding differs from evaluation in being what Judy calls a "shared reaction" (3). It is here-and-now feedback. It is not a list of things the writer should do next time, but an immediate response to what the writer is saying, now.

The goal of the responder is to help writers discover what it is they want to say, and then challenge them to say it as powerfully as possible. Modeling is very important at this point. Showing them good examples from their own papers encourages them. Take those papers home and look for good things: a word, a phrase, a fresh idea. Then mark it; circle it; say, "I like this because..." Excerpt the part you like and bring it to class on a ditto. Show the excerpts to your students. Say, "Look what I found in your writings."

Yes, you will have to look through a world of chaff to find the kernels. Yes, there may be far more bad writing than good. But you start by rejoicing over the good rather than haranguing over the bad. I try never to lie to my students at this point. I tell them I had to "mine the slagheap looking for the gems." Sometimes we laugh together about the lengths I will go to to find something good in their writing, but this positive psychology in the writing class changes dramatically the students' willingness to work at the job and improve.

If you have not tried "mining the slagheap," wait no longer. Look at this example by an eighth grader.

If I Were Older

I would like to be older than I am now. Because when I get sixteen I could drive a car. When I get eighteen I could buy beer. When I get twenty-one I could drive a transfer truck. I want to become a trucker because I have been on trips with my daddy and I had fun talking to all those trucker's. Once I talked to a lady trucker. Her handle was "The Lady Buttermilk." She had came from VA. headed toward Big 'A' town (Atlanta) with a load of frozen food. We was her frontdoor until she got behind schedule and she put the pedal to the metal. Then she passed us and she became our frontdoor. One other time I was with daddy on a trip and we was in the rockin' chair. The old "Yellow Jacket" was at our frontdoor and the old "Halk Eye" was at our backdoor. We was just riding along because when ever a smokey was coming, my good-buddies would call for me over the old radio. Then we would slow down to double nickles (55 m.p.h.). We stayed in the ol' rockin chair until we got up to ol 'Sparkle City (Spartenburg South Carolina). Boy we had fun that day.

Maybe all those run-ons and fragments and usage errors catch your eye first. Maybe you're tempted to label this a hopeless case. But you took the pledge. You said you would look for potential. Plunge in. First look for *anything* you like about this writing. There's a lot to like. Personally, I like the CB language and the fact that the kid is the expert and I'm the novice. He seems comfortable with the writing process. I could suggest the writer give me a dialogue between "The Lady Buttermilk" and old "Yellow Jacket." Point out the expressions you like. Skip the bad stuff. Listen to what the kid is trying to tell you.

I watched a teacher listen to a spastic kid telling her a story about his adventure at the circus. He stuttered and slurred words and labored with his speech. The teacher listened with relaxed attention. She didn't take his story away from him nor did she give up. Use the same approach for your beginning writers. Stay with them. Let them stutter and stammer. Point out the good things in their writings and be patient.

As we discussed in Chapter 7, "good" in writing is not a static quality. "Good" is a growing thing. "Good" for the halting writer is different from "good" for the fluent writer. "Good" for the unpracticed writer is different from "good" for the effective writer. Goodness in writing is not an absolute standard and does not have a moral equivalent.

Teacher's Response

There's no way to escape it; your response to your students' writing remains very important to them. In a traditional class, your response is important because you control the grade. Whatever your response ("Write this over in ink"), students who want a good grade do what you tell them and the rest check out. Moffett and Emig have both been critical of the teacher as audience for all student writings, suggesting that this power as absolute arbiter of what is good writing is inhibiting and even damaging to student development. There are certainly enough horror stories around to illustrate the point, and there are surely some Ghengis Khan types who teach writing out there somewhere. But I don't think teachers as insensitive responders do irreparable damage. One writing class with a Murray or a Macrorie type can restore confidence and awaken latent language talent even in the oppressed. My point is that the teacher's response is absolutely critical to student writers, and such response does not necessarily stifle and enslave them. My observations of successful writing teachers confirm this. They move students to insightful observations and helpful criticism of their own work and the works of others by example, by talking them through the process.

As Macrorie says, "student writers need your sophisticated and experienced judgment. . . . Talk *about* writing clearly and authoritatively but never as an authoritarian. Don't deny your writers your expertise and opinions" (4).

What Kind of Response Is Helpful?

The writing teacher has to be willing to play a number of different responder roles, changing these roles as the writer develops. At the fluency stage, the writer needs attention, encouragement, and support. Responding at this level means seeing potential, drawing out, spotting future topics, learning more about the kid—rescuing nuggets from the slagheap. Responding to beginning students' writings demands more than gold stars and smiling faces. Almost immediately the teacher must respond as an informed reader, pointing to things that work in the students' writing: For Macrorie, strong verbs, vivid detail, inventions of all kinds, a strong, personal voice, ironies, oppositions are signs of development (4). For Peter Elbow "cooking" is hopeful (5). For Murray an abundance of information, sense of order, clarity, and an air of authority are the most important initial indications that a writer has potential (6). See Chapter 7 for our list of good stuff. Better yet, make your own list. Create your own examples of these. Publish excerpts and demonstrate to students what you're talking about. Look for things that work at the word, sentence, paragraph, and whole discourse level. Keep the classroom awash in examples of good writing.

Ruth gives her students the task of making their own list. She asks them to work in small groups with a stack of examples of student writing that represent the full range of stammering to confident voices. Students sort through the writings, identifying and categorizing the criteria for good writing. Ruth feels that all of the arguing and questioning that occurs through the disagreements helps students find their own voices for responding to one another's writing and helps prepare them for peer responding. Each group composes a classroom chart that represents the criteria. These charts are displayed in the classroom as reminders of response topics.

Later in the year, Ruth will ask students to compare their categories with the Kirby-Liner chart when the peer groups need new stretches. She says, "If students compose their own criteria, I've found they refer to these during their writing and peer editing sessions. While student labels for the criteria may vary from teacher models, it has been my experience that students identify the same broad categories—interest and technical expertise—as well as many of the same sub-points. I think it's valuable to have the list generated from the students' own understanding of good writing. It prompts them to articulate and emulate the qualities they admire in a piece of text."

As the student writer gains confidence and a sense of personal voice and worries less about getting words on the page, your role changes gradually to that of editor: not an insensitive authoritarian who wants you to write it only one way. Rather, you become a supportive editor whose goal is to help writers express as powerfully and effectively as possible what they have to say. Your responses should often be phrased as questions or as take-it-or-leave-it advice. The writer is in control of the writing; the responder sees alternatives or offers a second opinion, being careful not to take the piece away from the writer.

This is not to say that there won't be times when writer and editor are at an impasse. Several summers ago I was working in the Whittenberger Writing Project in Idaho. One of my favorite kids, crazy Ed, was struggling with a piece about growing up in Northern Idaho. Basically he had a strong piece about riding up in the cab of his dad's log truck and how that gave him such a sense of importance and power as a kid. Nice piece. But in the opening paragraph, Ed describes the scene of coming into town in the truck; and right in the middle of this rather solid descriptive stuff, a panther runs across the road. Now, the panther never returns in the story, plays absolutely no role in the guts of the piece, and I find it distracting, a random detail. I say to Ed, "Oh, this panther doesn't really work for me, Ed." I give him some other feedback and he wanders off to the computer to grind out another revision. He's back in twenty minutes with a new draft, and the panther is still in there. Repeat scene one. "Ed, about the panther, I think he ought to go." Ed does eight or nine drafts and the panther never leaves that first paragraph. Finally I'm adamant. I'm ranting, "Ed, the damn panther is hurting this piece!" Calmly Ed replies, "I read it to four other kids and they all liked it."

So much for the teacher-as-editor. The important point to make here is that the teacher-as-editor is not the same as the teacher-as-God. The give and take—the healthy dialogue between teacher and student writers about specific stuff in the kids' writing—is a worthwhile activity regardless of where it takes the piece of writing.

With confident writers and advanced writing classes, your role as responder may be more to function as a critic, arguing fine points of diction, asking for a more consistent point of view, and challenging the writer to return to rework the piece. Even as critic, the teacher-responder realizes that the writer and the writing are closely related. The criticism must clearly be to improve the piece, not punish the writer. It will be much easier to function as careful critic if you yourself are a writer. Teaching writing from inside out builds expertise and credibility, but more important, such inside experience gives you a knowing empathy for the difficult task of the writer.

So far this chapter sounds as if all writing classes consist of one writer and one teacher. Thankfully and painfully, this is not the case where you teach. You've got the usual 150 kids a day in five or six motley classes, and you're leaning back on your heels saying, "Well, sure, I could teach writing if they would put overachievers in my class, etc. etc. etc."

We hear you...this book is about teaching writing well in impossible situations. The key to providing enough response to student writers is, of course, to involve the students themselves as responders. Student response is often more forceful than your own and certainly may carry more weight. Okay, you tried that and nothing happened. You brought in some student papers and said, "What is good about this writing?" And the kids looked the other way. Macrorie calls that the "look-down-and-shuffle-period." Responding takes practice, and this is new to kids. Don't be surprised if it takes a little time to get them going. Model the kind of response you're looking for. Lead them. Cajole them. But don't give up on them.

Helping Circle

Students can become expert responders to the writings of fellow students if you take the time to train them carefully. I'm not talking choke chains and doggy biscuit stuff here, but training by demonstrating to kids using your own writing. When students are first asked to talk about each other's work, it's basically one incompetent talking to another incompetent. "Well, wha'd ya think?" "Oh, I liked it." So slap a piece of your own writing up on the overhead and ask them to give you some help. Tell them to point to good stuff first and then ask you some tough questions about your piece. What does it need more of? What to leave out, what to leave in? Bring in successive drafts of the same piece showing them how you have incorporated their suggestions and invite further response and questions. It doesn't take much of this kind of modeling to have a dramatic effect on the quality of student response in peer editing.

Macrorie has made great use of student responders in an approach he calls the "helping circle." Whatever you call it, leading a group of students through public responding to other students' writing is a bit frightening the first time or two.

It's important to begin with some rules or structures and then be prepared to enforce them. My basic rules are simple: be positive; be helpful; assume nothing—if you're unsure, ask the writer, be as specific as you can.

Sharing a piece of writing with a large group is definitely growth-producing, but it may also be very frightening. Spot good writing in the student's folder and write a note encouraging the student to share it with the group. Some students are understandably reluctant in this setting, but if you can get them to try it once, the thrill of seeing 28 heads bobbing up and down in response to their writing will get them hooked. The key to the "helping circle" is the teacher's skillful enforcement of rules and sensitive attempts to help the novice through the experience.

Excerpts

The best way to get the group trained as responders and to point out good writing is to publish weekly or twice-weekly excerpts. I frequently begin the week (because I can type the excerpts on dittos over the weekend) with dittoed cuttings from student writings. I read quickly through the writings for the week looking for particular pieces that work. The excerpts are kept anonymous. I read them aloud and ask for comments. The group members feel free to open up because they do not know the writer. We focus our comments on what makes the piece work and what if anything the reader might do further with it. Students look forward to the excerpts and take genuine pride when they "get published."

Partners

I have gone almost exclusively to response partners in my writing classes. Partners are so much more efficient than larger groups. I let kids choose their own partners and work together as long as they're being productive. Of course, there is always one kid left over whom nobody wants for a partner and he becomes my permanent partner. I don't like the kid either, sigh. I dodge most of the tough questions kids ask me by saying, "Check with your partner on that." We give "partner of the week" awards and generally celebrate good collaborations. Of course, as always some kids prefer to work alone and that has to be OK too.

Standing Groups

Small supportive groups that function well together can be a comfortable place for a writer to get helpful response. The key is to build groups who have confidence in one another and then keep them together for the tenure of the class, letting them meet on a weekly basis. The group gives the individual writer a home base and a comfortable audience to try something on before it goes "public."

Editorial Boards

If you're a well-organized type who doesn't mind an involved set of procedures for responding, the editorial board approach may be helpful. Appoint groups of five or so students who are responsible for selecting good writing and suggesting editorial changes. The board's problem is to publish an excerpts edition by a certain deadline. All student writers are required to submit a finished piece to the editorial board. The board reads the submissions, selecting pieces that have potential and notifying authors of their editorial decisions. Authors whose pieces are not selected are sent "rejection" notices. By simulating the actual process writers go through to become published, the teacher takes some of the mystique out of it, and students learn at first hand the joys and pains of getting published.

Rotate the editorial responsibilities among your writers so that each of them can experience the responsibilities and pressures of "editing" someone else's writing.

For Editing and Rating

Tom has experimented quite successfully in his advanced placement classes with a structured approach to responding and rating. He divides his class into groups and appoints a group leader. The groups read the papers from another group, responding and rating with a holistic rating guide. Specifically, each member of the group reads each paper, underlining examples of good writing and writing helpful and positive comments in the margin. The reader also makes general comments on the effectiveness of the piece, suggesting changes to the writer or simply asking the writer questions.

The entire group rates the paper on a five-point scale. The rating is assigned to the paper, and the group writes a brief defense of the rating. Such cooperative response develops the students' ability to recognize effective writing and shifts much of the burden of careful response from the teacher to themselves. In effect, they became responsible for their own writing.

Maybe none of these response strategies appeals to you. Responding is, after all, a personal style. What we suggest, however, is that you work out a system you are comfortable with which gradually involves the students in more and more responding practice.

* * *

I still like this chapter, and I think most of it still holds in writing classes. Learning to shift more of the responsibility for response and help to the students themselves is not only good pedagogy, it is absolutely critical to your survival as teacher. My goal with kids and writing is to make them more independent of my help and more reliant upon the community of writers in that classroom. I do think it's important that you vary response modes and strategies to keep the whole business as fresh as possible. Kids can get lazy as responders or they can get into ruts with formula responses. Jog them every once in awhile with a look at the quality of their responses. Spend some time evaluating student response as a whole class, talk again about what kind of responses are helpful, and challenge them to read closely and ask good questions of the writer.

Notes

1. Barbara Esbensen. *A Celebration of Bees.* Winston, 1975.
2. Rita, Shirley, and Sheri are fictitious names of students.
3. Stephen N. Judy. *Explorations in the Teaching of Secondary English.* Harper & Row, 1972.
4. Ken Macrorie. *Writing to Be Read.* Boynton/Cook, 1984.
5. Peter Elbow. *Writing Without Teachers.* Oxford, 1973.
6. Donald Murray. *A Writer Teaches Writing.* Houghton Mifflin, 1985.

CHAPTER NINE

Different Voices, Different Speakers

You will find the pronoun "I" used in this book a great many times. When overdone, this is considered bad taste.

I have overdone it.

Another much-used word in this book is "you." This is in better taste, I understand, but I suspect that I have run "you" into the ground as well.

Taste be hanged.

In this book, "I" am talking to "you" just as directly as if you were sitting in my parlor toasting your feet at my fire and eating my cheese and crackers. If the polite folks don't care for that, let them buy their own cheese and crackers....

To write, a person must think for himself. Unless he does this, what he produces is nothing.

You hear me?

—GENE OLSON (1)

Voice is at the heart of the act of writing. As I move from talking into writing, I try to hear clearly the flow of language in my head, capture it on the page, hoping you will hear me talking to you and be moved by what I have to say. That tension between "I" as writer and "you" as audience, created by the distance between writer and reader, is the dilemma and the generating force of every writing act. I write because "I" have something to say to "you." This chapter concentrates on the "I" of the writer.

When you read good writing, you "hear" the sound of another human being talking to you. A writer's *style* is the "sound" of a voice on the page. The natural place to start with a beginning writer is with his or her own voice. The first thing beginning writers should learn is how they "sound" when they write. And our job as teachers is to help them find a voice in each piece they write. Ken Macrorie gives this advice to young writers about finding a voice for a piece of writing. "Before you write your next paper, sit still a moment and listen to yourself speaking inside. If you hear a voice that takes on a clear tone—happy, calm, humble, arrogant, loving, irritated, enraged, soothing, or ironic—listen as you write and get it on paper" (2). Alice is a young writer who has found a voice with a clear tone in this moving and personal piece.

> I once felt like writing a poem about the moonlit door. Or the wooden lady whose face holds more secrets than her mind can speak. Or since silent spring never leaves, spring will always come.
>
> I once felt like writing about broken colored glass lying on a clear floor with the sun sparkling. I thought of mysteries with passwords to unknown hideouts. And human detectives with houses of dreams where there lives an old-fashioned girl that is someone's little princess. And when she glimpses that girl in her mirror, her wonderland through the looking glass will hold love for little men and little women.
>
> I once felt like writing about closing doors and opening windows, learning to pretend, to live in fantasy, of courage and war and love that I have not felt but that will be tomorrow's poem. For then it will be today and I will learn of love to come. For tomorrow is the future of today.
>
> —ALICE (3)

Alice is able to use voice very effectively for so young a writer. And there's more involved here than just using the first person "I" in the writing. Unlike Alice's "Babysitting" in Chapter 7, this prose poem has a more serious subject—pondering the mysteries of growing up—a little melancholy, but hopeful—even though her irony flickers in places in this one too. The pieces are very different, but Alice has been able to find a voice for each that we "hear" clearly when we read them. The voices are individual and identifiable as Alice's in both writings, and she has found the right voice for each experience.

Hal demonstrates his sensitivity to voice in this short piece.

Staying Alone

> I know when I left that I left the light on. And that paper wasn't on the floor. Someone is in here, I know it.
>
> Oh, don't fool yourself, no one got in.

I guess you're right. I'm just nervous. I'll just lock the door, the windows, and check under the beds and in the closets. No one got in.

I know I heard a voice when I finished washing my face and hands. And I know someone is here.

Ah, you're doing it again, no one got in.

No one got in. That's easy for you to say. You're just me, I'm you. And I'm scared. I guess I'll just watch *Saturday Night* and fall asleep.

No one got in.

—HAL (3)

He talks to himself—one voice afraid, the other reassuring—and both his. "You're just me, I'm you." And we hear throughout the piece the sound of a fallible, very human person.

The developmental approach to writing instruction that Dan and I have been describing helps students to discover and strengthen their individual voices in their writing. A great deal of practice writing about things close to them and important to them is necessary. Giving them choices in the writing class, the freedom to explore their own expressions in their own way, is also important. Your genuine, positive response to the good in their writing is essential, more important than anything else you do. And in your responses to their writing you need to be sensitive to, and point out for them, indications of an effective voice in what they have to say on paper. You should watch for opportunities to say things to your students like—"This is *you*"—and—"This *sounds like you talking*"—as you read their work. Mark their papers to indicate where they sound real, genuine, like themselves. Use every opportunity in class to point to passages in their writing that clearly reveal their voice. And have students ask themselves after they have completed a piece—"Does this sound like me? Can I hear myself in this paper?" Do whatever you can to create an environment in which students are aware of, and encouraged to use, authentic voices in their writing.

Because being aware of their voices in writing is so important to young writers, we don't believe you should try to move kids away from personal expression too early in their development as writers. Don't be too anxious to get them through the "personal stuff" and on to the "serious business of *real* writing." Any writing *real* to the good writer is personal stuff. Accomplished writers do not remove themselves from what's important to them. Even a writer as formal as Henry James had this advice for young writers:

Oh, do something from your point of view; an ounce of example is worth a ton of generalities...do something with life. Any point of view is interesting that is a direct impression of life. You each have an impression colored by your individual conditions; make that into a picture, a picture framed by your own personal wisdom, your glimpse of the American world. The field is vast for freedom, for study, for observation, for satire, for truth. (4)

Encourage students to write from their own point of view, to use the colors of the individual voice to make their picture of experience with the written word.

Tuning Your Voice

Although mature writers have a voice on the page that's relatively constant throughout their writing, they adapt their voice in a particular piece of writing to their purpose and to the anticipated demands of their audience. In a way, the workings of purpose, audience, and voice are so inextricably mixed in the act of writing that they can't be separated. However, it's important for us to focus on voice as the aspect of writing closest to the writer. And young writers, once they begin to find their writing voices, need to find out what those voices can do.

It's more difficult to talk about a writer's use of voice and exploring ways of using voice than to show it in operation. Listen to this:

The legend of Junior Johnson! In this legend, here is a country boy, Junior Johnson, who learns to drive by running whiskey for his father, Johnson, Senior...and grows up to be a famous stock car racing driver....Finally, one night they had Junior trapped on the road up toward the bridge around Millersville, there's no way out of there, they had the barricades up and they could hear this souped-up car roaring around the bend, and there it comes—but suddenly they can hear a siren and see a red light flashing in the grille, so they think it's another agent, and boy, they run out like ants and pull those barrels and boards and sawhorses out of the way, and then— ggghhzzzzzzzhhhhhhggggggzzzzzzeeeeeeeong!—gawdam! there he goes again, it was him, Junior Johnson! with a gawdam agent's si- reen and a red light in his grille!

—TOM WOLFE (5)

There is no mistaking the voice of Tom Wolfe. The excitement, the feigned innocence, even the sound effects make us hear the experience as though we were sitting around in a North Carolina country store listening to a backwoods orator tell us about "The Last American Hero" and how he fooled the revenuers that time. But when Tom Wolfe talks about Las Vegas, his voice changes.

> This is Raymond talking to the wavy-haired fellow with the stick, the dealer, at the craps table about 3:45 Sunday morning. The stickman had no idea what this big wiseacre was talking about, but he resented the tone. He gave Raymond that patient arch of the eyebrows known as a Red Hook brush-off, which is supposed to convey some such thought as, I am a very tough but cool guy, as you can tell by the way I carry my eyeballs low in the pouches, and if this wasn't such a high-class joint we would take wiseacres like you out back and beat you into jellied madrilene. (5)

This time the pace is slower, and we hear the deliberate sarcasm of a jaded crap dealer, a "very tough but cool guy."

The voice is always Tom Wolfe's, his trademark and not to be duplicated. Yet he alters his writing voice to put us closer to one experience or the other. He adapts his voice automatically to suit his purpose.

Exercises for Tuning Your Voice

Too much of what we teach in school is not a voice people want to read—it's only one expository voice, and a limited one at that. Compare, for example, the five-paragraph formula theme with the exposition of Tom Wolfe. The activities Dan and I suggest here will encourage your students to grow stronger in their own voices, to be more aware of what their voices can do, and to move away from that impersonal school voice James Miller calls "the prose in the gray flannel suit" (6).

One caution is in order, however, when you use these activities. They're not merely clever things for kids to do that you take up to read and return with a grade. The emphasis in the class should be on "hearing" the sound of the voice in the writing. And that means that the writings need to be shared *aloud,* and they need to be *talked about* in class. A great deal of reading aloud and much open discussion about what is distinctive and interesting, moving or funny, personal and unique are necessary if these activities are to be helpful in showing students what their own voices can do.

A supportive atmosphere in the classroom is absolutely essential when you talk with students about their voices in their writing. Remember that the point of all the activities in this chapter is exploration and experimentation, not a finished product. We'll talk about this first short exercise in some detail to show you how we approach the subject of voice with our students.

Mad Talking, Soft Talking, Fast Talking

This exercise had its beginnings in *Writing: A Sourcebook of Exercises and Assignments,* a useful little book by Gunther, Marin, Maxwell, and Weiss (7). The purpose of the activity is to let students experience something of the range their writing voices are capable of, and to see inductively that they use a variety of stylistic devices in their writing, automatically adjusting them to the use to which they're putting their voices. It shows them how purpose influences voice in specific ways.

Unlike most activities, we don't begin this one with an example of the kinds of writing we ask students to try. The idea is to show students the techniques they use automatically and intuitively in their own writing. We want to start with what they do, and we draw examples from their papers. The three short writings in the activity are done quickly as free writings.

Mad Talking

We ask students to think of someone or something that makes them very angry. "Who is someone who really makes you mad? Don't say the name out loud; just *think* of the person. Or maybe there's some *thing* that makes you madder than any person—your neighbor's aggravating dog, that lawnmower that refuses to crank when you need to use it, something like that. Think of it. Or maybe it's a *situation* that really steams you—like some rule here at school, or maybe something you've seen on the news that's going on in the country or the world. Think of that." We give them a few minutes to pick a specific subject. And then we ask them to close their eyes for a few seconds to see their subject and feel mad about it. We even ham it up a little—"Concentrate *hard!* Grrrr—Oh, that makes you sooo mad!" Then we give them five minutes to say in writing the angry things they feel about that person, thing, or situation.

Soft Talking

Then we ask the students to think of a person or thing in need of comforting. "You know, someone who's been hurt or is in trouble, or who's suffering in some way. Or maybe it's an animal—a pet hit by a car, or sick—or even something not alive you feel sorry for. I feel sorry for my old car lots of times. Concentrate on that person or animal or thing and feel sorry.'' We have them close their eyes again and visualize their subject for a few seconds. Then they write for five minutes to comfort that person or thing.

Fast Talking

The third writing we have students do during the class period is to persuade someone to do something or to believe something. "Think of somebody you want to talk into doing something—maybe you want your parents to buy something for you—or maybe there's somebody you need to argue over to your side. Maybe you need to explain that last grade report. Be irresistible. Be seductive.'' We have them visualize their subjects and concentrate on winning them over. Then they write for five minutes their most persuasive argument to that person.

Follow Up

With this exercise, talking about the writings is the key to its success. We call for volunteers to read aloud at least two of their papers, and we talk about how the papers change from one mode to another. We make three columns on the board for *Mad Talking, Soft Talking,* and *Fast Talking,* and list under each the stylistic devices used in each kind of writing as they appear in the papers as they are read. We concentrate on only one or two outstanding examples in each paper, and try to include as many students as possible in the sharing and discussion, without intimidating the shy students. Our point here is to show students inductively that they all use a variety of techniques as part of their writing voices.

Some of the stylistic devices you can expect to hear in the three kinds of writing follow. The examples are taken from a ninth grade class that recently did the activity.

Mad Talking: loaded language, abrupt sentences, repetition of key words and phrases, sometimes profanity.

> I hate you, you little shrimp. You think you're so good at everything, but everyone knows how stupid you are. You're always trying to copy someone else, but it never works. Everyone hates you because they're saying things behind your back and always talking dirty about you.
>
> —KEVEN (8)

> I hate this person. I think he's a pain in the butt. He makes me downright sick. He is so ugly, and he has greasy hair. He never takes a bath. He stinks all the time. I hate him so much. I think I'm going

to puke. Just thinking about him makes me sick. He thinks he's really cool. He even thinks he's good looking, and he also thinks I like him. *Yuck!*

—KAREN (8)

Soft Talking: repetitious, rhythmical sentences linked with conjunctions and little punctuation, a slower pace.

Bill, you don't need to run! You broke the law and you need to admit to that. You're old enough to understand what I'm saying. I've tried it and it doesn't work. Please confess to the court and I'm sure that they'll understand. See, if you stay then the judge will know for certain that what you say to him is true. Just tell him what really happened and he'll understand, I promise. Everything will work out and I know it will if you'll just face it. Please...

—LISA (8)

Pussycat, it's going to be all right and your leg won't be broken forever. It will heal. Now you lie down and rest for a while. I'll bring you some food later after you wake up again. It's OK. The cast will be off in about two more weeks and by then you will be able to walk on it. You just stay right there and go to sleep now.

—PATTI (8)

Fast Talking: logical, parallel sentence patterns; strong, active, or imperative verbs.

This is only a mid-term progress report. It will get better by the end of the quarter. I will start doing more homework. You don't know how hard it is. Just because you're so smart doesn't mean I should get straight A's. Teachers are a lot harder now. I've been trying real hard. I can't try much harder. Just because my sister has so much homework doesn't mean I should. I have different teachers, you know. I promise these grades will be better at the end of the quarter. If you ground me, it won't help my grades.

—DAVID (8)

Momma, please let me go out with him. You said yourself he was a nice guy. If he's such a nice guy, why don't you let me go out with him? Don't tell me I'm too young and I can't go out until I'm 16. I know, but I still want to go out with him. We won't do anything. He just wants to take me out. Please let me go, *please!* Well, what if

Sheila and Jill and their boyfriends go out with us? Then will you let me go? Please, you just got to let me! *Please!*

—KAREN (8)

As you do this exercise be aware of metaphor, kinds of repetition, rhythms, onomatopoeia, sentence length, and verbs. Ask your students to listen to differences among the kinds of writing and the various voices of their classmates and to describe the differences in their own way. Often they'll catch things you miss.

Evaluation

Because we deal with students' personal voices in a quickly done first draft in this activity, we don't grade the papers. However, we do take up the writings and point out more of the outstanding stylistic devices in our written comments. Or sometimes we simply underline examples to share with the class the next day.

Talking Back to Yourself

Read Hal's "Staying Alone" to your students and talk about the two voices he uses—one afraid, one reassuring—rather, the *two sides of his own voice* arguing with each other. Tell the students they're to write a dialogue in which they say something and talk back to themselves. Help them brainstorm ideas for the dialogues. Here are a few ideas to get them started:

1. You're about to do something you know is wrong.
2. You have just wrecked your father's car.
3. You're going to ask him/her for a date to the school dance.
4. You have money for a new album, but which one will you buy?
5. You skipped English class yesterday. Debate with yourself what you'll tell the teacher today.
6. Your parents expect you home at a certain time on Saturday night. You're *two hours late.* The lights are on, and you know they're up waiting for you.
7. You've just been kicked out of class and are waiting in the assistant principal's office.
8. Your girlfriend is pregnant.
9. The police have just pulled you over for speeding. The officer is walking up to your car.

Here's a dialogue with herself that Tami, a ninth grade student, wrote on a different subject.

Here comes the teacher, she's passing out the report cards now.

I know I'm gonna get an *A*, I've gotta get an *A*.

What if I get a *B* or *C?*

Naw, I'll get an *A*. I did all of my homework. Most of it. Well, some of it. Homework's not important anyway. Besides, this class is a snap and the teacher likes me, I think.

She's coming over to this side of the room. It's gotta be mine. Whew! Thank goodness. But here she comes again. She's coming toward me, she's looking straight at me. It's mine!

She handed it to me folded. Should I look at it?

Yeah, I better. What if it's bad? I'll die.

It's gotta be good, at least a *B*.

If it's good why did she fold it?

I'll look, good or bad. I gotta look at it sometime.

An *F!* I got an *F!* I knew she hated me. God, what am I gonna do?

I'll lose it on the way home.

Naw, with my luck my little brother would find it and take it home.

Man, I'm getting out of this class next quarter. My dad's gonna kill me!

—TAMI (8)

Have students write the papers quickly (thirty minutes is usually sufficient to draft them) and use the remaining time in the class to follow up by having some of the papers read aloud. Talk with the kids about the two voices in the papers and how they are different, and how they shift registers as they change point of view.

Save the papers for possible revision later.

How to Say "I Love Thee"—Let Me Count the Ways

The idea of this exercise is to explore ways of saying the same thing in different forms and media. Ask students to express "I love you" in these forms—a poem, a song, a brief essay, a letter, a telegram, a drawing, a greeting card, a film script, a collage. Share some of the results, and talk about how voice and form change with the medium.

An alternative is to say "I hate you" in the same media.

Trying on Other Voices

I said in the "Tuning Your Voice" section of this chapter that Tom Wolfe's writing voice could not be duplicated. That's true enough.

However, a time-honored method of good writers in perfecting their own style is imitating authors they admire. I'm not suggesting that we go back to the copy books of an earlier age, nor that we insist that students learn to write by following the examples of Milton, Swift, or Franklin. But there's nothing wrong—and much to be learned—with students' trying out the techniques of the masters.

Contrasting Voices

Another technique accessible to students for stretching their voices is putting on the voice of someone else. Ease them into creating a *persona* with this exercise. Remember that the point is again the experience and not a polished, professional product.

Give students these instructions.

Write about a *situation* twice, as two different people in that situation would see it. Each time you are to be one of the persons in the situation and speak with that person's voice. You may put your people into any situation you like, but here are the choices of characters for you to use:

1. A black kid, a white kid.
2. A man, a woman.
3. A young kid, an old person.
4. A far-out dreamer, a down-to-earth realist.
5. A worker, the boss.

Your students, of course, should be free to suggest their own contrasting characters. Tell them first to visualize each person in the situation and to hear that person talking in their heads before they begin to write. They'll also find it helpful if they use the first sentence of each contrasting voice to set the scene and get into the character. As they write, check to make sure they're using the first person. Often "I" will switch to "he" or "she" before they finish a piece. Emphasize again that they're speaking with the character's voice.

The finished papers should be read aloud in groups of three or four. Instruct the members of each group to underline words and phrases that they're speaking with the character's voice.

Don't have your expectations too high. Even professional writers find it difficult to keep a *persona* in character and sounding authentic. Your students will enjoy this kind of writing, but they'll require a great deal of practice before their characters begin to have a personality of their own. The point is for students to stretch their own writing voices, not to become novelists.

Getting into Another Speaker

Ask students to interview an older person whom they know (a grandparent, aunt or uncle, family acquaintance). Brainstorm with them a brief list of questions to ask to get the interview started before they go hunting with their tape recorders.

Once the interviews are taped, tell the students to write a *monologue* based on the tape, or at least part of it, in which the *speaker* is the older person interviewed—and which tries to capture the personality of the person by trying to catch the sound of the speaker's voice.

This exercise usually works best when students work in pairs—one to handle the tape recorder and one to conduct the interview. Sharing ideas and perceptions also helps in writing the monologue.

Collecting Dialogues

Another exercise for partners, this one concentrates on careful listening to speakers and writing for an audience. Send students out in pairs to do some eavesdropping around the school. Instruct them both to take notes for better accuracy and to collect several real *dialogues* that are funny, interesting, or bizarre. Then they're to write up their best dialogue. They may make it longer, more dramatic, funnier, stranger than it was in reality. But they're to write only the dialogue, leaving space for needed exposition to be filled in later.

The next step is for each pair of writers to read their dialogue to a listener recruited from the class. As they read the piece, they're to supply information the listener needs to understand and enjoy the dialogue. Groups can cooperate with one another by swapping listeners and taking turns reading dialogues for reactions.

The fourth step is for the partners to add to their dialogue whatever explanatory notes, scene setters, speaker identifications and descriptions, and stage directions that are needed by an audience. In essence, they turn the dialogue into a little drama by adding whatever exposition is needed.

Finally, the finished products may be performed for the whole class. The object is to observe, collect, and create authentic conversation, not to write a play.

On the Phone

This activity is a different slant on *Collecting Dialogues* that Dan has used successfully with his students.

Give your students a week to collect one side of a telephone conversation. Tell them to position themselves unobtrusively near a phone at home, in a cafe or some other public place, near the pay phones at school—anywhere the phone is likely to be used a lot and they can eavesdrop without being obvious. Suggest that they have paper, pencil, and books with them so it will appear they're doing a school assignment. They should sit with their back to the phone if possible so they can listen and take notes without being observed.

At the end of the week, the students bring their collected conversations to class. They are to select their best and put together a complete one-sided phone monologue to read to the class. Tell them to add whatever exposition is needed for the piece to be clear and effective (e.g., scene-setting descriptions, pauses or long silences, mannerisms of the speaker—"She listened breathlessly," "He twisted the phone cord nervously"). However, they should take out or change any names in the monologues to avoid identifying their subjects.

Share the papers, reading them aloud and talking about the way authentic voices are captured in writing.

This activity, like others in this chapter, can be used as a preliminary to more sophisticated writing tasks later. And students usually enjoy doing it. But more important, as they listen carefully to the sounds of voices around them, try to capture voices authentically on paper, read their attempts aloud, and hear the voices again in the reading, they're building their own intuitions as writers through practicing the basic skills of writers.

Who Owns the Voice?

This exercise leads students into the rather sophisticated techniques of "tagging" a character. It requires the skills of detail selection, repetition, dialogue, and pacing. For that reason, we suggest you use it after your students have had a good deal of practice with voice in writing and are beginning to have an intuitive feel for voice when they write.

Have students write a brief piece trying to capture the voice of someone known to the entire class (e.g., the school principal, the football coach, the Latin teacher, a TV personality, a famous politician, or a local disc jockey). Ask them to pick someone with distinct speech mannerisms. They're to write the piece as a short monologue using "I" and assuming the voice of their subject. Then read the papers aloud without identifying the speaker. The class tries to guess who owns the voice.

Follow up the exercise by selecting two or three of the best or most interesting monologues and asking *what the clues are* to the speaker's identifty in each case. Make a list on the board of key phrases and word choices that identify the speakers, and point out important uses of repetition in the writings.

Then use a recording or a video tape of an impressionist such as Rich Little or Frank Gorshin, and talk about how an impressionist works. Point out how they *select* and *emphasize* certain voice qualities and mannerisms. And talk about the things impressionists do to create a character that a writer can use—selection, repetition, and exaggeration.

Next, read your students the following scene involving a "tagged" character.

The tub was old and massive, one of those iron-looking things with claw-feet. I filled it with water almost to the top. The stereo was so loud I could hear it through the walls.

> "Colors surround them
> Bejewelling their hair
> Visions astound them
> Demanding their share
> Children of Orpheus
> Called by the dove
> Off on a trip
> Accompanied by love..."

I stepped into the tub with one foot, thinking—This is really going to be good—when the door banged open, and Bird Man came bouncing in. There I was, naked as sin, one leg in the bath and one leg out, and he comes in all smiles and sits on the commode with the lid down and crosses his legs.

"Hey, wait a min——"

"*Some* party, Man! Wow!" He had changed clothes, and the fuchsia outfit was gone. He was now wearing what looked like white leather pants and a matching vest without a shirt. Both the pants and vest were trimmed in scarlet sequins. He had a can of beer in each hand, which he waved around precariously. His eyes flickered—that's the only way I can describe it—they *flickered* like a flame. Maybe it was all those sequins. There was no help for it. I got in the tub the rest of the way and sat down.

"Hey, look, Bird Man, I'm in the tub and I would appreciate——"

"Wow, Man, I can *see* that. Man, that's some Far-Out Tub! That thing's got *Feet!*—it can walk around the room, Man!"

"I'm trying to take a bath."

"Yeah, Man, it sure looks *Good*. I think I'll join you." He started taking off the vest. I thought he was going to do it, just climb in the tub with me.

"NOW WAIT A MINUTE!"

The startled innocence of his face when I yelled at him was so surprising that I laughed. He looked like a little boy. He smiled without knowing what I was laughing at.

"Bird Man, I didn't think that was your kind of trip—taking baths with guys."

His smile grew wider. "Man, *Everything* is my trip. *Everything!*

"Get out of here, will you. That's not my trip."

"O sure, Man." He noticed the cans of beer in his hands as if they had just appeared there. He thrust one at me. "Have a *Beer,* Man! *Coors Beer!* Best *Beer* in the whole *United States of America!*" And he was gone, leaving me with a beer and leaving the door to the bathroom wide open (9).

Ask the students how they "see" Bird Man and his bizarre behavior. What's distinctive about the way he talks? Point out to them that the scene is really very short, yet they get a clear impression of this strange character mainly because of the way the writer uses repetition of words and phrases in his speech (e.g., "Man," "far out," "wow") and how only a few details are chosen and *exaggerated* (his dress, his "flickering" eyes). Also, Bird Man's sentences are choppy and sprinkled with interjections, exclamation marks, and overemphasized words ("Wow, Man, I can *see* that. Man, that's some Far-Out Tub! That thing's got *Feet!*—it can walk around the room, Man!") to create a rhythm that is fast, jerky, frenetic. His mannerisms are like his speech—he "bounces" into the bathroom, he "thrusts" a beer into the narrator's hands. A few repeated and exaggerated characteristics are used to *tag* the character in a short space.

Finally, ask your students to write about a character they know, including dialogue, in a few pages. Tell them to be particularly aware of the person's voice and mannerisms, to concentrate on *seeing* and *hearing* the character as they write. After they have the character "captured" on paper in a first draft, then they can go back and *emphasize* the characteristics of voice and action to make their creation stand out. That's the way I wrote Bird Man.

Share the finished characters aloud with the class.

Multiple Self-Portrait

The idea for this activity is from Miller and Judy's *Writing in Reality* (10).

The point here is for students to try to see themselves as others see them, and to explore different perspectives at the same time. Ask them to write a multiple portrait of themselves in several sections from the points of view of these people—their mother, a brother or sister, a close friend, an ememy, a teacher, and one other person who knows them well. Ask them to write each section in the first person as though they were the person describing them, and to conclude with a brief section on "the real me" from their own perspective.

Collect the papers and read aloud excerpts of the voices. The class will enjoy guessing who the subject is, and it gives you an opportunity to point out examples of well-done voices and the way voice changes with perspective.

As your students tune their writing voices and try on other voices, as they practice and stretch themselves, they naturally will speak as the "I" of the growing writer to the "you" of their audience. This chapter has concentrated on the "I" and ways to make it stronger and more flexible. The next chapter looks closely at the "you." Working with these two related and basic demands of writing helps students to become skillful and versatile writers who are confident of their ability to tell you what they know on paper.

*   *   *

I have been uneasy with this chapter since it was first drafted. I started to cut out all of the exercises, and reduce it to about three pages, except they are fun and they do demonstrate voice to students in obvious ways. They also show students powers they have as writers. Still, the longer I teach writing the more exercises like these ring hollow. Voice is easy to demonstrate in your kids' writing if you are sensitive to it. It's part of the whole fabric of writing and doesn't need to be isolated. All you need to do is point it out to them.

Dan recently commented on how important narrative is in all of this business of teaching writing. "Narrative is the language of world making." That's the way he put it. Each year it is more important to me as a writer and a teacher. What I really want to do is to tell you a story. That's what we all want. That's what your kids want. Writing starts with telling stories. And in those stories is where you will first discover your students' voices. Show them the power they already have where their voice is genuine and strong.

We struggle with voice in their writing because they don't read enough, or so we think. And because we still give them bad models. Maybe the video generation doesn't read as much as we do—or as much as we want them to. (Our teachers said as much about us, remember?) Given the state of the art of teaching reading in our schools, I don't see why we're surprised. It amazes me anybody reads at all. Nevertheless, I suspect our problems with voice—or the lack of it—in student writing really stems from the fact that they don't *write* much before we get them. They simply don't have a chance to find and use their voices. The neglect is regrettable, and I wish it were otherwise—but my job is to do something about it.

I am always amazed, and a little amused, at the relief in kids' eyes when I tell them, "You can say *I* and *you* and use contractions when you write." Of course they can. The question is, who has been telling them they shouldn't—and why? Forget those tired models of writing. Formal essays are written only in English class and only then as an excuse to "get them ready for college." Who are the writers you most enjoy reading? Bring them into class—when you can and still keep your job. Who are the writers your students like best? What are their voices like? When you share favorite writers, you enhance writing and reading. Try it. It works better than a basal any day of the week.

Notes

1. Gene Olson. *Sweet Agony: A Writing Manual of Sorts.* Windyridge Press, 1972.
2. Ken Macrorie. *Telling Writing.* Boynton/Cook, 1985.
3. Alice Murray and Hal Silcox were students at Gainesville High School, Gainesville, GA.
4. Henry James. "A Letter to the Deerfield Summer School," 1889.
5. Tom Wolfe. *The Kandy-Kolored Tangerine-Flake Streamline Baby.* Farrar, Straus and Giroux, 1963.
6. James E. Miller, Jr. *Word, Self, Reality: The Rhetoric of the Imagination.* Dodd, Mead, 1972.
7. Deborah Gunther et al. *Writing: A Sourcebook of Exercises and Assignments.* Addison-Wesley, 1978.
8. Keven Davenport, Karen Smith, Lisa Toler, Patti Tyson, David Van Laeys, and Tami Beaver were students at Stone Mountain High School, Stone Mountain, GA.
9. Tom Liner. *1969* (novel in progress).
10. James E. Miller, Jr., & Stephen N. Judy. *Writing in Reality.* Harper & Row, 1978.

CHAPTER TEN

Growing Toward a Sense of Audience

I think the writer ought to help the reader as much as he can without damaging what he wants to say; and I don't think it ever hurts the writer to sort of stand back now and then and look at his stuff as if he were reading it instead of writing it.

—JAMES JONES (1)

One of the most desirable sensitivities to cultivate in growing writers is a heightened ability to "feel" an audience out there as they write. Students develop distinct voices as they learn the control they have over their readers. The classroom can provide opportunities for them to develop a growing sense of audience. It's part of learning the craft. Writers experiment with their ability to control readers through their words. Dan and Ruth have shared excerpts of Italo Calvino's *if on a winter's night a traveler* with students as a way of emphasizing the point.

In the opening chapter of his novel, Calvino makes us squirm as we begin to recognize how clearly he manipulates us as readers:

> You are about to begin reading Italo Calvino's new novel, *if on a winter's night a traveler*. Relax. Concentrate. Dispel every other thought. Let the world around you fade. Best to close the door; the TV is always on in the next room. Tell the others right away, "No, I don't want to be disturbed!" Maybe they haven't heard you, with all that racket; speak louder, yell: "I'm beginning to read Italo Calvino's new novel!" Or if you prefer, don't say anything; just hope they'll leave you alone.
>
> Find the most comfortable position; seated, stretched out, curled up, or lying flat.... (2)

154

Control over the reader is absurdly obvious in Calvino's opener, yet it provides a vivid example of the writer's awareness of reader. I use the metaphor of filmmaking with my students as they become sensitive to the control they exert on audience. We view film clips and discuss how camera angles, lighting, and lenses affect our reactions as viewers. We look at excerpts from progressive drafts of both student and professional writing and take note of how writers re-vision their images and scenes to create effects with words.

Michael Ondaatje, as both professional writer and filmmaker, offers a marvelous study in holding scenes silent, in building momentum, in sharpening angles of action, and distilling images through language (3).

While the tools for writers and filmmakers vary, the camera lens, light bars, and filters work in the same way words do to create implicit messages through images, figurative language, momentum, or tone. Words create implicit messages that transfer to the reader. Writers need to test the effects of their words on readers. That is the way they develop a sense of audience.

As students look beyond themselves, they signal their readiness to explore and experiment with writing for audiences beyond their immediate context. As you work with students and bring them through journals and jottings to memory writings or poems, you notice their growing sense of confidence in their own voice and an increased willingness to share their writing with others.

Remember, they are not expert yet. Each writer is in the process of making discoveries about his control over audience. Each must keep writing, trying out and testing the results. Each will begin exercising independence as he develops confidence in predicting the ways readers will respond to certain effects. That's where you come in.

Begin by reminding yourself and them to think again about the communication process. When a writer begins to write anything, that process is set in motion. The piece of writing is written to be read by someone. As Britton describes it, a writer enters into a contract with an audience (4). The writer promises certain things to the audience, and the audience in turn agrees to read the work with an enlightened eye. The writer, the writing, and the reader are linked in a cooperative relationship that inevitably changes each of them.

Successful professional writers have a well-tuned sense of audience. They don't know the individual minds of their readers, but they have a feel for shaping language that connects with that audience. That "feel" often seems almost mystical to the novice. You can help student writers understand that there is more than mystery by bringing into the classroom excerpts from published writers' discussions of their work.

Professional writers trust that an audience will imagine, laugh, cry, and live momentarily through their words. An acute sense of audience is the mark of a mature writer.

A well-developed sense of audience comes through experience, and you can't hope that a chapter or five exercises on audience will do much for young writers. Your goal should be to provide many opportunities for students to adjust their writing for real audiences, letting this interplay of writing and audience teach indirectly what no direct teaching can do. Encourage students to practice and fool around with audience, and be patient as they learn by doing.

It's getting mileage with audience; gaining experience counts. Ruth's student, Jana Nelson (5), is a good example. At the beginning of her sophomore year, Jana was disappointed when her poem did not receive rave reviews from her response group:

At Night

> At night larks sing sweetly
> calling to the nearby trees.
> I'm sick at heart tonight
> wanting something I can't
> have. It makes my heart
> ache to hear the birds
> sing sweetly.

John Stevens fidgeted. Susan Levi stared hard at the poem in front of her. Becky Ray chewed her lip. We'd worked hard as a class to encourage constructive, concrete suggestions that help writers know what effect their language has on a specific reader.

But the poem sparked criticism from John. "Jana, there's nothing in this poem I care about. I can't see anything or feel anything because everything is general." John fell into the trap with Jana—generalization on top of abstraction.

Jana was crushed. She loved her poem. Becky added her voice to moderate. "Jana, you hear the birds and know what *you're* feeling, but that doesn't help me as a reader. I can't get inside your head unless you give one concrete thing." Jana nodded politely and said her thank you to the group. The poem was printed in our first class book in its original form.

Jana grew to trust audience response as the year progressed. She learned that the reader depended on her to deliver the meaning and visions from her head to the page. I watched her grow. It was time.

"Jana, let's take a look at the first poem you wrote this year. Read it to me, please." Jana read and sighed.

"Hopeless," she waved her hand through air.
"Take the challenge, Jana. Try it again."
Jana brought in this draft the next day:

Lark song rolls in like
a thick comforter. One low
note, oboe rich, vibrates
against a feeling tonight—the house
empty of people. I wait,
alone, for the front door
to open, to hear Mom's
voice comforting as the lark
song. "Jana, we're home!"

Jana learned from her encounters with a variety of audiences an important lesson: readers need concretes of sound, vision, and emotion. We finally understood what Jana had tried to say in the earlier draft. She'd grown enough as a writer to realize that what was in her head didn't necessarily transfer to the page automatically. Encouraging Jana to share her writing with others helped her sharpen her awareness of audience.

In this chapter we give you some ideas and activities for widening the audience for student writings. The very structure of schooling limits the possible audiences. Most school writing is written *for* the teacher. Furthermore, the teacher often functions only as an examiner or grader. For this reason, many writing theorists have been critical of the teacher as audience. These critics believe that the teacher-as-audience should be deemphasized to take the pressure off writers. The teacher will always be an important audience for student writings, but teachers can become more sophisticated audiences who see many possible roles to play as readers of student writings. No matter how confident student writers may have become, they almost always want to get our opinions first. Such opinion seeking need not be growth inhibiting. Students need to write for a whole range of audiences, testing and building intuitions and strategies for connecting with those audiences, but teachers need not apologize for their role as primary audience.

Initially, beginning writers should write for themselves as audiences in journals and personal writings, listening for the sound of their own voices. They may choose to share these writings with friends and helpful teachers to see if what pleases themselves also pleases those close to them. Beginning writers also can experiment with audiences less well known and further from them. You should encourage these audience experiments, but your evaluation should be gentle and positive.

Adjusting subject, language, and voice to other audiences is sophisticated writing behavior, and our approach to developing such sophistication is simply to encourage experimentation and explorations.

James Britton has suggested a helpful set of writer-reader relationships that span the range of audience options (4). His continuum, like Moffett's earlier work, is helpful for planning writing assignments and assessing the level of audience sophistication of your students. In simplified form, Britton's audiences include the *writer; the teacher* both as trusted adult and in the more traditional role of examiner; *wider known audiences* (i.e., peers, younger children, older relatives); and *wider unknown audiences,* (i.e., congressional representatives, corporations, and the general public). If we use Britton's continuum as a guide, here are some potential audiences:

Peers

- in class—notes and messages, persuasive papers, explanatory papers
- in other classes—letters, journal entries, inquiries
- in other schools—letters, class magazines, surveys, opinion polls
- pen pals
- famous peers—fan letters, question letters
- generalized peers—children of the world
- school newspaper—editorials, opinion letters

Teachers

- to encourage a teacher
- to request from a teacher
- to share personal information

Wider Known Audiences

- parents
- parents' friends
- principal

Unknown Audiences

- newspaper editor
- heroes
- authors
- athletes
- TV and movie personalities
- corporations

- unknown offenders (the person who threw all the trash on the highway)
- citizen groups
- governmental bodies
- information sources

Imaginary Characters

- in books
- on TV

Talking Directly to an Audience

In addition to varying the kinds of audiences students write for, many other audience experiments are possible. Some students have a flair for talking directly to their readers as they write. Use the following models to illustrate the technique:

The Author's Voice

> Or is the author trying to ease you into something here, trying to manipulate you a little bit when he ought to be just telling his story the way a good author should? Maybe that's the case. Let's drop it for now.
>
> But look here a minute. Over here. Here's a girl. She's a nice girl. And she's a pretty girl. She looks a bit like the young Princess Grace, had the young Princess Grace been left out in the rain for a year.
>
> What's that you say? Her thumbs? Yes, aren't they magnificent? The word for her thumbs has got to be rococo—rocococototo tutti! by God.
>
> Ladies. Gentlemen. Shh. This is the way truth is. You've got to let those strange hands touch you. (6)

That's Tom Robbins, involving you personally with Sissy Hankshaw, and with himself. Kurt Vonnegut also knows his audience. He touches us with his fine and scathing irony.

> [This book] is so short and jumbled and jangled...because there is nothing intelligent to say about a massacre. Everybody is supposed to be dead, to never say anything or want anything ever again. Everything is supposed to be very quiet after a massacre, and it always is, except for the birds....

I have told my sons that they are not under any circumstances to take part in massacres, and that the news of massacres of enemies is not to fill them with satisfaction or glee (7).

Ask your students to try talking to the reader directly in their writings much the way they may have been doing in their journals. Tell them to use their author's voice to inform the reader, to cajole the reader, to involve the reader.

Anticipating Audience Response

Writers' choices of voice, language, and content are often influenced by their informed guesses about audience response. Particularly when the writer's intent is to influence or persuade a hostile audience, the writer tries to anticipate possible audience rebuttal. My son, Matthew, when he was younger, tried to convince me for some time that he needed a minibike. Partly from frustration and partly from his knowledge of parent psychology, he put the following note on my desk. Notice how his intuitions about audience response guide his word choices, his specific information, and even the organization of his piece.

Dad—

This is about a minibike. Chris is only nine and his parents let him have one.
[Peer pressure—anticipates my "you're too young" argument.]

I would be real careful and only ride it when you're there to watch me. I would always wear a helmet and watch out for cars and trees.
[Anticipates my concern for his safety.]

I will always put it in the garage. And I could ride it to soccer practice and I wouldn't bug you about being bored and I would learn how to take care of something.
[Anticipates my concern for responsibility.]

I'll save my money and maybe we can find a used one cheap. I'll read the want ads. It saves gas. Dad, you could ride it to work.
[Anticipates my "we can't afford it" final line.
And involves me in the last line.]

Ask your students to draft an appeal to one of their parents. They should try to persuade their parents they need something. Tell them to anticipate parental response. Suggest that they actually write anticipated responses in brackets as they write their papers. Have the writers try out the piece on the parent and report to the class how accurate their hunches were about their intended audiences.

Writers also alter their voice with strategy that is based on their perception of their audiences' vulnerability. Sometimes a writer moves an audience with an emotional, evangelistic appeal. Sometimes a writer shames the audience by choosing accusatory and preachy language. Sometimes a writer supports the audience by using warm, understanding language.

Ask your students to draft three different pieces asking a teacher to change a grade on a recent assignment. Tell them to blame the teacher in one piece, to be humble and ingratiating in another, and to be coldly logical and businesslike in the third.

Speculate with your class as to what kind of teacher would be influenced by each piece. Compare the three pieces, talking about similarities and differences. Which voice are they most comfortable with? This follow-up time is important. Involve your writers in a discussion about their audience strategies and ask "why?" questions.

Profiling an Audience

You may find that a more direct approach to audience awareness works better with less sophisticated writers. Prewriting discussions about a potential audience and their uniqueness is certainly always appropriate. Asking students to think about and even describe their audience may help them refine their intuitions. Koch and Brazil suggest that you ask students to answer specific questions about their audience before they begin writing:

- What age is the audience?
- Where do they live?
- What are their educational backgrounds?
- What are their political and philosophical beliefs?
- What kind of jobs do they have?
- What kinds of leisure activities do they participate in?
- Is there anything atypical about them? (8)

Rewriting for Different Audiences

Advertisements and commercials are interesting sources for a consideration of audience strategies. Most of us have heard of or used the old commercial analysis stuff, perhaps without thinking about how all that is related to the writing process. Survey your students to find some particularly effective commercials. Videotape them for classroom use if possible, and analyze them with your students. Discuss the assumptions these advertisements make about their intended audience. Discuss how a particular commercial might change if the product were directed to another audience. Ask your students to rewrite a commercial for a different audience: they might sell sugared cereals to older people or Exxon stock to environmentalists, or Kennedy to conservatives, or pick-up trucks to college professors, or bubblegum to grandmothers. Discuss audience strategy with your writers, focusing on audience-directed changes they made in their sales pitch.

Follow this frivolity with a real writing assignment. Ask your writers to design and write ads for a class publication or design a commercial to sell the principal on what a great class they have, or the PTA on the need for an improved ballfield, or the county commissioners on the new recreation center, or the local theater manager on the idea of offering student discounts, or the city council on the feasibility of building bikeways. Brainstorm with your students for real products, real potential audiences, and effective audience strategies. Complete the activity by videotaping or recording the final products and presenting them to their intended audience.

Writing for Younger Children

Your writers need direct contact with their audience. If you can work out the logistics, elementary school children are an excellent potential audience for student writings. Find a second grade teacher somewhere and take the class over for a visit. Have them interview the younger children to find out what kinds of stories they like. Help them analyze their second grade audience, and then turn them loose to write some children's literature. You can make this experience as elaborate as you want to. Some teachers ask students to illustrate and bind their "books." Some teachers spend time talking about picture books and their importance in the education of children. But the most important follow-up is the chance for students to read their stories aloud to the younger children so that they can experience their audience personally.

Audience Adaptation

Good writers make subtle, often almost invisible, adjustments for their audience. Maybe an unsubtle and obviously rigged assignment will illustrate the point. Richard Gebhardt suggests the following activity as a way to create different audiences for a piece of writing (9). Ask students to write letters giving the details of a motorcycle accident, in which the writer was hospitalized and the cycle destroyed, to the following audiences:

- a relative or someone likely to be worried.
- the friend from whom you borrowed the cycle.
- the motorcycle company to discuss their bike's performance.

Follow this role-playing demonstration with real letters to real people. Have students try writing three letters to people they don't know well. For the first letter, they should find something around their house that has never worked properly or that has failed recently because of a manufacturer's error. Have them draft a letter detailing the product's defects and ask them to suggest a reasonable remedy. For the second letter, have students locate people around school or town who seldom receive recognition. Have the students write letters of appreciation to them. Send copies to the local newspaper and the persons' employers.

Finally, have students try a "Why?" letter. "Why?" letters ask people to explain a position or a recent decision. Why does the swimming pool close at eight? Why are students never invited to the school board meeting? Why did you vote against reduced bus fares for the elderly? The intent of such letters should be to give the addressee an opportunity to state fully a point of view. Letter writers need to choose a voice and a vocabulary that do not create defensive responses. The intent is to draw out the addressee and open a channel for dialogue.

Ask students to share their letters. Discuss specific audience strategies: voice, syntax, word choice. Talk about problems inherent in writing to people you don't know very well.

Real Audiences

It's not easy to design writing assignments that specify diverse, real audiences. Many so-called audience assignments are not real writing situations, and they don't teach kids very much about actual writing problems. Two important sources for real audience experiences are all around you: performance and publication. Students need to read their writings aloud to other classes, to PTA meetings, on local television and radio shows, and even in local shopping centers. Publish their stuff in classroom magazines, in school newspapers and newsletters, in local papers, in children's magazines, and in literary magazines. Encourage them to submit their products to contests and commercial publications. Be constantly looking for new outlets. Remember, nothing you can do in class will teach them as much about audience as a firsthand experience in performance or publishing. Going public with writing broadens audience intuitions and builds motivation. Design occasions that open the dialogue between writers and readers.

Endnote

This audience stuff still troubles me, and I guess I should confess that I'm still not sure that young writers get better at massaging readers by "working on it" or by performing rhetorical gymnastic exercises. I'm more and more convinced that writers always write for themselves first. As I struggle with this paragraph, I'm trying to make sense of "audience" for myself. Maybe what "communicates" here is my struggle, not my words. Meanings are personal, self-constructed, homemade. Maybe the best kinds of practice in writing for other audiences we can give our kids is lots of practice struggling with tough ideas and lots of opportunities to share those struggles with other writers. We can do that in our classrooms. We can help students find important things to write about, and we can encourage them to test those ideas by reading and sharing with fellow writers. It's that community of writers in our classrooms that will ultimately teach our students about audience.

Notes

1. James Jones, interview from *Writers at Work: The Paris Review Interviews,* 3rd Series, ed. George Plimpton. Viking, 1967.
2. Italo Calvino. *if on a winter's night a traveler.* Harvest, 1984.
3. Michael Ondaatje. *The Collected Works of Billy the Kid.* Penguin, 1974. *Coming Through Slaughter.* Penguin, 1984.
4. James Britton et al. *The Development of Writing Abilities (11-18).* Macmillan Education, 1975; NCTE, 1978.
5. Jana Nelson was a student at Boise High School, Boise, ID.
6. Tom Robbins. *Even Cowgirls Get the Blues.* Bantam, 1976.
7. Kurt Vonnegut. *Slaughterhouse Five.* Dell, 1969.
8. Carl Koch and James M. Brazil. *Strategies for Teaching the Composition Process,* NCTE, 1978.
9. Richard Gebhardt, "Imagination and Discipline in the Writing Class," *English Journal,* Vol. 66 (Dec. 1977), pp. 26-32.

CHAPTER ELEVEN

Writing About Literature

In the first place, as a born hider, I have been fascinated all my life by disguise, camouflage, shape-changers, and by everything that has to be approached backwards or sideways, while one pretends to be thinking of something else.

—PETER BEAGLE (1)

Literature is the first love, the *suffisaunce* in Chaucer's term, of those of us who teach English. We got in this business in the first place because we were touched by the Great Words and stirred by the Great Ideas of the Master Writers down the centuries. We've spent a great deal of time in libraries, and we've had to read a lot of books, explicate a lot of poems, analyze a lot of plays, hunt a lot of symbols, and interpret a lot of motifs—before they would give us a degree and a certificate so we could teach.

Most of us spend most of our day teaching literature of one kind or another, because the majority of the classes we teach involve literature in some way. We are trained in it. We've studied, and even written, a great deal of lit-crit in term papers and such for our college profs and we think that's a good thing, so long as we don't turn our high school classes into miniature lit-crit seminars. There's no excuse for literature teachers who don't know their stuff. That's the first and the minimum requirement for the job.

So this chapter is not going to tell you *how* to teach literature. (If you're looking for good ideas about teaching literature, the source we've found most helpful is Alan Purves's little book *How Porcupines Make Love* (2). What this chapter does talk about is *writing in the literature class*, writing about literature. We begin by giving you some ideas to think about, but most of the chapter suggests experiences with literature and writing for you to try with your students.

165

Things to Think About When Your Students Write About Literature

1. *Our job as English teachers is to help our students* experience *literature through* writing, *as well as reading.* As John Dixon has pointed out, the important use of writing in the literature class is for students to use it to discover *what* they know about the literature they read. Writing is a way of exploring ideas, of organizing perceptions, of expanding intuitions about experience—including *reading* experience. And we need to make more use of this exploratory and clarifying role of language in helping our students understand and relate to what they read. Writing is a way of approaching meaning in literature backwards or sideways, for more understanding and more enjoyment.

2. *One of the best ways for students to experience literature through writing is the now classic "creative response."* (See the CR sequence in the exercises for this chapter.) There's something almost magic about encouraging kids to react personally and honestly in writing to a piece of writing that moves them. The creative response helps students grow as writers and grow as readers at the same time.

Like free writing, the creative response takes time and patience to begin in the classroom. It will take a while for most of your students before you'll get the kind of insightful and sensitive writings you would like. But the important thing in teaching literature *is* the kids' response to what they read. For students to become perceptive and willing readers of literature is what we're working for.

Students will like the creative response once they're used to it. And you'll find that they'll read with more understanding and write about literature with more perception than they have before. Student examples will help you get them started, but the important thing with this kind of writing, like any other, is that they practice it regularly.

3. *Students in your literature classes should* write every day, *just like students in your composition classes.* I know that one reason you like to teach literature is so you won't have all those stacks of papers to grade, and I'm certainly not suggesting a five-paragraph theme in literary criticism every day. But daily responses in writing to what students read is essential for their growth as writers and readers.

The *journal* is a good way to encourage daily written responses, and I have had some success using the first ten minutes of the class for quick journal responses to the literature we're talking about that day. It's better than the threat of the dreaded pop-test to keep my students up with assignments (they look forward to the writings, for one thing). And it has the extra advantage of giving me a daily monitor of their understandings, or confusions, about the material the class is studying.

You might even consider substituting a variety of responsive writings about the literature your students are reading instead of fact-recall tests (with maybe a discussion question thrown in). I've taught very successful American literature classes in which students read a great deal and wrote every day, and in which there were *no formal tests at all*. Yet I feel my students were rigorously examined on their reading and performed better than those in classes in which I've given weekly tests, unit tests, and a final exam.

The fact that the syllabus for the class we teach has *literature* instead of *composition* in its title does not release us from our responsibility to the growth of our students as writers.

4. *It is important that you* model *writing for your literature students just as you do for your composition students.* Use student examples for responsive writing about literature, but remember that *your* example is the most important one to your students. After all, you're the literary expert in that room. As often as you can, write with them about the same literary works—and *share* your writing with them.

5. *Writing in the literature classroom and sharing writings with one another allows students to compare insights, perceptions, attitudes, and even problems about what they read.* Instead of only the teacher's interpretation of a difficult poem or obscure passage in a story, there are many interpretations to consider. Also, because I give my students many choices of what they read for class, we share through our writings the things we particularly like to read. The students experience a variety of stories by Poe or Hawthorne or Hemingway, for example, instead of just one read by the entire class. If someone in the class likes a book or story or poem, others are more likely to read it than if I recommend it.

6. *Variety is essential in any class but especially in the literature class.* I don't want students to get in the rut of looking at a piece of writing from only one perspective. Given the limitations of literature anthologies and the school library, I give them as many choices in *what* they will read as possible; and once they are used to writing responsively to literature, I give them as much freedom as I can in *how* they will respond to it in writing.

Give students concrete suggestions for their writing, and show them examples. But give them lots of choices. And encourage their own suggestions for writing. "Only by making writing natural can you allow it to come naturally." That's from Purves (2). And it comes most naturally from what the students themselves want to say about what they're reading in class.

Other Things to Think About When Your Students Write About Literature (2)

If you want students to write interestingly and well about literature:

- Don't give them writing assignments to accompany each selection.
- Don't give them lock-step writing assignments.
- Don't judge their writing by the standard of what the professional critic might say about the selection.
- Don't grade all their writing as if you were trying to decide whether they should go to hell or heaven.
- Don't make everyone in the class do the same assignment.
- Do allow the students the right not to write sometimes.
- Do let the assignment grow out of the talk you have been having; let it be an extension of the classroom conversation, a setting-in-order of the students' thoughts and impressions.
- Do let students modify assignments in the light of their understanding.
- Do make clear what you expect from student writing.
- Do read and respond to the students' writings as you do to the writing of established authors—somewhat humbly, somewhat tentatively.
- Do make writing a process of pleasure, not a punishment.

Writing Responsively About Literature: Backwards and Sideways Exercises

The exercises we suggest draw on students' responses—their insights, feelings, perceptions, even negative reactions—to what they read. They are *backwards* and *sideways,* in Beagle's phrase, not because they are distorting, but because they begin with the student rather than with the traditional interpretation of the literary selection. You probably have already noticed that we haven't had anything to say in this chapter about Writing Themes about Literature, or about the New Criticism, or about any kind of Literary Criticism for that matter. Well, we left that kind of stuff out on purpose. Although writing Critical Essays about literature may be all very well and good for advanced placement classes—and later for graduate seminars and such places—there are many more profitable (and less painful) ways to stimulate and nourish students' written responses to literature. These exercises give you some of those ways. In parentheses following most exercises, there are specific suggested literary selections that we have found work well with that exercise. These come from American literature.

CR Sequence

I use the creative response with the students in my literature classes the way I use free writing in writing classes. I usually begin the class with this kind of writing, and I return to it often, especially when we're working with difficult and unfamiliar material—or whenever the students seem to be having trouble finding things to say about what they're reading.

The class begins with the free response, and from there I lead them into guided responses of various kinds (some of the most successful are listed here). It's a good thing to do in the journal, but I recommend that the first responses be taken up and responded to individually to give students the immediate feedback they need to get a good start with writing in the class.

I've found the creative response to be the best way for students to explore their understanding of a piece of literature. Like free writing, often it's the beginning of some very good writing.

Free Response

I begin the literature class with a short selection. I like to use a song that is related thematically to the other reading the class will be doing, but a poem or very short story works just as well. I play the song for the class, supply them with copies of its lyrics, and give them these instructions: "You're to write a creative response to this selection. You may write anything about it you wish—except you may not say 'I like it' or 'I don't like it' or anything like that. It's a creative response, which means I'd like you to *create* something of your own. Write a poem, write a short sketch, draw a picture, tell me how it makes you feel, write the daydream you had while listening to it, free write while I play it again—respond to it any way you wish, but try to get something on paper this period."

Be patient with students at this point. They will be confused at first by the freedom of the assignment. Reading to them examples of creative responses to the same selection done by another class will help, and read them your own creative response.

I take the first few sets of free responses and "mine the slag heap," just as I do with free writings, looking for the good things to praise and ignoring their errors in usage and mechanics. When I think they're comfortable doing free responses, I start them on guided responses. (Favorite songs of mine for initial writing are by Bob Dylan, Don McLean, Harry Chapin, Carole King, Joni Mitchell, Jackson Browne, Bruce Springstein and others in the folk-rock genre. I don't necessarily try to use songs popular with my students, although we sometimes use those too. I share what *I* like with them.)

Guided Responses

Quotable Quotes

After we finish reading and talking about a piece, I put several quotations from the work on the board, choosing ones that are especially evocative. Students are told to write a creative response to the piece, starting with one of the quotes, and to use it in their writing in any way they wish. Often the papers that grow out of this exercise are interpretive. It's a good approach to use with literature the students are having trouble with.

A variation of this exercise I like to use a little later in the class is to have students pick their own quotations, swap them with one another, and then write creative responses to them. (Literature by such writers as Hemingway, Tennessee Williams, Faulkner, Longfellow, Thoreau, Welty, McCullers, Kesey and Tom Wolfe is good for this one. Any clearly stated theme works well. I've also used this device successfully with movies.)

Dear Author

"This is your chance to ask writers questions, to complain about their writing, to talk back to them, to tell them what you like," I tell the students. And we all write a letter to the author of the story or whatever it is we've read. I like to use living authors for this one because we can mail the letters when we finish them—or make up one class letter from all the things we want to say, and send it. This exercise stimulates *real* writing and revision activities, and it stimulates a great deal of thinking about writers and how they work. Actually I stole the idea from David Muschell, who taught in Greene County, Georgia. He had his slow kids write fan letters to their favorite rock stars or TV personalities or movie stars. (Any living author is fair game for this one. Some, like James Dickey, may even graciously take the time to reply.)

Imitation in Kind (Vignettes)

I watch for pieces of literature that lend themselves to student imitation. Quite simply, the assignment is to do *the kind of thing* the author did, but *in each student's own way*. It should be a try-it-and-see kind of exercise.

One imitation-in-kind exercise that has been successful in my classes begins with Hemingway's vignettes from *In Our Time*. After reading and talking about them (and it takes a lot of talking—they're not easy reading for most students), I ask the students to try three or four vignettes of their own. I encourage them to draw on their *memories* and write about episodes that involve *action*. "I want you to put us in the action," I tell them, and I suggest car wrecks, sporting events, fights as possibilities. And I encourage them to *lie* when they write the vignettes. The results of this exercise are usually good enough to follow up with revisions. (The model here is from Hemingway, but brief, self-contained episodes from other writers work equally well: Brautigan, Lopez, Flannery O'Connor, even J.F. Cooper—of all people! Kafka's riddles are good for advanced classes.)

Tall Tale Telling

I use this exercise when we're reading Mark Twain and other authors who write from a strong oral tradition. I point out that most families have their own legends—most of them exaggerated memories —that they like to tell when they're together. I illustrate briefly with my grandmother's stories of "panthers" in the North Georgia mountains when she was a girl, and the tale my dad liked to tell about Shine Peacock, a state trooper and friend of his, who lost control of his patrol car one night chasing a bootlegger and ran through a farmer's chicken house.

The student's assignment is to think of a family story (or make up a convincing lie), and *tell it* to a partner or a small group. Sometimes we write them down afterward; usually we just enjoy the telling. (Twain is mentioned here. I've also used Irving, O'Connor, Faulkner, Thomas Wolfe.)

Spooky Tales

Everybody likes to tell, and listen to, ghost stories. When we study Gothic writers, one assignment I always give my students is to tell a real live ghost story—one they have actually heard themselves. We close the blinds and turn off the lights and share our stories as a class (I don't push kids who are shy and don't want to talk, and I begin by telling a story myself). Then I ask them to write their stories: "Tell me about it just as you did now." (Poe and Hawthorne are useful, of course, and also Frost's "The Witch of Coös," Beagle, and Mary Shelley.)

Shopping for Poetry

Once my students are used to writing creative responses, I like to use this exercise to break the routine of a class when things seem to be dragging. I make copies of several very short poems and cut the pages so that each poem is on its own small square of paper. I've done this for some time and have a collection of these little poems. I spread about twenty of them out on display on desks or bookselves or some other convenient place before the class comes in the room. As the students enter, I invite them to shop in my Poetry Supermarket. They can take as long milling around and reading the poems and talking about them as they like. Finally, they must choose at least three for creative responses. (I like poems by Brautigan, Cohen, and Plath for this exercise, and I include one or two of my own and some by students.)

Strange Poetry

This is strictly a Friday kind of exercise. I find three of the *strangest* poems and/or songs I can. We play the songs and read the poems aloud, and I give the students these instructions: "I want you to write something *really strange*. It can be a poem, a song, a sketch, or something else—but *it must be weird.*" The results are always entertaining. (Favorite strange songs are Kottke's "Morning Is the Long Way Home"; Dylan's "Changing of the Guard"; Crosby, Stills, and Nash's "Winchester Cathedral"; Carly Simon's "De Bat." Favorite strange poems include Francis's "Summons," Monro's "Overhead on a Saltmarsh," and selections by Corso, Ginsberg, Ferlinghetti.)

Alternatives to the Book Report

The time-honored and time-worn book report! Kids hate it, and teachers are bored reading it. But your students ought to read books, right? So what we suggest here are some alternative exercises to make the chore more tolerable for your students and for you. Whenever possible, of course, students should have several exercises to choose from. Many of these suggestions also work well with short stories. Most are good exercises to use with films.

Advertise the Book

A suggestion from Kate Kirby is to have students write advertising blurbs (like those on the back of paperback books) and put them up in the room. Encourage students to make them as racy as possible, just like the real thing.

This exercise is quickly done and generates talk about books and reading. A variation I have frequently used is to have students make advertising posters for the books they've read, with a drawing and a blurb, and display these around the room.

Continue the Story

One of the most successful writing exercises on novels I've found is to have students continue the story for a page or two. I encourage them to keep the writer's style and approach as much as possible when they do this, and to include some dialogue if they can. The point, of course, is not to get them to write like professional novelists but to generate thinking about the writers' techniques and the whole business of storytelling. (Many novels lend themselves to this activity. Favorite authors of my students are Hemingway, Steinbeck, Robbins, and Potter.)

A Family Tree

You're probably familiar with the elaborate diagrams of family realtionships among characters in Faulkner's novels (Cleanth Brooks's *Yoknapatawpha Country* has the most detailed and accurate examples). On a smaller scale, novels like *The Grapes of Wrath* lend themselves to this way of looking at characters. I have students construct a family tree with brief notes on each character. The graphic representation helps students to clarify character roles in a long novel. (A family tree of the Joad family in *The Grapes of Wrath* has worked well in my classes. I've also used this exercise with novels by Leon Uris and Frank Yerby and, modified for relationships of military rank, even Heller's *Catch 22*.)

The Newspaper Interview

I sometimes have students conduct an imaginary interview with a character from a novel: for example, "You are an Atlanta reporter, and you are to interview Ed Gentry after he returns from his ordeal on the Cahullawassee River. Plan your questions to probe his actions and his character." A good approach with this exercise is to have students who have read the same novel pair up, one acting as the reporter, one the character. They can make a taped interview, or write it.

The results are remarkably insightful, sometimes hilarious. (The example is from Dickey's *Deliverance*. I have also used this exercise with *The Great Gatsby, Go Tell It on the Mountain, The Pigman, The Outsiders,* and *Ordinary People.*)

Shifting Points of View

A simple but effective exercise is to have students rewrite a brief version of a narrated novel from another character's point of view. It promotes a lot of talk and thinking about characters and values. (A favorite of mine is Catherine Barkley as narrator of *A Farewell to Arms* instead of Frederic Henry.)

Obituaries

I often ask students to write obituaries for characters who are dead at the end of a novel. I bring the most sensational obituaries that have been written before to class as models, and tell the students to write their own obituaries for one of those scandal-mongering, yellow journalism papers. We get started by brainstorming together as many sensational headlines as we can think of. A variation of the assignment is to write an exposé news story for a tabloid. Some very funny ones have been done on *The Scarlet Letter*. (Suitable novels are almost endless. Authors frequently kill off characters at the end of their books. Favorites of mine are Heinlein, Styron, Vonnegut, Kesey, Wambaugh, and Jones.)

Don't Forget the Little Guy

I save one book report assignment to talk about *minor characters* in novels. The exercise is simply to forget main characters for a while and "tell me about the unimportant characters, the ones you usually don't put in a book report." It's a good sideways assignment for getting students to look at a book from a different perspective. (Favorite books of mine with many interesting minor characters are *The Electric Kool-Aid Acid Test, The Starship and the Canoe, I See by My Outfit, Dune, Exodus, Sometimes a Great Notion, Wise Blood,* and *The Heart Is a Lonely Hunter.*)

Nonwritten Responses to Literature

The response to the book of Genesis shown on page 175 is a valid creative response in the literature class. Encourage students with drawing ability to respond visually to what they read whenever it seems appropriate. (And remember that there are some "artistic" exercises that don't require much artistic talent.) Visualizations help keep things interesting in the literature class. They stimulate talk about how we *see* the things we're reading. "That character doesn't look like *that,*" someone in the class says about an illustration we put up. "I don't know," I say, defending the artist, "I kinda see the person like that." And the class is off, talking about their *perceptions* of the work.

Visualizations, like drawings, should always be only one choice of several that are open as responses to literature.

TRACY TATE (3)

Character Portraits/Illustrations

I've always gotten good results giving students the choice of responding to a story by drawing an illustration or drawing a character's portrait from the story.

The Illustrated Map

This exercise is one of my favorites and one of the most successful with literature classes. Students work in pairs. Their task is to trace the action of a story by drawing an illustrated map (it does not have to be elegantly done—stick figures will work just fine) and labeling important actions. (Steinbeck's "Flight" and London's "Love of Life" are two stories that work well in my classes. Many novels are also suitable.)

Draw the Neighborhood

A variation of the *illustrated map* idea, asking students to draw the neighborhood where most of the action takes place in a novel or story, has produced some interesting results. (Alfred Brooks's neighborhood from *The Contender* and Bumper Morgan's beat in *The Blue Knight* are two of my favorites.)

Book Jacket Design

The idea of this exercise is for students to design an original and, it is hoped, an attractive and interesting book jacket for a novel. I encourage them to stretch their imaginations and be as sensational and bizarre as any book ad designer. The finished products are put up for display around the room, and they stimulate a lot of book sharing.

Slide Show Characters

This exercise comes from Hugh Agee, who used it to teach the Prologue of the *Canterbury Tales* (of all things!) to a Basic English class. You need a copy stand and camera, slide film, and a collection of magazines.

The assignment is for a small group to present the characters in a long story or novel to the class by making slides of pictures of the "characters" from magazines. These are selected by the group and shot with the copy stand, the film is developed, and each character is introduced to the class with his or her picture and a brief oral profile.

One side effect of this exercise, by the way, is that students remember these characters longer than they do others they read and write about.

* * *

The thing about teaching literature *and* writing is that what I'm looking for are *connections*—points of contact between the writing and the reading, and between the kid and both of them. You hear a lot about integrating the language arts these days. If you look for ways to teach your literature (and reading) with writing and your writing with literature, you will have done the job already. It never has made much sense to me to teach them separately anyway.

You may want more structure than you find in this chapter. Ed Youngblood gives us a scheme for using the journal to teach literature and writing together in "Reading, Thinking and Writing: Using the Reading Journal" (*English Journal,* Sept. 1985). If you haven't seen that article, read it. It is directly out of Ed's experience in the high school classroom. In a more recent article (*English Journal,* Feb. 1988), Susan Reed illustrates how to use parallel entries in a reading log and what to do with the entries once students are writing them. Like Dan and me, both Ed and Susan's point is to put students in touch with their reading through writing and to produce better writing and more perceptive reading in the process.

What I want to do with literature is to make lifetime readers, just as I want to make lifetime writers. I hope the point is clear in all of this that there is more to literature than what is in any high school literature series. Do something real with your students. That is every bit as true for reading as it is for writing. With every selection to be read, the question is—What's in it for the kid? And how can I put the student in touch with it, bring the experience of an adolescent and the written word together. One way to do it is to give them a lot of choices. Nancie Atwell, in her book *In the Middle,* has an excellent description of an eighth grade reading/literature program. It is based on students' choosing their own reading from a lot of options, with gentle "nudges" from their teacher, and writing about what they read to her and to each other. The same kind of thing works in high school and in elementary school and college, when I quit making all of the choices for my students.

At the same time, I bring my reading into the classroom just like I do my writing. I read and share with my students what I like. I give them short excerpts from things I've read, and I read to them. I read to them a lot. None of us outgrow the pleasure of being read to.

I'm going to give you something that will be outdated by the time you see it. It's just a reading list of favorite books of mine. It's a private list with nothing special about it, except most of the things on it are outdoor books and they sometimes get the attention of adolescent boys. You may find it useful for the dreamer in the corner by the window who won't read anything you suggest. The list is at the end of this chapter.

A Literary Conversation:
One More Literature/Writing Lesson

This lesson is about rubbing experiences together. It is about reading well and writing well and enjoying each more because of the other one. It comes from having fun with a favorite writer, Barry Lopez. (You can choose a favorite author of your own.) Kate Kirby and I worked it up a few years ago. It's one of my favorites because it explores several possibilities with the reading, taking me back to the work again and again. It starts in the journal but will not stay there. It has removable parts, and it's simple. What more can you ask?

1) *Setting the scene.* Write about a favorite place. Jot-list or cluster details about this setting before you write. Try to visualize the place at a particular time, maybe when something special happened there.

2) *The slide show.* More scene setting. We put together a tray of slides with nature shots. Ours were all more or less about rivers. The music to go with them was modern electronic jazz, certainly music our students had not heard before. Other good choices are Tim Weisberg or Dave Grushin. No words. We were getting ready for Lopez's *River Notes,* the work we were introducing in the lesson. Even if you do not put together a slide show, use something visual, even if it is just a poster you display during the lesson.

3) *Reading aloud.* Next we chose a lot of short excerpts from Lopez's writings and read them in a kind of "conversation," each taking a turn to read and then swapping. We liked the male and female voices in the reading. Borrow the history teacher or PE coach to help you with this.

4) *Short reading.* Then we gave them a copy of "The Log Jam" section of *River Notes* to read. We read it out loud too. There are six vignettes in this section. (We silently censored one of them for the classroom.) We read and talked, sharing what we liked about them informally, inviting students to do the same. We didn't push them. The point was to make contact with the writing, not to explicate it or find the true interpretation. We did not point out symbols or explain the elements of fiction or any of that stuff. We enjoyed Lopez's clever and beautiful prose as readers experiencing it together for the first time.

5) *Summary.* We all wrote a summary of one section. We were looking for literal understanding. (Comprehension, if you will.) And we were looking for students with problems. There usually are some. Lopez is not easy.

6) *Character.* Next we asked them to tell us about a character and to briefly "sketch" that person in their journal. I am surprised at how differently we see people.

7) *Mister Author.* Then we asked them to read the piece again and think about the kind of person who wrote it. After a five minute free write about Lopez, we shared our insights of him.

8) *Creative response.* As usual, the point here is to create something of your own suggested by or modeled after the piece. This section from *River Notes* is particularly good for this.

9) *Wrapping up.* Then we shared our drafts of the responses, looked over our other writings for other good things that had presented themselves, revised, edited, and published our writings.

10) *Finally we circled up and read to each other.* Some of us read some more Lopez and kept talking to ourselves about him in our journal. Some opted for other writers.

The point is to consider the writing on as many different levels as possible. You can even get analytic if you want to, but do analysis last. It takes a good, interesting piece to sustain interest through all of these activities. That's a matter of feel, but push your students not to turn a piece loose too soon. There is always something else in there I haven't seen yet.

Good Stuff from My Book Shelves

I have resisted the temptation to annotate these titles, as much as I like to talk about them. You can read them for yourself. And I have stayed away from all that "literary" stuff. You already know it. The list is incomplete, of course, and still growing.

Edward Abbey. *Beyond the Wall.* Holt, 1984.
_____. *Desert Solitaire.* Ballantine, 1968.
_____. *Down the River.* Dutton, 1982.
Kenneth Brower. *The Starship and the Canoe.* Holt, 1978.
Richard Brautigan. *Trout Fishing in America.* Dell, 1967.
    And many others!
Leo Buscaglia. *The Fall of Freddie the Leaf.* Slack, 1982.
Russell Chatham. *Silent Seasons.* Dutton, 1978.
Annie Dillard. *Pilgrim at Tinker Creek.* Bantam, 1974.
_____. *Teaching a Stone to Talk.* Harper, 1982.
David James Duncan. *The River Why.* Sierra, 1982.
Charles Elliot. *Gone Fishing.* Stackpole, 1953.
_____. *Gone Hunting.* Stackpole, 1954.
Paul Hemphill. *Me and the Boy.* Ivey, 1987.
Gene Hill. *Mostly Tailfeathers.* Winchester, 1975.
Aldo Leopold. *A Sand County Almanac.* Oxford, 1949.
Barry Lopez. *Arctic Dreams.* Scribner's, 1986.

_____. *Crossing Open Ground.* Scribner's, 1988.

_____. *Desert Notes.* Sheed, Andrews, McMeel, 1976.

_____. *Of Wolves and Men.* Scribner's, 1978.

_____. *River Notes.* Andrews and McMeel, 1979.

_____. *Winter Count.* Scribner's, 1981.

Patrick McManus. *A Fine and Pleasant Misery.* Holt, 1978.

_____. *Never Sniff a Gift Fish.* Holt, 1983.

_____. *They Shoot Canoes, Don't They?* Holt, 1977.

John McPhee. *Coming into the Country.* Bantam, 1977.

_____. *Pieces of the Frame.* Farrar, 1975.

Norman MacLean. *A River Runs Through It.* University of
    Chicago, 1976.

William Least Heat Moon. *Blue Highways.* Little, Brown, 1982.

Farley Mowat. *Never Cry Wolf.* Bantam, 1963.

_____. *A Whale for the Killing.* Bantam, 1972.

Sigurd Olsen.*Songs of the North.* Penguin, 1987.

Robert Pirsig. *Zen and the Art of Motorcycle Maintenance.*
    Morrow, 1974.

Burton Spiller. *Fishin' Around.* Winchester, 1974.

Hyemeyohsts Storm. *Seven Arrows.* Harper, 1972.

Charles Waterman. *The Part I Remember.* Winchester, 1974.

W.D. Wetherell. *Vermont River.* Winchester, 1984.

Craig Woods and David Seybolt. *Waters Swift and Still.*
    Winchester, 1982.

And two magazines with excellent writing and wonderful photography.

Gray's Sporting Journal
Sports Afield

Notes

1. Peter S. Beagle, ed. *The Fantasy Worlds of Peter Beagle.* Viking, 1978.

2. Alan Purves, ed. *How Porcupines Make Love: Notes on a Response-Centered Curriculum.* Xerox, 1972.

3. Tracy Tate was a student at Gainesville High School, Gainesville, GA.

CHAPTER TWELVE

Revision: The Student as Editor

Tony [Lucardo, Venetian sculptor] explained to me all the steps that have to be taken between the clay and the finished bronze. They were too many, it seemed to me. Unless the art were very great, it could not be worth the trouble.

—MARY WELSH HEMINGWAY (1)

Revision. It may be the most frustrating part of writing to teach, and to learn.

Your kids have been writing for a long time in their journals; their entries have grown from only a sentence or two to a page and more of writing each day. Good things are happening in there. Their writing in the journal and in class is spontaneous, alive, creative, self-revealing, often entertaining, sometimes very good—*but* their writing is also sloppy, plagued with spelling errors, punctuated indifferently if creatively, often one rambling paragrpah, usually too fat, and in dire need of cutting. Verb endings have evaporated, sentences run into each other, verb tenses and pronouns are errratic, conclusions don't conclude, introductions don't introduce, descriptions don't describe—in short, the writings are first drafts and need to be *revised*.

OK, you say to yourself, it's time to get *serious* about this writing stuff. The fun and games are over; it's time to bear down and get to work. These kids can obviously write—they're just lazy.

So you return that last batch of papers, make your students a little speech about cleaning up their act and maybe even getting ready for college English. You tell them to write the papers over in ink and correct their errors. You even generously offer to help them make corrections, not wanting to be too much of an ogre.

The kids groan but get to work readily enough and rewrite the papers in a suspiciously short time. They ask only two questions while they work—one about how to spell a word, the other about writing on the back. When you face the batch of "revisions" that night, the results confirm your worst suspicions. Most of the papers are very neatly copied over in ink, carefully preserving every error in the original draft. A few kids have made a halfhearted attempt at correcting misspellings and punctuation—their papers get worse about as often as they get better. Only two kids seem to have done any effective revision of their papers, and they always do the best writing in the class anyway. There's even the kid in the back of the room who wrote his over in *pencil*—you wonder if he ever used a pen in his life.

You wonder where you can go from here and think maybe kids are just too irresponsible to do any really good writing and maybe you'll take that job at K-Mart and forget the whole business. Or that's how it looks right now, late at night, fatigued, frustrated, and feeling dead-ended.

But keep in mind that revision in writing is more than eliminating surface errors in spelling, puncutation, and usage. And before you sigh and reach for the grammar book and those *serious* writing exercises, remember that revision does not have to be drudgery either. Revision, as Donald Murray has said, is just that—*re*vision, "seeing" it again (2). When we revise our writing and do a good job of it, we see it anew, and from a different perspective. We become our own reader, and we become critical and questioning—at least as much as we are able. We also read with appreciation and enjoyment. But this, too, is something we learn. Kids aren't lazy because they don't revise in detail a paper given back with the impatient command to write it over and make it better. They simply haven't been taught *how* to revise yet.

Learning to revise writing is part of the larger developmental process of learning to write. Because it's a growth process, it needs to be approached systematically and with some knowlege of how the process is likely to take place. Our job is to make students competent *revisers,* and therefore better writers, rather than to turn them into error correctors. In this chapter Dan and I suggest some good places to start the process of revision with students once you have them writing, and we point out some things about revision that will help you teach this potentially frustrating part of writing more systematically and with more success.

1. *The revision process is really a series of closely related activities.* A term describing writing, and especially revision, you will hear often is *recursive.* Writing is recursive because the writer keeps circling back on the writing, tinkering, changing things, rethinking, rearranging mentally and on paper, anticipating what is coming up. It complicates writing

wonderfully, making it practically impossible to describe with any authority. But to set aside the theorists and researchers for a moment and say it another way, when I write I also read and fix. I read in chunks behind myself, dotting an *i,* checking a spelling, adding a word, moving a sentence, putting things in, throwing things out—trying to get it to "sound right." And I run ahead of myself down the page, already thinking of what I will say next. Without this recursive capacity, writing would be virtually impossible—so would talking, thinking, and even reading.

So writers do many things all at the same time, and they should. So how do I teach revision? Knowing students are going to be all over the place at once in a piece of writing does not mean I cannot point out to them parts of the process that will most help them make their writing better. And my job is to simplify their job and chop it up into pieces for them so they can handle it in manageable chunks. Because you are doing a lot of things at once does not mean I cannot teach you. Fly fishing is a pretty complicated activity too, but I can teach you how to do it. You see what I mean? When I teach writing as *craftsmanship,* and not a body of knowledge to master, the job becomes doable.

It helps me to think of revising writing in four steps, knowing they overlap and can happen at the same time—in-process revision, re-vision, editing, and proofreading. At some point I will focus attention on them separately, coaching young writers in the tricks of the trade, demonstrating to them how they work for me.

In-process revision takes place as the writing is going on, and it is one of the things that makes writing such a complicated business. Writers ask themselves as they go along questions something like—Is this what I really want to say?—and they make adjustments to try to get closer to their intended purpose. They add words and phrases and sometimes sentences; they cross out things; they change things. They listen to the *voice* of the writing and make adjustments so it will "sound right." They become their own *readers* even as they write, often stopping to reread part of the paper from the beginning. They look back to see what has already been done, and they look ahead, anticipating what will be said next.

In-process revision is hard to observe, probably impossible to measure, and certainly as individual as the writer; but we do know that it grows with practice. As writers reach maturity, they probably interrupt the writing more and more and spend more time as readers and in-process revisers than they actually spend writing.

Reading out loud is one way to enhance in-process revision in the classroom, but reading aloud does so many things for growing writers it is hard to isolate its effects on revision. I try to teach students to "read with a pencil" like I do. In a reading session, I always have a pen in my hand, marking my journal as I read from it. And I try to make my thoughts visible to them, interrupting to tell them what I'm doing to the writing as I read. And we talk about our struggles, writer to writer, and our efforts to "make it sound right."

Re-vision: I write it like this to remind me that a good bit of revision is seeing it again a different way. Donald Murray has helped me understand revision in this sense more than any other writer and teacher. There is value in trying a piece or a subject from several different perspectives, of literally writing whole drafts from scratch. I have never encouraged enough of that in my classroom, always too anxious that the job get done by Friday. Deadlines are necessary. All writers have them. But I also need to teach my students the option of trying things a different way.

One place you can put this notion to work immediately is writing leads. Students can have better papers instantly if they will just do something about how they start them. You grab me or lose me in the first paragraph or half page. It's a simple matter to write three or four leads for a paper that has trouble getting warmed up. No, I'm not talking about topic sentences. I teach writers, not little English rhetoricians.

My job here often is simply to be alert to possibilities they might have missed and to ask a lot of questions. Have you thought about doing it this way? Are you satisfied with this order? How will you end it? Where does it really start? What are you trying to say really? Does it do what you want it to do?

Editing, in my lexicon, involves at least two people working on the piece of writing, writer and editor. The relationship is a special one, supportive, helpful, nonthreatening, probing, sometimes challenging. I work as an editor with my students, but I prefer to train them to be editors for each other in groups.

This takes time early in the class, but it saves me time later. And the rewards go far beyond teaching writing. I use Response Groups, the way the National Writing Project folks taught me; and I recommend that model of editing groups to you. Each group has a leader, responsible mainly for seeing that each member reads and participates. When I lead a group, the first question I ask before each member reads is "What help do you need from this group for this piece of writing?" I want them to put into words how the group can help them specifically before they read. This keeps us from shotgunning, and it keeps us from saying vague things like "That was nice." After the reading I will make sure each person around the table responds to the reader's request for help. At least I want them to try to speak to the reader's stated problem with the piece. At first this is not always easy. But we keep at it, and it doesn't take us long to become pretty good editors for each other. And because we all take part, we all have ownership in the group.

At the same time, as the teacher, I rotate from group to group concentrating mainly on modeling responses after members read. Sandra Worsham at Baldwin County High School, Georgia, taught me a simple way to train response groups. She pulls a group of experienced kids into the center of the room, their five desks facing in a tight circle. The other kids circle close behind them. She simply leads the group in reading and responding, pausing now and then to point out to the audience at their backs why they are doing certain things. It looks weird at first, and the first time in the center sure feels funny. But it works.

Proofreading sometimes takes place with editing. It's the job of cleaning up the paper, eliminating surface errors. It's the least important activity of revision, until the final stages of the paper. Following the lead of college freshman profs and such people, some writing teachers have taught only this kind of revision, leaving their students with the impression that learning to be a good writer is learning to avoid or correct errors. It's a narrow and narrow-minded approach to teaching writing, and alone it produces properly correct and uniformly unreadable prose.

2. Revision should be taught in terms of what we know about the processes of writing and in terms of what we know about the growth of young writers. We don't get frustrated and angry when the novice violinist saws out squawks and screeches. We encourage the novice to practice, and we endure the assault on our ears with patience, knowing this racket will grow into sweet music with time, regular effort, and proper direction.

A lot of our problem is solved when we quit thinking of revision as correcting mistakes and start to *teach* kids how to revise. When we do that, we discard the old prejudice that kids are lazy and have to be forced to make their writing better, and we become able to see just what they do when they write and revise—if we are willing to take the time to watch them. And we start to see how they develop as writers and how revision fits into that development.

Kids are not lazy. They want to write good papers, and they work hard at it. Dan and I both have done a lot of formal and informal research on students' writing. We've watched a lot of kids writing and revising papers. I'm amazed at how hard they work. I watched and documented one high school senior who planned, drafted, revised, and rewrote a paper in one class period, after instructions, and made fifty-three effective changes from the original to a revised draft! And her work is not unusual.

I have seen students do a wonderful job revising and editing their writing when it has been clearly demonstrated to them what they are to do—and when they work in an atmosphere that is not threatening. I have seen them grow from halting, damaged writers barely able to fill part of a page with unreadable prose into good writers with style and sometimes brilliance, and always with excitement and joy, in one semester of work with a well-trained editing group.

Forget the notion that kids can't revise, and take some time to watch them. Then structure your class to help them do a better job. Show them how and plan ways for them to help each other. And make sure what you ask them to do is appropriate, for them and for the writing job at hand.

3. *Revision cannot be successful until students are practiced in a particular mode of writing.* They cannot be confident enough to tinker with a piece of writing until they have practiced enough and know they will not destroy what they have worked so hard to get on the page. If you're getting resistance from normally willing students when you try to get them to work on revision, then you may need to go back to writing assignments such as those in Chapter 4 for more practice before pushing revision too hard.

And remember, when your students begin with a new mode of writing, they need time to practice this new experience before they can be expected to be able to revise it with any success. Students who happily write and revise personal narratives into flawless form cannot be expected to write and revise well a movie review the first few times they try, although both are legitimate kinds of writing for your class. Let them get comfortable with the new kind of writing first. Let them get the feel of it and find out what they have to say before you expect them to do a good job revising it.

4. *The piece of writing to be revised needs to be important to the student.* The usual situation in the classroom is that students want to finish papers as quickly as possible and turn them in so they'll not have to fool with them anymore. That is especially true when your students feel that their papers are not good enough. School has encouraged this get-it-done-fast approach to writing with days neatly divided into hour-long class periods and teachers insisting, "Turn it in at the end of the period." Because we're not willing to take the time with a piece of writing, we get hastily done and shoddily produced two-draft papers (one class period for the assignment, prewriting, and first draft; then one more class period for the rewrite—and older kids get to do *both* drafts in one period!) We teach our students to write fast, and we teach mediocrity. There is no reason why we can't spend more time teaching revision on fewer papers.

One of our jobs is to recognize promising pieces and encourage our students to keep them going. Dennis was a big, lumbering boy in my second period class (3). He was state champion and an All-National wrestler, and he had trouble with his writing all semester. I trotted out my best, most creative, and strangest assignments—and he sweated and suffered and wrestled the pencil across the page. Early one week I assigned one of my more bizarre flights of fancy. The class buzzed with prewriting talk for a few minutes and fell to work writing. Dennis chewed his pencil.

The class was working on experiences (see the *Two-Day Writing Workshop* at the end of the chapter). "Just write me a *memory,* Dennis. Tell me about it." And the end of the period he was writing. He stopped precisely five minutes before the bell rang with that uncanny sense of timing students seem to have.

"Here. This is about my uncle. It ain't too good." He grinned as if he was glad the ordeal was over. Dennis was right. It ain't too good.

> I'm going to tell you about a man that lives in Chicago. He has a 6th grade education and is an elevator repairman. He quit school and went to work because his parents were very poor and he stopped caring about education. He lived in the ghetto and was in a street gang. When he was about 18 or 20 he was learning a lot about mechanics. Finally he started working on elevators and he was doing great. One of his biggest jobs was working on the elevators in the Sears building. He is the best man in the business. They want to move him up higher, but he refuses to take the written test. He could take an oral test, but he is too proud to tell them the reason for an oral test. So he hasn't moved up in a long time. He now has a 10 year old son that reads as good as him.

He was reluctant to go back to work on the paper the next day. Like most students, he figured that one period and one page ought to be enough to satisfy any English teacher. But we talked for a while about his uncle. I wanted to read more about him (and I thought that possibly a good piece of writing was there), and Dennis was certainly interested in *talking* about him. Then we talked about the writing. I told him to concentrate on *seeing* his uncle in the writing and to "tell me about him." Dennis added this part quickly on the back of the first paper.

> he is a short stocky man about 30, he is Italian always has hair greased back, he is always dirty, he is considered a dago, he lived in the mid western part of the city, I'm not sure what the neighbor-

hood was called, except for don't go through there all the dagos will kill you.

I told him I liked the details. We talked some more about his uncle. Dennis's ideas were really cooking. "Okay, Dennis, now put it together, and how about some paragraphs this time?" So he wrote a third draft.

I'm going to tell you about a dago from Chicago. He has acquired a 6th grade education and he is a elevator repairman. He quit school to get a job because his parents were poor and life was hard.

He lived in the ghetto in an all Italian neighborhood. He belonged to a street gang. He was now about 18 or 20 and learning about mechanics. He got a break and started working on elevators in the Sears Tower. They want to move him up in the business, but he refuses to take the written test. He is too proud to tell them he can't read to take an oral test. You can still picture him sort of short, stocky build, hair greased back, dago t-shirt, tatoo of a heart and an old girl friend's name, he is always dirty. His house is filled with comic books of his sons that he reads for practice. His 10 year old son now reads and writes better than him. He is now about 35 and makes the same pay as when he was 30, and he does a better job.

Well, the paragraphs almost got in. Dennis knew that it still didn't say what he wanted it to, but now we had a piece of writing we could work with. And he was willing to work at it to get what he wanted. We went over the draft carefully together, talking about what was good, how to use particular details to say some things better, where paragraphs might go, how to punctuate it, some points about spelling. We talked some more about his uncle, and he wrote his fourth and final draft.

I'm going to tell you about a dago from Chicago. He has a 6th grade education, and he is an elevator repairman. He quit school to get a job when he was a boy because his parents were poor and life was hard.

He lived in the ghetto in an all Italian neighborhood. He belonged to a street gang. He was 18 and learning about mechanics. He got a break and went to work repairing elevators, and he was doing great at it. His biggest job was the elevators in the Sears Tower. They want to move him up in the business, but he refuses to take the written test. He is too proud to tell them he can't read.

I can still picture him—sort of short, stocky build, hair greased back, dago t-shirt, tattoo on his arm. It is a heart with an old girl friend's name. During the day he is always covered with dirt and grease.

His house is filled with his son's comic books, but he reads them too. His 10 year old son reads and writes better than he does. He is about 35 and makes the same pay as he did five years ago.

Dennis's paper still doesn't capture the feeling he has about his uncle when he talks. And in many ways it's not a good piece of writing from a high school junior. But it's much better than his first try, and he learned by working with it. He and I felt good about the paper when he finished. He also recognized that most readers would deeply resent his using the word "dago," even if it was a neutral term to him.

If the piece of writing is meaningful to them, most students are willing to revise extensively and will seek your help in making it better. Your interest in what they're writing and your encouragement of the good things you find are the most important factors in keeping them going through the work of several drafts, but there are a few other simple things you can do to encourage revision.

Choosing from several pieces to edit is one way of getting something the student is willing to work on longer. After all, *selecting* is an important form of editing. If I expect my students to take a paper through more than one draft, I always try to make sure they can choose from at least three things they have written.

When a piece is revised to be published, the student is more interested in getting it right. Publishing makes the writing real to your students, no longer only an exercise to turn in to the teacher. In-class publishing is essential to any meaningful work on revision because it gives students a valid reason to revise their writing.

Working together in groups to revise papers is another way to give students an audience for their writing and, therefore, a reason to revise. Reading aloud the papers they are working on is an important tool in revision work, but you'll have to structure opportunities for it in your classroom carefully. Students need to hear their writing, and the immediate response of a group of classmates can be very valuable in editing a paper.

I don't hesitate to use the grade to get students to revise their writing. Part of Dennis's willingness to work so hard on his paper instead of turning in the first draft and forgetting it was that I promised him a good grade if he would improve it. Notice, I say *improve* it, rather than correct its errors. I wanted him to do more than proofread it. I have found that my students do a better job and work harder when I tell them the good things in their writing and ask them to expand on those, rather than telling them, "This is what you did wrong." There are times when I withhold the grade for poorly done papers from capable students until they try again, but my best success with revision in the classroom has always come when I've emphasized what they're doing right.

5. *The three minute conference can be very effective in teaching revision.* You need to see Nancie Atwell's *In the Middle* for this one. She describes how she conferences with her eighth graders *every day!* No, a good writing conference doesn't have to take more than three minutes.

Just like in the response group, I ask the student, "How can I help you?" The writing belongs to the writer, not to me. I do not take papers out of their hands and show them how to fix them. I do not talk first, unless it is to ask them to tell me about the piece and the help they might need.

If they draw a blank and don't know what help to ask for, then I ask them to read the piece to me quietly. I tell them what I hear and ask them again, "What help do you need?" Usually that gets us going. Sometimes I send them back to their response group, and in some classes I will not conference with a kid if he hasn't tried the piece out on his group. They own the writing. I don't want them dependent on me. "Is this good?" and "Read this and tell me what you think" get no response from me.

I teach a lot in conference, and I see some real growth in their writing from it. I enjoy it. But what I like best about this teaching is that it is directed by the student according to what each one needs for a particular piece of writing at a particular time.

6. *You're the first model for your students. You need to write with them, and you need to revise with them.* Let them see you struggle with writing. Talk to them about what you're doing as you revise. Go through the whole process with them, talking about your problems and the way you try to solve them with each step. Show them the different drafts of your work and the way it changes from one draft to the next.

7. *Remember that there are individual differences in the way students revise.* When you teach revision, you need to allow enough flexibility for these differences in your classroom.

You've seen the drafts of the paper Dennis produced, each time getting a little closer to what he was trying to say. Look at this original and revised paper by Lynn, from the same class.

Original Draft

The jumps are coming and the horse breaks into a dead run. Low again the rider prepares for the jump. Up and over, the horse's legs stretch outward and down for the ground making a huge arch.

Revised Paper

The jumps are nearing and my horse breaks into a dead run. Staying low on its back I prepare for the jump. Up and over. My horse's legs extend. Stretching and reaching for the ground on the other side. Making a huge arch in the air (3).

It's a very different kind of writing, of course. But Lynn is also a very different reviser from Dennis, as this paper illustrates. Two drafts usually do it for her, but she does a great deal of in-process revising. She does little editing (she changed point of view here on my suggestion), but she's a near-perfect proofreader.

Being able to do a good job in two drafts is rare in the high school classroom, but you'll have a few students who work well in a short time. Cary, a senior, did this remarkable job of editing a creative response to a song from only a series of impressionistic notes. He did the whole job from listening to the song for the first time to the final essay in less than an hour.

Original Draft

There Only Was One Choice

"Strum your guitar, Sing it kid"
"Just write about your feelings, not the things you never did"
You can hear your footsteps shuffling in the dust
Rustling of shadows tells you secrets you can trust.

—HARRY CHAPIN *(Dance Band on the Titanic)*

An attempt at a modern American ballad, but also a stream of consciousness, dreams and subconsicous thoughts. The story of his life? yes but also a returning cycle. He begins as a young boy playing a guitar on the street corner, and as he grows learns the secrets of life through his music, that he can use his music to make other people happy and to give his own life meaning that he might otherwise have missed, "Strum your guitar, Sing it kid/Just write about your feelings, not the things you never did." An expression of individuality, a stab at being different and getting the most out of life. He, through music, discovers the little secrets that life offers, "You can hear your footsteps shuffling in the dust,/the rustling of shadows tells you secrets you can trust." He has been happy with his work and his accomplishments, that "his journey has been worthwhile." And he passes on his knowledge to his son, "Just write about your feelings, not the things you never did." But the one question is whether he is singing about himself, his son, or maybe the two are actually one and inseparable. Maybe he and his son, and his son, and his son, etc. will always continue, throughout eternity, mortal, yet immortal through time, synonymous with his/their music (3).

Revised Paper

There Only Was One Choice
HARRY CHAPIN

Chapin makes an attempt at a modern American ballad, creating a folk hero in the music field, but the song is also a stream of flowing dreams, aspirations, and conscious and subconscious thoughts. Maybe the story of *his* life, but also a recurring cycle of generations past and yet to come.

He begins his story as a young boy playing a guitar on the street corner, and as he grows, he learns the secrets of the trade as well as some idea of what life is about through his music, travel, and dedication to his calling. He learns to live in reality, "Strum your guitar; sing it, kid/Just write about your feelings, not the things you never did."

The song is an expression of a young man's individuality, a stab at being different, in a search for the most living life has to give. Music is the young man's form of self-expression, but also a close friend and advisor, "You can hear your footsteps shuffling in the dust/The rustling of the shadows tells you secrets you can trust."

Chapin also makes a point about his age, and the fears of growing old without some great accomplishment, but he wants to pass his knowledge on to his son, to start him on the same road he passed as a growing boy. And so the story ends, and so the story begins again. He sings of the mortality of his self, but his dreams and hopes, through each preceding and each following generation, each revolution of the wheel, starts an old journey all anew. Each individual is not really separate, but each entity is only one being, striving as a whole toward perfection. The only problem is that there are so many footsteps to take, and each foot is unaware what the other is doing until the results can be analyzed and the next move made. Only experience counts, and to gain this, inexperience must be overcome, only to reveal more inexperience to be overcome again.

"Strum your guitar; sing it, kid/Just write about your feelings, not the things you never did."

Although I don't encourage it in my students, I'm usually a two-draft writer like Lynn (or three sometimes if the piece is for publication). But Dan is a multidraft writer, which leads to all kinds of complications when we work together on something. He and I both go through the *agonies* of prewriting. I think that is universal if you write. And we talk a lot about what we're going to write before we start. When he's finally ready (and it seems to take him a long time to get ready), Dan writes what he calls a *zero draft* straight through without stopping. It's handwritten very fast in his blocky calligraphy and is almost free written, without pauses for corrections, rephrasings, or changes in order. It awes me a little to watch him. My first draft is always handwritten slowly and painfully, and I do a great many in-process changes as I go. I reread, I tinker, I write notes to myself in the margin, I write alternate words and phrases between the lines, I strike out and rewrite, I chew up the tops of my pens. Dan wrote the zero draft of the chapter on expository writing in two hours; this chapter's draft so far has taken me nineteen days, writing a little each day.

After I've typed a copy and proofread it, I'm ready to be through. I hate the drudgery of typing, and I'm a bad editor. At that point Dan is just really getting down to work. It's not at all unusual for a piece of his to take six drafts, and more, before he's satisfied with it. Dan says he's afraid he'll lose it before he can get it on the page. Once it's there, he's ready to play around with it. Writing as slowly as I do, I don't really have that fear. But once I've finally got it down, I'm afraid I'll spoil it if I play around with it too much, although now word processing helps a lot.

The point is that there will be both kinds of writer/revisers in any writing class you teach, and both of them (and all those somewhere in between) need your suggestions and encouragement to get better at writing.

8. *Students should have the choice not to revise.* Remember that students can't really do a good job of revising unless the piece is important to them. If they are not ready for revising, or not really involved in the writing, then pushing them to edit in depth and proofread in detail will be a frustrating experience for them and an exasperating one for you. As you work on revision, you need to be sensitive to when students have had enough. Dennis and I could have continued with his paper, but he was tired of it after four tries—and so was I. We may return to it later, but we've done enough for now.

Remember, also, that sometimes the piece of writing itself is not worth the trouble. The art of the clay is not always worth the steps to make the finished bronze.

Keeping It Going

With me, it gets to be very practical. Most students I teach come to me knowing nothing of revision beyond hunting errors in a first draft, and they're not very good at that. The first thing I have to do is get them to work on a paper more than a class period. Sometimes more than fifteen minutes.

Students want to finish the thing and turn it in. I want them to write something real for them and me and turn it into a quality piece of work. How do I keep them at it?

First, the writing must be important *to the student.* I've said it already in this chapter and through this book in different ways, but it won't hurt to tell you again. *Their writing belongs to them.* You will save yourself and your students a lot of grief if you can accept that idea—and they will write better.

Response groups in an inviting and encouraging atmosphere show my students possibilities and let them know that their writing is appreciated and taken seriously. For most of them their peers' approval makes the difference between writing that is merely a class exercise, something to get done and turn in, and writing that is an expression of who they are.

I push them. Nancie Atwell "nudges" her students. I shove mine. "Tell me more. Tell me more." They hear that more than anything else from me. God bless Don Murray and the three minute conference. I tell them frankly, "You are used to finishing it and turning it in. I want you to try to stretch it. There's something here you haven't said yet."

Dan is more organized than I am. His students, like mine, write a lot of short, exploratory pieces, looking for important writings that will grab them. Then he has them work with a partner on what he calls "elaboration" and individually on "crafting," giving them specific instructions for two revisions. Take a look at his notes on the personal narrative, the kind of writing done in the "Anatomy" suggested at the end of Chapter 2.

Elaboration: First Revision Options for Personal Narrative

Read your piece aloud to a partner. Listen for places where you can add more stuff. Mark these places as you read it.

Try at least two elaborations. More is better.

1. *Character.* Flesh out a person in your story. Describe the character in more detail. Select one or two things about the character and develop them like a cartoonist would. How do his hands look? How does her mouth work when she smiles or talks? What about hair, eyes, clothes? Favorite sayings? Where do you see the character when you close your eyes?
2. *Dialogue.* Let them talk. Don't tell us what they say. Let's hear it from them. Don't worry about how you punctuate it now. Just use real voices.
3. *Scene Setting.* Develop scenes in your piece in more detail. Look for parts where you mention a place but don't give us a picture of it.
4. *Looping.* Find the best parts in your piece and take off on another free writing from there. See what else you know about this memory. Run the movie in your head again.
5. *Write More.* Finish it. Tell it all. Pick up the story right where you left off and ride it to the end.
Remember, the key is to write more.

Crafting: Second Revision Options for Personal Narrative

This is the tough part. You have to work alone, and you won't always know what you're doing. You can try these revisions out on somebody later, but right now you have to hack it out alone.

Begin first with chunks, pieces of text that are several sentences long. Choose at least one of these to work with.

1) Beginnings. (Try at least two.)

1. The Hook: "I should have known Mrs. Swartz hated kids."
2. Scene setting: "It was a dark and stormy night."
3. Telling detail: "There on the pavement was a small child's tennis shoe."
4. Character throwing: "Teddy Howland was the skinniest, ugliest kid in Eureka."
5. Walking: "Giving credit where credit is due, if it hadn't been for my mother, I never would have gotten him in the first place, mainly because my father didn't like dogs."
6. Dialogue: "I'm not even sure I like you."

2) Endings. (Try at least two.)

1. Circle: End where you began.
2. Ah ha!: Sadder but wiser, or gee look what I learned.
3. A feeling: Stuck in Mobile with the Memphis blues again.
4. Drawstring: "And that's how it happened."
5. Surprise: The strange twist at the end.

3) Moving Chunks. (No limit. Cut and paste.)

1. Movement: Pacing readers, making them play your game.
2. Paragraphs: Have some. Keep them short unless they have pictures.
3. Scenes: Shuffling the story.

4) Deleting Chunks. (No limit. Follow rules.)

1. Nice but doesn't fit. Save it.
2. Not nice and doesn't fit either. Cut it.
3. Chaff words. "ly" words, "being" words.
4. Compact and compress. Cut the "telling."

Now that the hard part is done, turn to some relaxing sentence level revisions. Make at least ten specific changes.

5) Sentence Level.

1. Concrete detail. Add sensory stuff.
2. Specificity. Name stuff.
3. Strong verbs. Get rid of those adverb props.
4. Search and destroy the *is*'s and *was*'s.
5. Cure a serious case of the *would's*.

Notice that whether you teach revision strategies like these in two formal steps the way Dan does or informally in conferences and editing groups the way I do, your kids are still writing and you haven't gotten to proofreading yet. Do it last, as we suggest; and you will find it is less of a problem than it once was. Try it. It may surprise you.

The Computer and Revision

I have a confession to make. I only recently learned to use the computer. Word processing is pretty new to me. Dan told me what it would do for my writing. I didn't listen. I was a stick in the mud. I didn't have time to fool with that stuff. It looked hard. I was doing just fine with my writing, thank you, and so were my students. Besides, all that talk of bits and bites and memory and floppies and disk drives and software scared me. Let the math teachers play with the machines. That was their area, after all.

While I was working on my dissertation, I spent a lot of time in Dan's home. While I was laboriously writing chapters out in longhand and typing them—and retyping and retyping and retyping and retyping —Dan was happily working on a couple of books in front of the green screen of his Apple. I was tearing my hair out over every revision, every correction in a draft. He was pecking away, moving things around in his chapters, throwing stuff out, putting things in, fixing things—and *smiling*! It took me a while longer, but it finally sank in that there might be a better way.

So if you are a little leery of the computer and word processing, I know how you feel. But it is more than worth your time to learn it. Today I don't know how I would get my work done without the magic machine. And it is a wonderful tool for a writer.

The first experience I had teaching word processing to kids was in a low-level ninth grade class at Albany High School. I taught the class with Becky Howard, a fine writer and teacher of writing. She had less experience with computers than I did. Fifth period in an unair-conditioned building in South Georgia in a hot September. We figured the kids would like the machines all right, and they had done some writing we liked. So far so good. Could we make it work and get some real revision done? Would they run amok in the library the first time we turned them loose? Would they run amok the first time something went wrong? Would we know what had gone wrong and be able to fix it? Were we in over our heads?

We checked ourselves out with the word processing program we were using with the Apple computers, paired the students up (we didn't have enough machines for everyone), gave them instructions as brief as we dared, took a deep breath, and marched them over to the library.

They were wonderful! Within a week they knew more about the program than we did. We could hardly get them off the machines at the end of each class. The librarian got mad because they were hanging around the library all the time. Almost nobody in the room could type. They spent hours hunt-and-peck writing, and more hours revising and editing. Nobody ran amok, not even when I dumped two days' work for five kids when I hit the wrong button at the end of class. Partners really helped each other. We all talked about writing and had a marvelous time.

With limited equipment, our rule was that you had to have a finished draft before you took a turn word processing. Our goal was to publish the best writing from their journals. We were thinking of one piece from each of them. They wouldn't let us stop there. They wanted to write more and keep on working.

I have not explored what word processing can do for students' writing and writing instruction. I have just gotten started. What I saw in that class and in classes since then are students I could not get to look at a paper twice willing to work on pieces for hours because of the computer. Revision, in spades! If you need convincing, the kids will make a believer out of you.

I pretend no expertise with the computer or word processing. I am a rank beginner. But I have written this section because I suspect a lot of English teachers are like me, and like me will find it almost indispensable once you begin using it with your own writing and with your students.

I can't talk the relative merits of different brands of hardware or software with you. I'm writing this on an Apple IIe, using *AppleWorks* software, because we use Apple computers in my school system and everybody in this building uses *AppleWorks*. That gives me friends to talk to when it does something I don't understand, like when my writing suddenly disappears. Oh, yes. They tell me this machine has an "80 column card" in it and will not do word processing without it. I take their word for it. Of course, you will also need a printer—not for every machine if there are several you have access to, but at least one in the room.

In case it's important to you, I like the Apple IIe, and I like the software. Dan likes Macintosh. We use MECC software in many of our classes because my system has a contract with the company and the software for the teacher is virtually free. Frankly, I don't like *MECC Writer* as much as *AppleWorks* or even *AppleWriter*, but we can make as many copies of the MECC program for kids to use as we want and it is easy for inexperienced kids to learn.

Don't worry about all the technical stuff. Like me, you'll use whatever machines are available. Start with a friend, if you can. This is hands-on learning—trying it, messing up, talking through what went wrong, and trying again. Use a word processing program with commands just as easy as you can find. Some are much harder to learn and use than others. I don't try to use any that take longer than a couple of hours for me to start writing. You will find that once you learn to use one of them, others are similar and easy to learn. I do not use pirated copies of software. Nobody should.

Like other things I do, I use the magic machine and word processing with my students because I use these tools in my own writing.

Notes

1. Mary Welsh Hemingway. *How It Was.* Knopf, 1976.
2. Donald Murray. Workshop on Writing at Georgia State University, Atlanta, GA, Spring, 1979.
3. Dennis Turner, Lynn Aaron, and Cary Quinn were students at Gainesville High School, Gainesville, GA.

CHAPTER THIRTEEN

Expository Writing

The young are taught expository writing and learn to keep in their places, growing up to stand before their computers, languishing for lack of a poetic touch in their day, their own stories finished before their lives....

—JOHN ROUSE (1)

If you glanced quickly past the earlier chapters of this book because they were referring to "creative writing" and you teach "real, hard-core composition," you're just the person we want to talk to. Many English teachers make arbitrary distinctions between writing about personal matters using descriptive and narrative forms and writing about more substantive issues using the expositional forms of comparing and contrasting, arguing, persuading, and explaining. We take a far less prescriptive, less form-bound view of exposition. When we look at a fine piece of nonfiction by Lewis Thomas or a well-crafted essay by John McPhee, we notice how these writers blur the sharp lines of form, putting all the elements of good writing to work. Contemporary exposition borrows heavily from narrative and descriptive writings. Teachers and students alike need to read and explore many examples of modern exposition to get a sense of how the form and its content are changing.

We don't mean to say we find exposition easy to teach, however. We're still puzzling over it and tinkering with our strategies. Our students, who seem eager to write in other forms, balk at essay writing. The same students who have found a voice in journals, in stories, or in poetry suddenly lose confidence when they undertake the dreaded "essay." Their voices turn stiff and lifeless and their writing turns timid and halting. We wonder why that happens and what we can do about it.

Ruth and I started some serious experimenting with the phenomenon this past fall. Ruth had a group of wonderfully bright and confident seniors. Somebody had told these kids that they were smart and could write well. We asked them to show off a bit by writing an essay for us in response to a literature selection. We expected lucid, confident, imaginative, well-formed prose. We got thesis statements, topic sentences which introduced new paragraphs and in some foggy way related to the thesis, and transitions formed with words ("Anyhowever and furthermoreover" as Dan calls them) rather than ideas. Almost without exception when writers came to the fifth paragraph, they concluded with a summary. Generally the papers were not very risky, ideas were tentatively and somewhat amateurishly advanced, and the conclusions told us what we already knew. Big disappointment.

These same students had wowed us on previous days with their humor, insight, and articulateness. We got to know these young people through their voices, both oral and written. Stephanie spoke with language rich in metaphor, as she likened Peter Caldwell, in Updike's *The Centaur,* to a "spider clinging to the filaments of his father's failures to justify his own life." And Darin, who saw with the artist's eye the "clouds marbled with snow" and the "night punch the sky black" in a story he'd written, and Alyssa's sense of rhythm and sound in her poetry (2):

> Passive consent is
> the first trick she learned
>
> cracking her fingers
>
> one
>
> at a
>
> time
>
> her eyes glazing over like
> copper pennies kept too long
>
> Her backbone's knife edge makes
> curling uncomfortable
>
> the best she can do is imitate
> a wilt

Where were those voices in the essays? They had disappeared along with the humor, insight, metaphor, and attention to language we knew these kids had in their heads.

We were frustrated. Dan gave them his "When is the last time you went to B. Dalton's and asked for the latest best seller volume of five-paragraph essays'' speech. They laughed but didn't believe we were seriously questioning a form they had fretted and sweated to learn.

We didn't back down. We talked about getting their voices back into those pieces and using their unique ways of seeing in exposition. We reminded them they could do it. We'd seen evidence in the stories and poems they had shared with us.

They sat silent, wide-eyed, and numb, a little shell-shocked, perhaps. After all, they'd worked hard to learn a form, had it down pat, and now we were asking them to consider its usefulness and effect. Most of all, they puzzled, wizened their brows, and thought us a bit crazy. Questions started to fly:

> But aren't essays supposed to give a voice of authority and straightforward information without any of the creative stuff?

> We were told you can't use "I" and now you tell us its OK. What will next year's teacher say?

> Don't essays always follow the five-paragraph format?

> I thought essays had to sound academic. How can I be credible as a writer if I use my own voice?

> Don't you need to give pros and cons in all papers?

> If you don't summarize in a conclusion, what do you write?

> What about introductions? What should they do?

We found that these students had listened carefully to their teachers. They had created products that demonstrated their mastery of ill-conceived notions and just plain bad advice about essay writing. We think there are good reasons why this happens and we want to explore those before we consider an alternative approach.

Problems with Expository Writing

1. *Past experience.* Most of us sat in desks during the days when little writing other than theme, report, or formal essay was taught. We use the word "taught" loosely. Most of us were simply told to write. The instructor set arbitrary standards that made the job of evaluating the paper easier—form, length, mechanics, spelling. But we knew that little attention would be given to content, voice, style, or to generating ideas.

Now in our more enlightened state, with the emphasis on processes of writing, we've found it easier to work expressive writing into our classrooms—journals, reaction papers, free writing. It's an impressive list and most of us feel comfortable assigning, discussing, and evaluating the expressive now. Essays remain a problem, however. Most teachers we talk to are still perplexed about how to juggle all the demands of teaching such a complex form. This transactional writing, as James Britton calls it (3), asks the writer to control a number of contrastive features all at once: the form, the language—both syntax and diction—the topic, and the voice. Student writers are like beginning jugglers, having trouble keeping all of the demands in the air.

Even for us processy types, "essay" remains a dirty word. When we assign essays, we still expect the procedure to be painful and unrewarding for us and our students. Preconceived notions of structure and prohibitions of language and form abound, but the genre remains illusive. Sometimes "essay" means reporting, sometimes persuasion, sometimes formal pieces explicating literary works, but always a confusing, confining, jumble of advice and prescriptions. We've created a history with "essay" that hangs like an albatross around the necks of English teachers in writing classrooms. The resultant confusion leaves teachers and writers uncertain about the constraints and freedoms associated with essay writing—especially the freedoms. Our process knowledge doesn't do us much good if we can't find ways to apply it to the teaching of exposition.

2. *Expository writing isn't form first.* Somehow students get the notion that the structure of what they have to say takes precedence over what is said. Teachers often talk too much about structure before students have a subject they understand well enough to write about in exposition. We haven't spent much time noticing what students have to say. They hear us talk, talk and talk about thesis statements, topic sentences, outlines, 500 words, and five paragraphs, but they hear little talk about collecting, percolating, generating information. Expository writing isn't a cookie cutter operation. Subject matter cannot be rolled out, stamped out, molded and baked at 350 degrees.

As writers we know subject seeks its own form in the best writing, but we don't trust students to go through the messy process of finding it. Rather, ideas fall into stilted structure, stilted language. Students say nothing in a structured way, and we praise them for the structure. We get idealess and voiceless papers with impeccable structure.

Form doesn't make up for the problems a writer might have. The five-paragraph essay does not take the place of superficial subject or the lack of interest or knowledge of subject. Form may be perfect and subject may lag. Form alone cannot carry feeling and caring and meaning.

Attempting to simplify the task for students by reducing composing to a formula promotes bad writing and bad thinking habits. The five-paragraph "theme," the topic sentence, and the well-tuned outline are all artifacts of formula writing that diminish student options and stifle the writing processes. The result is often form without meaning, "correct language" without power, and rhetoric without audience appeal.

3. *Lack of experience with fine nonfiction.* Students don't see good writing in exposition. Models in composition books, and especially literature anthologies, are often stuffy or uninteresting. These texts traditionally emphasize organizational structure (i.e. Comparison/Contrast, Classification, Cause/Effect, and Definition) over subject, language or style. Students and teachers just don't encounter much good expository writing.

In Burton Hatlen's "Old Wine in New Bottles: A Dialectical Encounter Between the Old Rhetoric and the New," he describes such texts as promoting "composition as essentially mechanical, a matter of selecting certain appropriate parts and putting them together in accordance with the 'rules' of composition. Second, all of them see the choices which the writer makes as 'value-free'; neither the commitments of the writer nor the values and beliefs of the audience should, these textbooks assume, affect the process of composition" (4).

The sterility of the approach to models comes from the mechanicalness with which we approach essay writing. We need a new way of using models. We must see them more as a way of eavesdropping into a writer's way of thinking or a writer's way of shaping and communicating subject than as blueprints for clones. We've recommended several nonfiction writers who have nurtured our students' imaginations in the Resources chapter. One last thing. Good models invite writers to imagine other ways of seeing.

What's to Be Done?

As we continued to work with this group of twelfth graders, and as we confirmed our sense of the exposition problem with other writers ranging from sixth grade through twelfth, we discovered approaches that help us make essay writing a more meaningful experience. We're developing a philosophy about essay writing behind the practices we advocate. It's worth sharing both.

We believe that fine exposition grows out of imaginings. Subject matter shifts and shapes as the writer, like any artist, builds minutiae upon minutiae until form and subject unfold and flower. We find figurative language, often reserved for poets, rich and full-bodied and alive in the best prose. Spend an afternoon reading Loren Eiseley and you'll see. Fine writing in any genre evidences care in languaging and in forming subject. Students should be encouraged to stretch for imaginative language.

We've come to believe that there is no essential difference in the strategies we employ when writing poems, short stories, or chapters for a book. First, we get excited about a subject and want to talk about it. We write exploratory drafts to think our ideas through, we talk them out with friends, we read whatever we can get our hands on that helps us clarify the ideas—all are ways of informing ourselves about the subject. We check to see if what we've written says what we're thinking. Subject, language, form work together when we get rolling. We move pieces of text around and try them out; we check out how the pieces fit together. As we make sense of the subject for ourselves, the pieces start to fit together naturally. We tinker with language and pother over expression until it feels right. It takes a long time and the writing gets messy and frustrating, but we work our way toward shape and meaning. Finally, we have something to communicate.

Exposition assumes an audience out there somewhere, but we have to write to understand the topic for ourselves first. I think we've made too much of audience constraints with exposition. Maybe all of these audience-directed heuristics only derail meaning-making. Conscious decisions about the effect of a piece on readers are important at some point, but these decisions require interest in and knowledge of our subject. Worrying about audience before we know what we think can certainly interfere with thinking. The initial processes for exposition must center on making sense of our subject, wrestling with ideas, and constructing texts that represent those ideas clearly.

Planning Expository Assignments

We've taken this bit of philosophy and applied it in careful planning and structuring of assignments. First things first, we find ways to get the students going.

Brainstorm Topic Options

Offering options means much more than giving students a list of topics. Warriner's tenth grade book, for example, offers several hundred expository topics (5):

1. The threat of Communism
2. The idea behind the UN
3. What is the balance of trade?
4. Why vote?

5. The tyranny of the automobile
6. Air pollution
7. Stream pollution
8. How to improve our schools
9. Will there always be wars?
10. Fewer and fewer farm jobs

The problem with such canned topics is that they simply do not invite students to begin the thinking process. Imposing arbitrary topics results in expository writing becoming unpleasant for young writers who get few opportunities to use their own knowledge and, even more seriously, their own voice in exposition. It's deadly dull to write about something you care nothing about. That's when we get "Man in all times faces death," or "If one were to consider the role of George in Steinbeck's *Of Mice and Men*." That's when students press their automatic pilot button and slip into the writing robot mode.

Brainstorming frequently "gets the juices flowing." The process generates enthusiasm and ideas. It engages the entire class in talking and thinking about approaches to the writing task. How do we brainstorm with a group? Sally is thinking about the prom Saturday night; Joe is worried about the track meet; and Joel worked until 2:00 a.m. at a local restaurant.

Dan and I find that it helps if we introduce controversies. We try to get kids fired up about a subject by introducing our own uncertainties and a variety of ways of looking at an issue. Students take over then and learn from one another's knowledge and experience, and discover ideas or concerns that they genuinely want to find out more about.

We've found our job is to provide the stimuli. We arrange problems and puzzles that can tie to the student's personal experiences. Media, fiction, poetry, personal experience, artifacts, and experts in the field invite students to shift their perspectives and see subject through a variety of lenses.

As with all writing, previous experience as reader, person, and thinker count. Experience precedes effectiveness in exposition. This means, of course, that students need time to explore a subject until they feel expert with the material.

Explore the Topic with Journals and Jottings

The second step in planning an expository piece is not the formulation of an outline. It's impossible to outline a topic until you discover what you know about it. Writers discover what they know by playing around with a topic, turning it over in their minds, jotting down ideas, and working them over in informal writing.

Students should live with their topic a while—a few days, a week—collecting and recording ideas, information, and opinions from anywhere they can find them. Getting an interesting topic and watching it grow and take shape in the mind is important groundwork for effective expository writing. Organization and structure grow naturally from such explorations because the exploration itself begins to suggest its own organizational scheme.

Dan and I have found that mini-writes provide opportunities for writers to explore a subject. Writers get control over their knowledge base when they write out what they are thinking, connecting, and questioning. These Here and Nows, as Dan has labeled them, give students a chance to practice and play with the subject. They find out what they know and need to know.

Here and Nows can be recorded in a thinker's log. Our job as teachers is to nudge them along. We try to keep their topics hot and lively by consistently bringing in new bits and pieces of information, contrasting viewpoints, or downright puzzling and confusing ideas related to their topics. By the time the students think about writing an essay they have ten or more pages in the thinker's log of resource material, their own reflections recorded in their own voices, that they can use. The Here and Nows have been the bait for them to nibble on. They have thought through their subject in a variety of ways and become rather expert and interested.

Use the Draft as Discovery

Students carry all of their preliminary thinking from the log into a draft. Because expository writing is more complex than other writing, students need to draft their ideas in tentative form to let the writing suggest how it might best be written. Dan prefers discovery drafts to outlines. Outlines enslave inexperienced writers, taking away the opportunity to discover spontaneously an organizational structure and an appropriate scheme for developing ideas. A discovery draft shows a student writer where the paper is light on content, where transitions are needed, and where more thinking is needed. The draft forces students to re-see the topic they are exploring.

Ruth labels these drafts the quick draft. She has found that a short burst, twenty minutes to write the draft through, forces the students to get their thinking out. They don't have time to panic. "I've found the word 'quick' frees students to take a chance on letting the material fall

together in a logical fashion. After all these students have worked with
their subject for days and know it well. I trust the mind to make sense
and connections; I trust the mind's capacity to organize ideas. Students
so often panic when it's time to commit themselves to a draft
of the essay. Fear keeps them from writing more than voiceless,
rigid prose. They freeze because of the baggage of past experience they
carry in their heads. They slip backward sometimes. Quick frees them.
It's just a psychological boost."

Call them exploratory drafts, quick drafts, or discovery drafts—they
function in the same way—it is a twenty minute to a one hour
commitment by students to get the ideas they have been working with
out there on paper.

Even more important, the discovery draft is a place where new ideas
are born and new information discovered. James Britton suggests that
"we talk ourselves into new understanding" (3). He likens the writing of
a draft to a person "pushing the boat out from shore hoping it will land
someplace." Confident writers push the boat out fearlessly because they
have been out before and know it will not drift indefinitely. Unpracticed
writers need more support and encouragement during the discovery
draft because they may be less sure where a piece is going.

Encourage Students to Use Their Own Language

We're not suggesting that expository writings be couched in teenage
slang, but neither should they be laden with adult jargon. The best
language for expository writing is the best language the writer knows.
To borrow the words of others or to falsify one's own language is to
doom the individual voice in expository prose. Arguments about
whether the "I" pronoun is appropriate are futile. The piece itself and
the writer's own language resources dictate appropriate diction. Inexperienced writers lacking in intuitions about appropriateness may merely
need suggestions and feedback from their audience. We need to support
and encourage attempts to find a unique voice. We cannot lock student
voices out of the writing. If language interferes with meaning, we need
to help, but we do not need to inflict our voice in their writing.

Encourage Students to Use Personal Allusions or Cite Personal Evidence

Expositional prose should not be impersonal, detached, and devoid
of expressive detail. Perhaps in our attempts to help our students
distinguish between informal and formal writing we have overstated
these differences or even described the division as a dichotomy.

Effective expository prose, the kind people actually read and enjoy, is impossible to dichotomize. As Nancy Martin suggests:

> Much effective writing seems to be on a continuum somewhere between the expressive and the transactional. This applies to adult as well as children's writing. What is worrying is that in much school writing, the student is expected to exclude expressive features. . . . The demand for impersonal, unexpressive writing can actively inhibit learning because it isolates what is to be learned from the vital learning process—that of making links between what is already known and the new information. The [effective] expository writing task asks the student to reconcile what he/she already knows with new knowledge or experience. As a student develops as a writer, he/she should be more able to bring appropriate inner resources to bear on knowledge of the outside world. (6)

At a conference on Learning to Write in Ottawa, Canada, in 1979, I was impressed once again by the British use of expressive writing and personal experience in scholarly essays. Their presentations were scholarly, often philosophical, but never pretentious or arcane, as so many American scholarly papers tend to be. Woven throughout the British papers were personal examples, narrative, and sensitive metaphor, always metaphor.

I'm convinced we've been teaching exposition as a nineteenth-century phenomenon, ignoring the new, more exciting directions expository writing has taken. We've been using the wrong models—models that do not represent the range of contemporary exposition. Such writers as E. B. White, Loren Eiseley, Kenneth Brower, Tom Wolfe have certainly found new ways to enliven expository discourse.

Discover New Ways to Introduce Traditional Assignments

Let's look at some of the traditional assignments English teachers make. It isn't that they are bad. It's the way we have approached them. Good student writing in the expository mode can happen only infrequently if we use the old "throw out a topic and ask them to write on it" approach. We want to free the constraints and the anxiety and peak the curiosity and interest. Here are some suggestions for doing old stuff in new ways:

Comparison and Contrast Assignment

The C and C assignment has always been an English teacher's favorite. Unfortunately, it's an easy assignment to formulate, and easy to get shallow, saccharine analysis from. Rather than writing a formula on the board and telling students to go to it, I've tried to use a more inductive approach, which also generates some good writing in the process. I've used the following example with my college-level student teachers, but the process is readily adaptable to writers at any level.

I don't begin the assignment by announcing, "Now we're going to do some serious comparison and contrast writing and it's very difficult . . . ." I simply ask them to take out pen and paper, as I do almost every day.

1. Jot down notes on the most bizarre, frustrating, absurd, nagging experience of student teaching to this moment. Be as concrete and specific as you can. Remember the details. See the experience in your mind.

2. Share the notes. Try ideas on one another. In large classes the sharing goes on in small groups. Take enough time for this step. New ideas and details occur to the students as they talk about the experience.

3. Jot down notes on the most rewarding, memorable, worthwhile, joyful moment of student teaching to this moment. Replay the experience in your head. Watch out for generalized feelings. Be concrete. What caused the feeling?

4. Share the notes again. Allow time for discussion.

5. Jot down notes on what you have learned about yourself that you didn't know before you began the student teaching experience. Sometimes these insights come to students immediately; sometimes they get stuck. If they get stuck, tell them to relax and work on this later. They may need to write more before the insights grow.

6. Write out a discovery draft. Begin at the beginning; begin at the end; begin in the middle. Don't interrupt the writing-out process. Give students plenty of time to struggle with their notes. Let them shape the piece, using their own intuitions.

7. Share the discovery drafts, reading them aloud. Talk about beginnings and endings. Talk about transitions. Talk about concrete detail. Talk about language and diction. Talk about anything that concerns you or the students.

8. Advise students to rewrite, revise, or file their piece, depending on the writers' own involvement in the writing and your assessment of its worth.

9. Now give your comparison and contrast lecture, although it may be quite redundant at this point.

Action Research Project

Breathing life into the old research papers is not easy. Almost no one enjoys them. The students hate them because they take planning and discipline. The teachers hate them because they have to read and grade them, and they're mostly dull. The librarian hates them because that means thirty kids in the library for two weeks misfiling encyclopedias. Parents hate them because it means driving their kids to the university or city library on weekends. There seems to be no way out of the dilemma, however. High school English teachers think they fail their college-bound students if they don't assign the research paper. For me the value of the research project is in the process rather than the product. Good research projects are problem-solving experiences that challenge students and leave them with a positive feeling when finished.

Students need a model of how to work through the research process. Ruth recommends giving students new to research an initiation period that works something like this.

1. *Generate a class topic of interest to most students.* You might bring in an editorial, lyrics from a contemporary song, a short story, a poem to get them started. Pick something that will generate mixed and rather complicated reactions: divorce, pros and cons; individual's responsibility to society; students' responsibility to the school community or teacher's responsibility to students.

2. *Check out the topic in subjective and objective ways.* Use fact and fiction in Here and Nows. Have students do short reaction writes and keep a researcher's log while they explore the topic.

3. *After several days of seeing the topic from a variety of viewpoints, each student or a group of students working together can formulate questions about the topic.* The questions should reflect the complexities of the subject and not encourage yes/no responses. Spend time with students helping them formulate questions.

4. *Ask students to answer these questions using their research logs for preliminary responses.* Fill in information with further investigation—readings, interviews with classmates and people in the community.

5. *If you are sold on notecards as a procedural way for students to compile information, now is the time to introduce it.* Notecards are made for summarizing the findings and drawing conclusions. Bibliography cards are compiled for all sources. Students use their research log reflections, Here and Nows, interviews, and information shared with classmates. No

slavish copying of ideas from books onto notecards. Students have thought through their ideas in their own language first. Cards are merely a way of separating out the pieces.

6. *If you don't use notecards, students may begin discovery drafts that explore findings and sort through ideas.* Students work their way toward a more formal paper through a series of short papers.

One thing we've found in following this procedure—students learn the process and can apply it for individual research at some future time. They have learned a way of collecting information and transforming it into an opinion paper.

The same process can be used with individual topics if your students have previous experience. It's tough for students and teachers when thirty students, covering thirty different topics, spread their books and notes out over a huge library. We get our jog for the day but the students get frustrated. They all need help at the same time. We like to have several students work on various facets of the same subject. Each provides expertise and helps the others. The collaborative effort helps them explore the topic more thoroughly and brings other viewpoints to individual ideas. They follow each other through the exploratories, discovery drafts, and serve as a response group through the final paper.

Writing About an Author

The problem in this assignment is to generate enthusiasm for finding out more about authors and getting kids into their work. Dan and I decided to introduce Loren Eiseley to a group of teachers using the Here and Now and exploratory approach. We think the process adaptable for any classroom:

1. *Place a basket near the door of your classroom where students can pick up handouts as they enter the room each day.* We compiled a series of one page handouts that contained short excerpts from Eiseley's writing, from his notebooks and journals, and interviews. We included photographs of him, biographical accounts, reviews of his work, and criticisms. We put one handout a day in the basket. Students are to read, talk, share their feeling, speculate as their knowledge and understanding of Eiseley grows.

2. *Ask students to find out more about the author.* Each student brings a fact about the author, a selection to read, or a review. Students share this information with the class.

3. *Keep an author log where students write reactions to what they find, write favorite quotes, write original pieces triggered by some idea or technique the author uses.* Ask them to react to content, style or whatever strikes their fancy.

4. *Read longer selections by the author.* Ask students to present interpretive readings to the class.

5. *Bring artifacts that represent the author's life and work.* For Eiseley, we filled the room with bones and skulls and seed pods. We wanted to accompany an archeologist on a dig. Do it if you can.

6. *Encourage students to choose pieces of writing from logs and develop these into an inquiry booklet for future classes.* This gives students a new audience for their imaginings. I have shelves of inquiry booklets that contain reactions, questions, statements, explorations, imaginings about many authors. As Julie, a former student, told me: "I got interested in so many writers by thumbing through the inquiry booklets. Other kids' writing tempted me to find out more about writers I'd never heard of. Many of us would go into the room at lunchtime and just thumb through the booklets. There was interesting stuff. I'd get curious and check out a book by John McPhee or Ivan Doig because they sounded worth reading. When I read *This House of Sky* I could hear Melissa's voice interjecting comments (I read her booklet on Doig). I could hear the short story she wrote on lambing season on her grandfather's ranch, and I remember she wrote a critique on *English Creek* where she brought the images right into my head. I hope the booklet I wrote on Lewis Thomas leads another student to Thomas's work" (7).

Thinking It Through

We've searched for years through the nettles of jargons and forms trying to think what it takes to coach students toward an authentic voice and form. We recognize it when we see and hear it. We think time, exploration, sharing, and reading strengthen a writer's determination to risk deviating from traditional structure and traditional voice.

We are carried back to one of those twelfth grade voices that sounded alive in poetry and dull in prose. We worked Alyssa out of her "smart kid, Men in all times language" and into the voice which throbbed through her poetry. Once she took the time to discover the strengths of that voice, we'd find paragraphs in her exposition much like the one we find in her essay on *Medea,* in "Poison, Lies, and Politics":

Medea was a believer (as all the best lovers must be), taking Jason's promises so tremblingly into herself that, entirely possessed, she could throw her flesh and blood piece by piece into the sea. Realizing this, thinking of all the tender words that Jason scattered carelessly over her, remembering that during the waiting time, when her hero wandered the earth, she would take these promises out and hold them close as rare truths, precious to behold. Knowing this we may better understand the tragedy that has come down to us, the story of the child-killing crazy woman. Small wonder she did not believe his story of becoming a better provider. Truths turned to lies are not flowers turned to dust. They are jewels that become the eyes of snakes, cool and hard—venomous. (2)

Good writing surprises us with its imaginative play. Good writing brings the voice of the writer to the reader.

Notes

1. John Rouse. "Write, Johnny, Write," *Media and Methods,* Vol. 13 (May/June 1977), pp. 20-24.
2. Stephanie Morris, Darin Weyrich, and Alyssa Harad were students at Boise High School, Boise, ID.
3. James Britton et al. *The Development of Writing Abilities (11-18).* Macmillan Education, 1975.
4. Thomas Newkirk, ed. *Only Connect: Uniting Reading and Writing.* Boynton/ Cook, 1986.
5. John Warriner. *English Grammar and Composition.* Harcourt Brace Jovanovich, 1969.
6. Nancy Martin et al. *Writing and Learning Across the Curriculum 11-16.* Ward Lock, 1976.
7. Julie Johnson was a student at Boise High School, Boise, ID.

CHAPTER FOURTEEN

Grading and Evaluating

My predominant impression has been that [writing classes] are fantastically over-evaluated. Students are graded on everything they do every time they turn around. Grades generate anxiety and hard feelings between [everyone]. Common sense suggests that [grades] ought to be reduced to the smallest possible number necessary to find out how students are getting along toward the four or five main objectives of the program, but teachers keep piling them up like squirrels gathering nuts....

—PAUL DIEDERICH (1)

Grading students and evaluating their progress is one of the toughest jobs in teaching. After twenty-three years of the classroom, I still find the whole process tiresome, frustrating, and often in conflict with my objectives. Nowhere is that grading frustration more problematic than in the composition classroom. Not only does the paper-grading crunch take up too much of my time and energy, the grading process itself is often a futile and defeating experience.

The teachers I talk to are frustrated by composition grading because they often see little improvement in student writing even after hours of hard work. Even worse, their students are negative about their writing classes because they find it difficult to accept the teacher's subjective criticism and critical marks on their papers. Some students view the whole process as a plot to make them feel inadequate.

Part of the problem is deciding just how evaluation and grading can help a writer. Do we evaluate to grade or grade to evaluate? Is the grade based on that final piece in front of us or on what we know about the work or lack of it that preceded what we have? Do we take into consideration that Joe works until 2:00 a.m. every morning? The issues don't sort out easily.

215

On top of all these perplexities, the teacher should represent only one reader of the text, one voice in the evaluation. We want to grade more than technical proficiency and form. We want to evaluate nebulous categories like quality of inquiry, risktaking, improvement through revisions, and control of language. Too many composition books ignore this subject altogether or dismiss it with a few simplistic suggestions, and the temptation to be glib or flippant is strong even now. But realistically, the grading of papers and students in composition classes will not go away, so I'm going to take a deep breath and plunge in.

First—Confession Number One

We don't have any sure-fire, simple answers. We wrestle with grading problems in every class we teach. A part of the problem is that our approach to teaching writing makes grading harder instead of easier. We have been encouraging you throughout this book to develop your responding skills. "Be a sensitive reader." "Look for the good." "Be positive." "Go to your papers with anticipation."

These attitudes and behaviors are absolutely essential to develop if you're going to get writers going. *But* it's difficult to make a smooth transition from reader to grader. Students who hear you say, "That's good. I like it," turn pale when they see the C go down in the grade book. Responding and evaluating are not mutually exclusive teaching activities, but it's not easy to work out the conflicts in those two roles.

First, let us suggest some general principles about grading in the composition class.

1. *Grading should be deemphasized.* Students have become very grade conscious, and they often bludgeon their teachers with the "Is this going to be graded?" question. If your answer to them is "yes," that's the universal signal that the assignment is important, and they grudgingly set out to give you what you want. If your answer is "no," they may decide that the assignment is not worth doing. At its worst, this grade-grubbing becomes a kind of "we won't work unless we're paid" statement.

Careful planning and deliberate strategies to deemphasize grading can do much to change the grade-grubbing syndrome. I begin all composition classes with my "not everything you do here will be graded" speech. I talk about the importance of practice and the establishment of a rigorous conditioning regimen. I tell them that practice pays off eventually in better grades because some major assignments will be graded, and the practice assignments lead up to and prepare them for the graded assignments. I know some of you have given the same speech. Such a speech works, however, only if you actually deemphasize grades in your class by finding a set of strategies to put it into practice.

2. *Drafts should not be graded.* The standard composition format— student writes paper; teacher takes papers home to grade—teaches students very little about how writers work and how good writing grows from draft to draft. One of the surest ways to involve students in a viable composition process is to withhold grades until a final draft has been completed. Comment and respond extensively to drafts without grading them. Don't use the grade as a threat or an ultimate weapon. Don't talk about grades much. Focus on the piece of writing itself. After a student has worked on several drafts of several pieces, ask her to pick one for careful evaluation.

3. *Develop grading criteria with students.* In Chapter 7 Tom talked at length about developing criteria for *good* writing. These criteria, when cooperatively arrived at, can become a grading scale that students can understand and accept. Furthermore, by using such cooperative criteria, students can see more clearly how to improve and grow as writers. It's more than showing them what you want. It's developing their own critical sense and evaluative judgment.

4. *Students should be involved as graders and evaluators.* There's perhaps no more dramatic way to help students understand the pitfalls of grading than to ask them to participate by grading one another's papers. I'm not suggesting, of course, that a teacher abdicate the role of grader. I am suggesting that students can and should *participate* in the evaluation process, not only to develop empathy for the grader, but also to become better readers of one another's papers.

5. *Grade process as well as product.* That letter grade on the paper carries meanings all out of proportion to its importance. We need to develop grading strategies that reward students for careful preparation, extensive revision, and practice.

6. *Focus your grading.* Begin with a few criteria. Grade only the specific structures of writing you've been working on. If you have spent all week on concrete detail or strong verbs or beginnings or transitions, let your grading of that week's assignment reflect your teaching emphases. Don't try to grade everything all at once. Start small. Slowly add criteria to your grading scale, carefully demonstrating to students exactly what you're looking for.

7. *Give ideas and inventiveness and content an important weight in your grading scale.* Most of us have tried the two-grades approach at least once. You know, A over C; A for content, C for mechanics. I've never found that very helpful. Students either average the two or see the A as a gift and the C as a shot.

If you follow our philosophy in this book, we propose that student writers experiment with ideas, explore options, and take chances. Remember, they are apprentices learning an art. They stretch further, try new tools, or follow an unlikely vision if they trust we are their supporters. Our evaluations should reflect their increased confidence, their willingness to tackle difficult subjects, and their ability to analyze the strengths and weaknesses in their own writing. This may appear to deemphasize correctness, but we want writers concentrating on shaping their subjects first. We honestly believe that the development of fluency through extensive writing practice brings with it growing control of the language.

The more students write and receive careful feedback, the better they become and the fewer problems they have with correctness. Not all things improve with practice. As Mina Shaughnessy pointed out, some usage errors stubbornly persist even in the writings of college students (2). Subject/verb agreement and pronoun reference problems seem to be with us in spite of practice. They're so much a part of the oral language process that students seem to have difficulty deleting them in written dialect. We'll certainly need to approach such usage problems directly. Yes, even with drills or whips and chains if necessary. But we make a serious mistake in the teaching of writing if we emphasize such surface considerations at the expense of real and powerful expression of ideas and feelings. Content and correctness are both important, but it makes a big difference to your success as a teacher of developing writers where you begin and where you put your emphasis.

There is a place for rigorous grading in the writing class: at the end of the process after practice, trials, and revisions.

A Little Self-Evaluation

A good place for any teacher of writing to begin thinking about grading is to engage in some self-evaluation. How do you grade your students' papers? What are your primary emphases? Have you worked out a grading scale? Does it overemphasize surface features? Do you respond to ideas as you grade the papers? What do you hope your grading methods will develop in your students?

Maybe you're not ready for an introspective look at your own grading procedures, but success in the teaching of writing demands that you have a grading system compatible with maximum student growth. Take a look at that stack of papers you've just finished grading and answer the following questions as honestly as you can. Write your answers down so that you can argue with yourself later.

1. Are they graded in the "deduct" manner? (You take off points for errors and sometimes the kids end up owing you points.)
2. Are there papers in that stack that make you feel uncomfortable (either good papers with bad grades or bad papers with good grades)?
3. What was your *primary* emphasis when you graded those papers? What were you looking for? Do the grades reflect that emphasis? Do your comments reflect the emphasis?
4. Is the grade *final,* or does the student have the option of improving the paper?
5. How have you responded to *what* the writers are saying? Do your comments question, confirm, and show interest in the content? What are the percentages of your markings that identify errors? Successes?
6. What do you hope your grading will accomplish with these writers?
7. What type of follow-up teaching have you planned after the papers are returned?

Perhaps the most seriously damaging habit we get into as "theme graders" is mindlessness. The sheer volume of papers and their frequent drabness have a kind of hypnotic effect that can rob the evaluator not only of objectivity but sensitive and insightful reading. If student papers are important enough to be graded, they deserve the best reading we can possibly give them. The rest of this chapter is dedicated to practical alternatives for making grading and evaluating a less loathsome activity.

Perhaps the most satisfactory answer to the grading headache is to present a number of grading alternatives and encourage you to take your pick. My guess is that you'll end up using all of them at one time or another, perhaps arriving at some personal, eclectic system.

The Nongrading Approach

Some writing theorists (none of whom work in the public schools) recommend strongly against any kind of grading in the composition class. Several teachers I know have tried the nongrading approach, focusing exclusively on constructive responses to student papers, carefully keeping each of the students' papers in a folder to serve as a record of progress. Several times during the quarter the student and the teacher sit down in conference and discuss the student's progress in concrete and specific terms, referring to the collected writings. The advantages of such an approach are obvious. The teachers spend most of their time focusing on writing behavior rather than agonizing over grades. The students are weaned away from writing for the grade and are encouraged to practice and experiment with their writing. Progress is emphasized; evaluation is positive and helpful.

Unfortunately, the realities of the schools demand that even the teacher who deemphasizes grading in the composition class give some kind of grade for the permanent record when the course is over. This means, of course, that the teacher must grade something. We suggest that at least with younger children you grade anything but their writings.

The disadvantages of the nongrading alternative are principally the hassles teachers face using such a system. Students exhibit withdrawal symptoms, parents think your course lacks rigor, and your principal thinks you're lazy. In the end you still face the difficult task of translating "progress" into a letter grade for the report card.

As a middle ground, we suggest that you have a number of assignments that are not graded. Call them "practice activities" or better yet "explorations" or "jottings." Train your writing students to expect frequent practice activities. Culminate this practice by responding to, sharing, or publishing the writings rather than grading them.

A Performance System

The performance system is quick and simple for the teacher and clear and concrete for students. If students do the assignment, they get the grade (or points); no value judgments are made about the quality of the work. You establish an acceptable level of performance in your class and students meet it. You may specify that you want five pages in the journal each week or two short writings each week with a revised piece every two weeks. Whatever your performance criteria, the student either does the work and receives credit or fails to do the work and receives no credit.

The advantages of such a system are its efficiency—it's easy to record who did what—and the psychological effect of transferring the responsibility of grading to the student. "You want to do well in my class? Do the work." Teachers can spend their time responding and commenting on student papers rather than counting errors or debating between a C+ and a B–.

The disadvantages are few but not unimportant. A performance system does not give the teacher the flexibility to recognize works of exceptional quality, bad or good. Such a system could lead to a lessening of incentive to do good work unless the teacher uses other things to motivate writing. Motivation comes through publishing class books that contain the best work on a particular assignment or by celebrating an outstanding piece through oral reading. Publishing excerpts on the bulletin board gives credit for excellence. A performance system can lead to the complacency of just getting the job done unless we find ways to celebrate excellence and quality.

Holistic Grading Strategies

Charles Cooper and Lee Odell, with characteristic clarity, explain holistic evaluation as:

> ...a guided procedure for sorting or ranking written pieces. The rater takes a piece of writing and either (1) matches it with another piece in a graded series of pieces or (2) scores it for the prominence of certain features important to that kind of writing or (3) assigns it a letter grade or number. The placing, scoring, or grading occurs quickly, impressionistically, after the rater has practiced the procedure with other raters. The rater does not make corrections or revisions in the paper. Holistic evaluation is usually guided by a holistic scoring guide which describes each feature and identifies high, middle, and low quality levels for each feature. (3)

Holistic grading is a system compatible with our philosophy. It focuses on the piece of writing as a whole and on those features most important to the success of the piece. It helps the teacher to evaluate more quickly, more consistently, and more pointedly. The rating is quick because the rater does not take time to circle errors or make marginal notations.

The rating is consistent because the rater uses the same carefully developed criteria on all pieces of writing. This consistency is evident not only from piece to piece rated by the same rater but also between different raters rating the same piece. This means, of course, that students can expect their English teachers to be more consistent in their grading, thus reducing the grading idiosyncracies that so often frustrate student writers.

Table Grading

Ruth uses roundtable holistic grading as a way of letting students into the evaluation process. Students read papers, establish criteria, and evaluate. Each student has a clearer idea of her own performance on a particular paper after the experience and is responsible, with the teacher's input and several markings by peers, to assign her own grade. If students take this role of evaluator, the most useful part is that they become better judges of their own work. They have a clearer idea of what they can do to improve their own piece in light of the features they established as rubrics. Students come up with categories for evaluation:

- a coherent plan is evident behind the text
- the writer resists tangents or straying from the subject
- focus is maintained
- explanations give the reader what she needs to know to be satisfied
- errors do not distract attention from content
- natural transitions grow out of content discussed

At times, Ruth and I ask students to design an evaluative schedule before they complete an assignment. We've found that writers are particularly sensitive to problem areas in an assignment while they are drafting. They have a healthy notion of the pitfalls and have good ideas about what might present problems or successes. Our advice is to develop the scale prior to final drafting and encourage students to revise after table evaluation.

The table grading model and the term itself come from the procedures the Educational Testing Services uses to rate student writing samples. Tom has used this approach with his advanced placement students with good results, but we have both learned the hard way that evaluation by peers must be thoroughly structured and patiently implemented. Even then, we have sometimes been forced to admit that in some classes it just didn't work.

Impression Marking

Perhaps the simplest and quickest approach to the holistic grading of student papers is to read them quickly without circling errors or suggesting editorial changes. The reader scans the paper and marks it based on some general feelings about the paper's effectiveness. The system is efficient and surprisingly reliable, particularly if readers have a clear set of criteria in mind as they read the papers. This set of criteria must, of course, be in the writers' minds as well as the readers'. So impressionistic criteria must be shared and illustrated for writers as a part of the writing process.

Following is a list of criteria used by Emily Gregory, a former colleague and an excellent teacher of writing. Notice that she uses this list as a guide to direct *readers'* thinking as they read student papers. She cautions against using the guide as a grading scale by converting various items to point values. This guide gives the reader a focus and suggests specific features in the piece of writing to key on, but the reader must read quickly and carefully to arrive at a "feel" for the piece and a grade.

Emily reads student papers using the guide as a reminder. As she finishes reading a paper, she places it in one of three or four piles without marking it. When all papers are read, she goes back to the piles to argue with herself a bit, sometimes moving papers from pile to pile. When she's satisfied with the relative value of the papers, she assigns grades by piles and rereads each paper, writing some notes to the student about the paper.

Emily uses the holistic approach sparingly during her composition class, preferring to focus more on developing fluency in first drafting and fine-tuning during revision stages. But like most of you she must grade her students, and she feels they have a right to know where they stand long before the mysterious grade appears on the report card.

She also involves students in the grading process and trains them in the impression system. A student's final grade in her writing class usually consists of several holistic grades given by the teacher and several given by the student's peers. Her students seem comfortable with the fact that their grades are in such humane and understanding hands.

Holistic Guide for Evaluating Student Writings

(Do not make a scale of these criteria, but use the list as a reminder of important characteristics of good writing. When you are providing opportunities for students to respond to peer writings, help them recognize and value excellence and experimentation in any aspect of the writing.)

1. Impact

The reader's interest is engaged.
The writer has something to say and is imaginatively involved.
The idea or experience is conveyed with fluency or intensity.
The writing is convincing. It may have a sense of immediacy, a completeness, or a rightness of content and form that makes it effective.

2. Inventiveness

The reader is "surprised"—finds that the writer has not followed the usual or the trite but has introduced elements that are new and unexpected.

Evidences of the writer's inventiveness may include:

- coined words (onomatopoeic, portmanteau, etc.)
- tag names (allusive or symbolic)
- unusual point of view (often to add humor or irony)
- figurative use of language (to clarify meaning, not to adorn)
- significant title—one that augments the meaning of the writing

- original, surprising, and appropriate element in content or in arrangement
- use of unconventional punctuation, spelling, or format to achieve desired effects

3. Individuality

The reader is aware of a distinctive speaking voice. This sense of persona, or individual flavor, seems to come from the writer's control of tone and point of view and/or distinctiveness in the ordering of ideas or in using the resources of the language (figurative language, vocabulary, syntax, etc.)

The sense of a distinctive persona is usually strong in good monologuing—expressive, expository, or dramatic.

In narration or dialogue the sense of control comes from the appropriate meshing of all parts into the whole.

Analytic Scales

If the idea of grading a paper by "feel" bothers you or your students, you may appreciate a more precise and carefully articulated grading scale. Analytic scales direct the reader's attention to specific features of the piece of writing and suggest relative point values for each feature. The grade for the piece is arrived at by summing scores on the various subparts. Such a scoring tool is more pointed than impression marking because the rating guide defines and illustrates the grading criteria to writers and raters alike and keeps raters on track during the marking procedure. Such guides, when carefully shared and explained to students, can demystify the final grade and highlight strengths and weaknesses in their writings. The guides also ensure that certain surface features in the piece (handwriting, spelling, punctuation) do not influence the rating of the piece out of proportion to their importance to the piece's effectiveness.

An example of an analytic scale is the famous Diederich Scale; many English teachers will recognize it. Diederich and his colleagues at the Educational Testing Service developed the scale to use in scoring SAT essay examinations. Because the essay exams are read by several raters, Diederich needed a scoring tool that would provide a quick and reliable evaluation. The scale itself was developed primarily to be used for staff grading, but many teachers have adapted it to use with their students.

Diederich Scale

1—Poor   2—Weak   3—Average   4—Good   5—Excellent

Reader _____

Quality and development of ideas 1 2 3 4 5
Organization, relevance, movement1 2 3 4 5

_____ ×5= ____
Subtotal

Style, flavor, individuality   1 2 3 4 5
Wording and phrasing   1 2 3 4 5

_____ ×3= ____
Subtotal

Grammar, sentence structure   1 2 3 4 5
Punctuation   1 2 3 4 5
Spelling   1 2 3 4 5
Manuscript form, legibiilty   1 2 3 4 5

_____ ×1= ____
Subtotal
Total Grade: ___ %

How to Interpret This Scale

1. This scale weighs content and organization 50%, aspects of style 30%, and mechanics 20%. The multiplication translates the 40 point scale into a 100 point scale.
2. The ratings for each item range from 1 to 5. Regard 1 as the lowest grade, 3 as the average, and 5 as the highest. Use 2 to designate below-average performance but not marked deficiency and use 4 to designate above-average performance but not marked proficiency. *Reading five randomly selected papers from a set before you attempt to grade the set will help you to form a realistic notion of 1, 3, and 5 performance for that particular assignment.*
3. Observing the following guidelines will also help to assure more uniform and consistent grading.
   a. *Quality and development of ideas.* Grant the writer his choice of subject matter. He was, after all, offered choices dictated by the teacher and should *not* be penalized by the value you place on one choice as compared to another. Look how well he has supported his subject and *his* point of view or attitude toward the subject.
   b. *Organization, relevance, movement.* A 5 paper will begin with a clear indication of its controlling idea, offer convincing relevant support, and come to a close. A 1 paper begins anywhere and

goes nowhere. A 3 paper may be skimpily but relevantly developed or fully developed but including some irrelevant material.

c. *Style, flavor, individuality.* Guard against the temptation to give a low score for the use of substandard English. Papers containing substandard English are often rich in flavor and individuality. Reserve 5 for the truly arresting paper. A single apt, precise, or arresting phrase can move a paper from a 3 to a 4.

d. *Wording and phrasing.* Here is the place to give a low score for an impoverished vocabulary and a high one for apt and precise diction and clear phrasing.

e. *Grammar, sentence structure.* Low scores should be given for frequent *and varied* substandard constructions like errors in agreement between pronoun and antecedent, dangling constructions, subject-verb agreement, etc.

f. *Punctuation.* Again, frequent *and varied* abuses of standard punctuation marks deserve a low score; occasional varied errors in common punctuation marks a middle score; freedom from common errors a high score. Errors in the use of the comma, the apostrophe and end punctuation should be regarded as more serious than errors in the use of the semicolon, quotation marks (especially double quotes), parentheses, and brackets. Regard the mistaken presence or absence of the apostrophe as a punctuation error, not a spelling error.

g. *Spelling.* Give a score of 5 if the writer has misspelled no words; a 4 for one spelling error; a 3 for two spelling errors; a 2 for three spelling errors, and a 1 for four or more errors. This is the *only place* on the scale where you are to assess spelling. Misspelling the same word is only one error.

h. Adherence to manuscript form and a clearly readable paper merits a 5. An unreadable paper without margins and without a proper heading merits a score of 1. Perhaps readers should attempt only a 1, 3 or 5 judgment on this item. Do *not* give a low score for neat cross-outs. (Remember that the students are writing their papers in class and that they have been encouraged not to waste time recopying.)

I have never used the scale more than once or twice during a writing class because it does not entirely reflect my own emphases in the teaching of writing. It is important, however, for students to be exposed to such a grading approach, and my students actually enjoy being graded by such a concrete and carefully articulated scale. I think they like to feel that their grades "add up."

Checkpoints

By far the most effective rating guides for student papers are the ones teachers themselves devise. These scales can be content-specific, focusing the evaluation on those things you've been trying to teach. Such guides should be used after you have demonstrated them, devised practice activities, and given students a chance to revise and improve their papers using the criteria in checklist form.

Below are two checkpoint guides I've developed for seventh graders (4). Checkpoint 1 comes after two weeks of writing practice and is used on a student's revised writing. Notice that in addition to numbers, some specific suggestions are included for improving the paper. If students are rated low on vivid, concrete detail, they are encouraged to add more specific detail. The checkpoint scale focuses on specific aspects of writing instruction and also allows the teacher considerable latitude by including an "overall impression" section that makes up 30 percent of the rating.

A further advantage of the checkpoint idea is that teachers can standardize their grading and instruction at particular grade levels. Seventh grade teachers could work to develop five or six checkpoints to use to focus composition instruction during the year. Eighth grade teachers could build on seventh grade criteria, and so on, thereby developing a cooperative and compatible schoolwide curriculum and a consistent grading system.

The checkpoint scales are quick to use (averaging about three minutes per paper), self-teaching, and positive. Using these checkpoints decreases the number of papers that need careful grading, and they free the teacher to work with students on first drafts and revisions.

For more technical discussions of holistic ratings, analytic scales, and primary trait scoring read Cooper and Odell's *Evaluating Writing* (3). The book is a good, long read, but it discusses clearly the theory and research practice behind these more sophisticated evaluative strategies.

Scoring Guide: Checkpoint 1

Your revised writing was rated as follows:

(1) *Honest Writing*

1	2	3	4	5	×4= _____
Try again. Write fast. Use the words in your own head.		You're moving. Keep working.		Yes! Fresh honest language. Good!	

(2) *Vivid, Concrete Detail*

| 1 | 2 | 3 | 4 | 5 | ×4= _____ |

Try again. Your writing is bare. Add more specific detail.	Some good stuff in your writing. Add specifics. Stay away from generalizations.	Surprising words. Concrete word pictures. Good!

(3) *Strong Verbs*

| 1 | 2 | 3 | 4 | 5 | ×4= _____ |

Try again. Use verbs that paint a picture.	I see you've been working at it.	Good. I like those words!

(4) *End Punctuation and First Word Capitalization*

| 1 | 2 | 3 | 4 | 5 | ×2= _____ |

Many sentences do not begin with capitals. Many sentences do not end with appropriate punctuation. See me for help.	Several errors. Proofread carefully.	All sentences begin with capital letters and end with appropriate punctuation.

(5) *Overall Impression*

| 1 | 2 | 3 | 4 | 5 | ×6= _____ |

You really haven't given this assignment a fair shot. Spend more time developing ideas for writing.	Yes. I see potential. Keep working.	I was touched by your writing. You connected with your audience.

Total _____

Comments:

Scoring Guide: Checkpoint 2

Your revised opinion paper was rated as follows:

(1) *Evidence*

1	2	3	4	5 ×4= _____
Ideas unsupported. Rethink your reasons. Back to brainstorming.		At least one of your pieces of evidence is strong. Support more completely.		Yes! Good. Solid support. Fresh, convincing.

(2) *Arrangement*

1	2	3	4	5 ×4= _____
Be sure you have each bit of evidence in a separate paragraph.		Check your conclusion or beginning. You can find a stronger arrangement.		Each paragraph fits with others. Your arguments build to your conclusions.

(3) *Language*

1	2	3	4	5 ×4= _____
Weasel words. Use more forceful language.		Better. Some words are strong.		Good, strong, concrete words.

(4) *Punctuation and Spelling*

1	2	3	4	5 ×2= _____
Proofread carefully. Too many errors. See me for help.		Still have a few errors. Check and double check.		Good job. Careful proofreading pays off!

(5) *Effectiveness of Your Opinion Paper*

1	2	3	4	5 ×6= _____
I'm not convinced. Develop your paper more completely. Use good evidence.		Yes. You're making progress. Keep working.		I'm convinced. Good support. Solid paper.

Total _____

Comments:

Evaluation by Peers

Grading by peers is controversial. Many teachers feel that they abdicate their responsibility as evaluators when they ask students to grade one another's papers. Other teachers feel that students are not capable of careful judgment of the work of their peers. On the positive side, we involve our students in the evaluation process with quite favorable results. We teach students to evaluate one another's papers not to make our job easier or lessen the paper crunch (although both are side effects of peer grading), but because the process teaches them many things better than we can.

First and foremost, grading by peers teaches students that grades belong to them. They come to realize that those letter grades do not flow out of the diseased mind of a cruel teacher. The grade represents a reader's estimate of the worth of the piece. A grade is simply a calibrated personal response. Second, careful reading of a number of student papers sensitizes them to problems in their own papers. As they offer editing and proofreading advice to peers, they are also teaching themselves. Perhaps even more encouraging is the fact that students use peer papers as creative sources for borrowing ideas, rhetorical and syntactic strategies, and even vocabulary. Taking students through the judgment process not only makes them better proofreaders; it also teaches them how to make critical judgments of written products.

We've found that students take the responsibility of peer evaluation very seriously and work as careful critics. Likewise, when they write pieces they know will be read and graded by their peers, they seem to take more care and work with real purpose on the assignment.

The key to the successful involvement of students as peer graders is the careful specification of evaluative criteria and careful modeling of the criteria so that all students recognize and understand them. It takes time to develop this kind of sophistication, but we think the results are worth the trouble. Here are two ways to structure peer grading.

Elbow's "Center of Gravity"

Peter Elbow suggested a method for giving writers group feedback on a piece of writing (5). Although Elbow did not intend such a system to lead to grading, we've found that students can and do use Elbow's criteria for evaluative judgments. Groups of five work best for this process, but groups of anywhere from three to seven members can function effectively. The groups begin the process by *responding* to a student's paper. Elbow calls this "pointing" and suggests that readers "point" to words and phrases that work well or have a unique effect in the piece. Responders may draw lines under these words and phrases or simply note them on a separate response sheet. Likewise, student readers may point to weak or empty words or phrases. As students begin this process, suggest that they limit their negative pointings to only a few serious problems.

Second, Elbow asks readers to summarize the piece, using the following steps:

1. First tell quickly what you found to be the main points, main feelings, or centers of gravity.
2. Then summarize the piece into a single sentence.
3. Then choose *one word* from the writing that best summarizes it.
4. Then choose a word that isn't in the writing to summarize it.

Once the pointing and summarizing are complete, students are asked to evaluate the piece, giving it a 3, 2, or 1. A "3" piece has a readily understandable center of gravity and solid supporting detail. A "2" has a center of gravity, but it's not powerfully stated and is lost among the verbiage. A "1" starts anywhere and goes nowhere. It's not a centered piece.

The point of this kind of peer grading is to involve students in animated discussions about what works and doesn't work in their writings. The pointing and summarizing format keeps the discussions on track and helps students to become more specific in their responses to one another's papers. The 3, 2, 1 scale gives the paper a relative value in a low-threat and helpful manner. The emphasis of such an approach is clearly on discussing written products rather than assigning grades.

Cooperative Grading

The cooperative grading process involves the teacher and two students. (Student readers are picked at random.) Each reader reads and evaluates a paper, assigning it a letter grade. Specific criteria are discussed prior to the grading. Tom suggests that readers consider surface conventions, arrangement, illustrations and examples, and the care the writer took. A simplified version of the Diederich scale might serve as a good guide.

After each reader has assigned the paper a grade, the three grades are averaged for a final grade. The teacher's grade counts as a third of the final grade. The student's paper receives a careful hearing by the three graders, and the weight of collective judgment is often more forceful as an evaluation tool than the teacher's grade alone would be.

Round Robins

Students sign up for or are assigned to round robin groups of three members. Each group member takes the responsibility for reading and responding in writing to the text written by the two other group members. We find that the procedure establishes a mini-community that provides keen evaluation along with sensitive understanding.

Each responder writes evaluative comments and assigns the paper a grade. The group holds a conference, after each writer has had time to digest the comments, for each individual's paper. When the group reaches consensus about a grade, the papers are given to the teacher with comments and grade attached. Ruth has found that the grades a group gives reflect honest and caring evaluation. Students receive the implicit message that their ability to evaluate is respected by the teacher. Students take these groups seriously and nurture one another's progress.

A Psychological Boost

Ruth tells her students that an 87 on a paper represents how much they already have done with the paper. The 13 points they didn't get represents the tinkering and tuning that they could still do on this paper. Thinking about a grade as reflecting what is still to be done with 87% complete helps the writer tackle the fine tuning with enthusiasm. For any of us, it's a boost to think that we've accomplished 87% of the task.

Self-evaluation

One of the important goals of my writing class is to make the writer feel more responsible for the quality of the piece of writing. One of the more unfortunate side effects of having the teacher as the sole grader is that students either prostitute their own writing abilities to please the teacher or they rationalize the teacher's judgment with a "I wrote a great piece, but he didn't like it" attitude. Real growth toward precision as a writer comes only when students are willing to look openly at their own writing, judging, evaluating, reworking, and tuning the piece in the light of such examination.

I've never had much luck asking students to grade their own writings, but there are many ways they can be involved in making judgments about the effectiveness of a piece they have written. Donald Graves suggests that student writers look carefully at first drafts, asking themselves two questions (6).

Question 1

What is this piece about? At the end of a first draft, a writer needs to be able to formulate a clear and pointed answer to this question. If she has an answer, the piece probably has focus.

If she's not sure what the piece is about, the drafting is incomplete. Many times I've seen first-draft pieces with real potential, either because of a strong personal voice or a patch of strong sensory description or a telling character sketch, but these good points have been submerged in circular verbiage. The writer has hit a few hot spots, but has not discovered exactly where the piece is going. By asking writers to answer question 1, you save yourself the trouble of telling them this, and the lack of focus becomes clear as they stutter and stammer about what the piece is about. We usually smile and the student says, "Looks like I need to write some more to find out where this piece is taking me." Sometimes just the act of talking through that question helps the students form the piece in their minds. As Britton says, "They talk themselves into new understandings" (7).

Question 2

Graves' second question, *What am I trying to do?* is rhetorical and stylistic, and asks the writer to examine purpose and audience. For instance, the writer is trying to evoke sympathy in a reader but is acutally turning the reader off by using overly dramatic or maudlin examples. Writers who can function as critical self-readers should be able to spot the problem as they answer question 2. Again, the discussion of the question helps the writer to clarify purpose and examine specific rhetorical strategies in the piece.

Steve Judy offers the following suggestions for engaging students directly in the process of assessing their own writings:

- Encourage the students to talk to you and to each other about problems while they are writing.
- Make it a standing invitation that any student can propose an alternative topic at any time in the class, thus reducing the number of lifeless papers.
- Let the students decide which of their writings is public and which is private. (In practice, most teachers find that the students are more willing to share their personal concerns with each other after initial phases of "testing" each other.)
- Describe the publication forms that are available. As the writing program develops and students catch on to the idea of publication,

they should more often write with a specific audience and form of publication in mind.

- Encourage the students to serve as each other's editors. One doesn't need to be an expert in composition and rhetoric to make useful suggestions about the clarity and effectiveness of writing. Although students may not know terminology, they are certainly capable of spotting editorial problems and talking about them in their own language: "Hey, I don't know what you're talking about." (Translation for teachers: "Lacks clarity.") "That's crazy." (Translation: "Lacks logical structure.") "I don't believe it." (Translation: "Needs more supporting evidence.") Students are highly perceptive in these ways, and when their editing has real purpose, they can take over the process and make genuinely helpful suggestions to each other.

- Leave proofreading to the students. In every class there are some students who have mastered most of the proofreading skills. Often such students are simply "good spellers" or "intuitive punctuators." Acknowledge their skill by setting them up as proofreading consultants to the class.

- Treat proofreading as something to be done quickly and efficiently, rather than as a climactic step in the process of composition. Only when proofreading is made a mysterious, complex part of the mastery of standard English does it become intimidating and therefore difficult for students.

- Help the students learn to react to each other's work. Small- and large-group discussion of completed compositions should be a regular part of any English class. At first you may find that students are a bit hard on each other, no doubt imitating previous teachers of their acquaintance. It may take some practice before the students can respond to the substance of each other's writing, but it will come with time and guidance.

- Encourage students to develop criteria of excellence, in advance, for the work they are doing by putting themselves in the position of the audience and asking questions it would raise.

- Encourage group and collaborative projects from time to time so that students can share both skills and critical knowledge.

- Read some of your own writing to the class, and share your own satisfactions and dissatisfactions with it.

- Encourage the students to develop lists of problems and pleasures that they associate with each project they do. (8)

Editing Checklist

A more concrete and less sophisticated way to involve writers in self-evaluation is to provide them with an editing checklist that they can use as they rework first drafts. Although it's possible for students to use the checklist in a cursory and superficial manner, it does give them a tool and an opportunity to improve their writing before the final grade.

Tom often uses the checklist for less motivated students, offering the potential for a better grade if the student wants to do a careful editing job. "The paper is about a C as it stands now. If you want to clean it up a bit, I could go a B. But if you're really willing to work on this thing, I'll consider an A. Get out your editing checklist and start working through the piece."

Conferencing

Throughout this chapter I've used examples of grading and evaluating that involve the reader and the writer in face-to-face discussion and negotiation. I honestly believe that the only consistently helpful and effective evaluation of student writings comes as the two of you sit down with the piece of writing, focusing directly on what's on the page. Extraordinarily successful teachers of writing have one thing in common: they spend very little time in isolation, reading and marking papers, and a great deal of time responding and discussing student writings with the writers themselves.

There is some disagreement here to be sure. Donald Murray uses the one-on-one conference almost exclusively in his teaching. Ken Macrorie prefers to work in a helping circle, using the writers themselves as a larger and more diverse audience. Macrorie feels that the one-on-one conference intimidates beginning writers. We prefer to run the writing class more like a writing workshop, getting groups together whenever helpful and holding many thirty-second conferences with working writers as we walk around the room. All of us agree that looking at the writings and discussing strengths and weaknesses is a far more effective evaluation strategy than taking stacks of papers home on weekends to grow blind and bitter as we puzzle over grades that many students will ignore or rationalize away.

And perhaps it is fitting to end this chapter with a reminder from the Senior Research Associate at the Educational Testing Service, Paul Diederich, a man who has been intensely concerned about the quality of student writing for twenty-five years:

I believe very strongly that noticing and praising whatever a student does well improves writing more than any kind or amount of correction of what he does badly, and that it is especially important for the less able writers who need all the encouragement they can get (1).

Notes

1. Paul Diederich. *Measuring Growth in English.* NCTE, 1974.
2. Mina Shaughnessy. *Errors and Expectations.* Oxford, 1977.
3. Charles R. Cooper and Lee Odell. *Evaluating Writing.* NCTE, 1977.
4. Miles Olson, Dan Kirby et al. *The Process of Writing: The Allyn and Bacon Composition and Applied Grammar Program,* Allyn and Bacon, 1981.
5. Peter Elbow. *Writing Without Teachers.* Oxford, 1974.
6. Donald Graves. Workshop at Georgia State University, Spring, 1979.
7. James Britton. Speech in Ottawa, Ontario, Canada, Spring, 1979.
8. Stephen N. Judy. *Explorations in the Teaching of Secondary English.* Harper & Row, 1972.

CHAPTER FIFTEEN

Publishing Student Writing

...and for the first time I learned another lesson which every young writer has got to learn. And that lesson is the naked, blazing power of print.

—THOMAS WOLFE (1)

Writing becomes real when it has an audience. Except in those isolated cases when we become our own audience in the diary or private journal, our purpose in writing anything from a note taped to the refrigerator to a Petrarchan sonnet is *contact* with other human beings. Their responses guide the growth of our writing. We learn ways to make it more effective by seeing its *effect* on others.

Dan and I talked earlier in this book about the importance of publishing in the development of student writers, and this chapter's purpose is not theoretical, but practical—to tell you the best way you can publish student writing in and out of the classroom. But first, a brief reminder of the reasons it is so important to publish student writing.

1. Publishing gives the writer an audience, and the writing task becomes a real effort at communication—not just writing to please the teacher.
2. Publishing is the only reason for the writing to be important enough for the hard work of editing and proofreading.
3. Publishing involves the ego, which is the strongest incentive for the student writer to keep writing.

Ways to Publish in the Classroom

Basics for the writing class: provide *regular* opportunities for students to publish their writing in class, and include all students. There are several relatively easy publishing methods. We recommend that you use a variety of them.

Reading Aloud

Sharing writing by reading aloud should be a frequent part of any writing class. It's the best way for students to get immediate reactions to their writing. It's a good tool for checking responses to a piece for editing, and writings simply need to be shared and enjoyed. Reading aloud grows writers.

Have students work daily with a reading partner with whom they feel comfortable and on whom they can try out their works in progress. They should also regularly form small groups for reading and responding. I like groups of four or six (two or three pairs of reading partners). Finally, there should be times when the entire class is the audience.

The Faithful Photocopy

Dan and I have both found that what our students look forward to most eagerly and read most carefully are the photocopied sheets we pass out at the beginning of class each Monday. Selecting and duplicating student writing should be done often. The selections from journals or in-class writing do not have to be long, but try to include as many students as possible. Select good writing, even if it's only a sentence or two with a vivid image, an unusual twist, the surprise of humor—writing with creative possibilities, not necessarily mechanically perfect writing. Talk about the selections to the class and tell why you picked them and why they're good.

Make sure, especially when duplicating selections from student journals, that you have a clear understanding with your students about the things that will be published in class. Always get their permission before sharing their writing with the class. I recommend publishing journal selections anonymously (their authors will take credit when others respond positively in class). A system my students and I have worked out for dealing with in-class writing selections is to identify them with the initials of the writers.

After you've selected and published excerpts from student writing for several weeks, turn that job over to the students themselves. Set up small groups as "editorial boards" (see Chapter 8) to pick writings and prepare copies each week. Rotate the responsibility from group to group so that all the students in the class have the regular job of editing during the course. Work closely with the editorial boards, but let them pick *what they like* to publish. Their selections, of course, will have to come from in-class writings and not from journals.

Word processing is an invaluable tool for classroom publishing. Printed text is easier to read and looks professional. And word processing makes editing easy. In Chapter 12 we talked about the computer and how it can help students become their own editors. It also will make it possible for you to publish their writings more often and with less hassle. Even if you are inexperienced and a little scared of the computer, *learn to use it.* It's really not that hard, and word processing will do a lot for you and your young writers.

Making Books

If you want to see your students' eyes light up with pride, have them prepare their best writings and bind them in their own books. Don Graves gives simple directions for bookbinding in *Writing: Teachers and Children at Work* (Heinemann, 1983). The directions start on page 59, but you will be interested in what Graves says about publishing in all of that short chapter. All you need for bookbinding are some wallpaper samples, Elmer's glue, dental floss, a large needle, construction paper, cloth tape, vinyl letters for the title if you want to be fancy—and patience. It can be messy, but it's worth it. Do your own first so you can show them how.

The bound books are attractive. A lot of schools keep them in their library where students can check them out. Talk to your media specialist.

A simple soft cover for students' writing can be made by folding a piece of wallpaper over the pages that is trimmed slightly larger than the sheets of writing. Then it's a simple matter to staple the "spine" two or three times and cover the end with cloth tape.

Illustrations and calligraphy of student made books are limited only by student imaginations.

What do you do if it's spring quarter and the principal informs you that the paper allotment for the school year is used up? What do you do about publishing then?

Having faced that situation almost every spring, I've found that a good alternative to publishing with photocopies is to put together a *Class Book* of the selections chosen by the editorial boards, edited when necessary, and bound together in a large binder. I keep these books on a table in the middle of the room, and during most classes they get passed around. It's not as efficient a system as providing each student with copies of class writing, but it works well enough.

Room Displays

You probably already have a place in your room to display student writing, and have found that a display of finished products attracts attention and stimulates talk and thinking about writing. But as Dan pointed out in Chapter 3, room displays have other possibilities. A "Works in Progress" section of the bulletin board—or wall or reserved corner table—is an easy way to encourage growing writers. And it helps to dispel notions that writing is quickly done in two drafts for the teacher and that what's important in writing is always the product.

With the cooperation of the principal, there's also the possibility of displaying student writing in the halls of the school. I like to do this with short writings such as name poems and cinquains, which are easy for students to put up on butcher paper. *(Never insist that students display their writing.)* And hang the writings high to keep them out of the reach of the curious. Displays are a fluid medium and should change often. Your writing should appear on display with the students.

Projection Publishing

Dan likes to make transparencies of outstanding student papers (or papers with particularly well-written sections), and he regularly uses an overhead projector to share these with the class. If you don't have the facilities for thermofaxing transparencies, the opaque projector, although more awkward, also works well for displaying and talking about good student writing.

Caution: Please notice that we're not suggesting that you slap a kid's paper on the opaque projector and begin criticizing its faults before the entire class. Use the overhead and opaque projectors to publish and share the good stuff your students are writing.

Ways to Publish Outside the Classroom

Publishing outside the classroom can be the most significant writing experience you and your students share. It should be approached carefully and should not be attempted unless the students are ready to move from the relatively safe class environment, where publishing is part of a common and shared experience, to the cold world of print read and judged by strangers. It's a scary transition but an important one—and your support and encouragement (and example) help your students to mature as writers.

The Literary Magazine

If your school already has a flourishing literary magazine, then count yourself lucky and enjoy its benefits. Encourage students to participate in it as fully as their inclinations and activities permit. Help them select and edit and polish their best pieces to submit to the literary magazine. Rejoice loudly with them when their stuff appears in it. Mourn with them when they don't make the cut. Use the literary magazine for its full effect with those students in your classes who are ready for a larger audience.

Unfortunately, the school with a literary magazine is relatively rare, and because you're a teacher who encourages and supports writing, chances are you'll be approached sooner or later to start one. So what we offer here is a very brief primer in doing the school literary magazine.

First, the basics of creating a literary magazine, from our experiences and prejudices, are as follows:

1. Everyone is creative and potentially has a place in the literary magazine. It's not just for the precious few.
2. The literary magazine begins in the classroom with the journal and the things students writer there. (It may stay there.)
3. An effective literary magazine is not a miniature copy of the *Kenyon Review* or *Poetry*.
4. Most students are shy about their writing appearing in print. Encourage them.
5. The literary magazine belongs to the students.
6. The literary magazine can be expensive, but it doesn't have to be.
7. If you do the literary magazine for money, you'll lose money.
8. Administrators sometimes don't like literary magazines.
9. The literary magazine is vulnerable to censorship.
10. The literary magazine is a lot of work.

How to Produce a Literary Magazine

There are three practical methods of producing a literary magazine. Each requires a great deal of time and work. Each requires the willing help of students. And each requires the cooperation and support of the principal.

Method 1: The Photocopied Literary Magazine

The cheapest kind of literary magazine is simply photocopied, stapled together, and passed around the school. It's spontaneous, easily produced by students, and given away. It's my favorite.

If you want to be fancy, get the class artist to do a silk screen design on heavy stock paper for a cover. It will be a very pretty product. And cheap.

Method 2: Offset Printing

The offset press is relatively inexpensive, and the result looks professional. The cost varies depending on where the printing is done and whether you include things like photographs and art work. It's often possible to get a local printer to give you a considerable price break. Many schools have their own graphics department with an offset press. Your school or one in your area may be able to print the literary magazine very cheaply.

With offset printing, of course, your copy has to be camera ready. So proofreading and careful typing are essential.

Method 3: The Full-Blown Technicolor Special

Color photographs and slick, clay-based paper and typeset printing —when you add these pretty touches, the literary magazine can become very expensive. It may cost literally thousands of dollars to produce.

That's out of the reach of most of us, but I have a fantasy that some day there'll be a public high school somewhere in America with a creative arts budget equal to that of a successful athletic program.

When to Begin a Literary Magazine

You begin a literary magazine when a group of kids says, "Hey why don't we put all this good stuff in a magazine of some kind?" In short, you begin it when the students want it and are willing to work together to produce it.

It's not an easy job, and students need to know that when they begin. Help them, advise them, encourage them—*but don't do the work for them*. It's their magazine and will be effective only as long as the students know it's theirs and take responsibility for it. It ends when students are bored with it, are tired of working on it, or want you to do the work of producing it.

When Not to Do a Literary Magazine

Never make the literary magazine a crusade. Suggest it as a possibility to students when you see that they're ready for a larger audience than the classroom, but don't insist on it if they seem uninterested. They may not be ready to move out of the audience of their peers with their writing yet. Or it simply may not be as important to them as it is to you.

If your principal—perhaps still smarting from too-fresh memories of the underground magazine that called him all those names in the 1960s—is opposed to the idea of a school literary magazine, then look for and suggest alternatives, such as those mentioned below. It's not going to help the cause of writing in the school if you lose your job.

Sometimes there's simply no way to find the money to produce a literary magazine. Literary magazines rarely pay for themselves, and you shouldn't go into debt assuming you'll sell enough copies to pay for it. You'll need some kind of financial support. Advertising, patrons, a deal with the school library or English department or school board or even the football coach—there are possibilities for paying the costs, and we've seen all of them (and some other pretty bizarre schemes) work in one school or another. But if there simply is no money, look for other possibilities for publishing student writing.

Alternatives to a Literary Magazine

Many schools have literary editions of a school newspaper that feature student writing. A better alternative is a regular *Literary Column* in the paper. Suggest this possibility to the editor or sponsor. Your classes may even volunteer to edit the column and, cooperating with the newspaper staff, provide a regular place for student writing to appear.

A similar alternative is the literary section of the school yearbook.

Publishing Outside the School

Your local newspaper may sponsor writing contests for students, or it may even regularly feature student writing in its pages. If it doesn't now offer opportunities like these for young writers, don't hesitate to approach the editor with ideas for regularly printing student writing. It's good PR, for one thing. If you live in a larger community, chances are that your local paper has an educational editor (or consultant) whose job is to work with the schools. You'll usually find this person receptive to suggestions.

If your community has a cable TV station, approach the manager with the idea for a program of students' reading their writings on the air. You may get a positive response.

In most towns and cities there's at least one literary group or group of professional or semiprofessional writers. They probably sponsor contests for young writers. Find out about them. These writers' groups are usually happy to offer assistance to student writers and teachers of writing.

Check with the professional organization in your state for writing contests and opportunities for publishing they may sponsor—many such organizations do. Also ask the language arts coordinator in your school system to send you any flyers on writing contests that come through the central office. There are many of these each year, but *examine the ones unfamiliar to you carefully and critically.* Be especially wary of any contest requiring some sort of fee for entering. Have a regular place in your classroom where you post notices of writing contests.

POETRY

1228 NORTH DEARBORN PARKWAY ● CHICAGO, ILLINOIS

60610

We regret that we cannot use the enclosed.

Although we should like to send an individual answer to everyone, particularly those who request special criticism, our staff and time are insufficient for detailed correspondence.

All contributions must be accompanied by a *stamped and self-addressed envelope.* Otherwise we cannot return them or make any other form of reply, and they will be destroyed. Stamps alone are not sufficient. Contributors living abroad should enclose a return envelope and international coupons.

THE EDITORS

Even those of us who've been writing for years grind our teeth in frustrated rage and hurt when we get one of these. Consider carefully before you expose any young writer to the writer's ultimate rejection— the rejection slip. And for those very few, very sophisticated young writers who you feel are ready to venture into the impersonal world of the adult writer, your role is to give them as much support, help, and encouragement as you can.

We talked about publishing outside the school in Chapter 6, but one point that needs to be reemphasized here is that *you* share the experience of submitting writing for publication with your students. Whenever possible, send something somewhere yourself when your students do. Most of the time, writing is rejected—in fact, almost all the time. Sharing the disappointments—and sometimes the triumphs—makes the experience easier, and more meaningful.

The so-called "little magazines" offer student writers the best opportunity to appear in print. Editors of the "littles" are usually individualistic and idiosyncratic, but most of them do take the time to respond *personally* to writers who submit work to them. Many of these editors are writers themselves and encourage the beginner. Besides, you can get the strangest letters from editors of little magazines.

Rusty Dog Press
Joseph P. Pentglass, Editor

Dear Joe:

Is your press accepting submissions of poetry and/or fiction? If so, what are your require-ments regarding form and length?

Thank you for your trouble.

                                        Sincerely,

                                        Tom Liner

                                        Tom Liner

*Tom —
Sorry for the delay. Your letter fell behind my desk and then a burglar broke into my house and subsequently I broke up with the broad I was living with. We just came out with 2 books and are now broke — not accepting anything. Don't give up!!!
Joe*

The *International Directory of Little Magazines and Small Presses* is the bible for noncommercial and avant-garde writers. It lists literally hundreds of addresses and descriptions of magazines. It's a supermarket of places to send manuscripts.

One warning about little magazines, however. Supervise your students carefully and be frank with them about the kinds of magazines that often print experimental—and sometimes antisocial—writing.

Finally, there are the commercial magazines. A few, such as *Seventeen,* offer some opportunities to young writers. All are highly competitive, impersonal in responding, and very difficult—sometimes impossible—to break into.

Writer's Market is the best source for addresses and descriptions of commercial markets. It's published annually by Writer's Digest Books, who also publish *Writer's Digest* magazine. Get your school librarian to order a copy. It's expensive.

Cautions About Publishing Student Writing

Whether you're involved in publishing student writing in your classroom, in the school literary magazine, in the community, or in the national press, remember that the printed word can be cold and terribly final. Keep these cautions in mind.

1. It's *the student,* and not the piece of writing *by* the student, that's important in this process.
2. Never publish a piece of writing without the student's expressed permission.
3. Don't try to move too fast with your students. Give them time and practice to get ready, especially before publishing for strangers.
4. Always prepare students carefully for what they can expect in a particular kind of publishing venture.
5. Watch out for harsh judgments, hurt feelings, embarrassing situations. Guard the young writer from scorn, ridicule, and sniggering remarks.
6. Protect the confidentiality of the student's journal, and the confidence and privacy of the student.
7. Be frank and honest and realistic about censorship, not prudish.
8. Even when publishing, remember that you are still the most important audience for your students.
9. Write, edit, and publish *with* your students.
10. Never forget the "naked, blazing power of print."

Publishing Information for Your Kids (and Their Teacher)

By the time this list is printed it will be out of date. It is also sketchy, nothing approaching a complete list of where your students can send their stuff. That is major research and takes more time than Dan and I both have spent writing and revising this book. But it will give you some places to start.

It is also unabashedly stolen (but with thanks) from the sources I have at hand, notably from Mildred Grenier's little book, *The Beginner's Guide to Writing for Profit* (Pilot Books, 103 Cooper St., Babylon, NY 11702), Deborah Valentine, and of course Nancie Atwell. And from other sources long forgotten. Photocopy this list and start yourself a fat file of places where your kids can send their writing, adding to it as often as you can from other publications, sources the kids themselves discover, and workshops you attend.

Robert Heinlein was right. The way you get into print is to type it up and send it off. When it comes back with a rejection slip, you take it out of the old envelope and put it into the new envelope, with a SASE (self-addressed stamped envelope), and send it off somewhere else. And you keep doing that until somebody takes it. That's it. That's the secret. And in a significant way, that's what becoming an author is all about.

What this list is for is to help your young writers become young authors.

First, three basic sources of informaton. Two of them we've already mentioned:

The International Directory of Little Magazines and Small Presses. Dustbooks, Box 100, Paradise, CA 95969.
   As I've said, use this one with care.

The Writer's Handbook. The Writer, Inc., 8 Arlington St., Boston, MA 02116.

The Writer's Market. Writer's Digest Books, 9933 Alliance Rd., Cincinnati, OH 45242.

I am going to include a few publications in this list for young students, because we know elementary teachers frequently use our book. All of these publications and contests accept writing from students.

Action. 901 College Ave., Winona Lake, ID 46590.
   For children 9 through 11.

Child Life. 1100 Waterway Blvd., Box 567B, Indianapolis, IN 46206.
   For kids to 14. Science fiction and mystery magazine for students.

Co-Ed. 50 West 44th St., New York, NY 10036.

Accepts poetry but wants a statement from the young poet and the teacher, on school stationery, telling them the writing is original. This is a common requirement.

Creative Kids. P.O. Box 6448, Mobile, AL 36660.

For kids 5 through 15. Accepts a wide variety of writing and artwork.

Cricket. P.O. Box 100, La Salle, IL 61301.

For kids 6 through 13. Poetry, stories, and drawings accepted.

Dash. Box 150, Wheaton, Il 60189.

For kids 8 through 11.

Discoveries. 6401 The Paseo, Kansas City, MO 64131.

For kids 8 through 12.

Ebony Jr! 820 South Michigan Ave., Chicago, IL 60605.

For kids 6 through 12.

The Friend. 50 East North Temple, Salt Lake City, UT 84150.

For kids through 12.

Highlights for Children. 803 Church St., Honesdale, PA 18431.

For kids through 12. Accepts a wide variety of writing and black and white art.

Jack and Jill. 1100 Waterway Blvd., Indianapolis, IN 46206.

For kids 7 through 10. Letters, poetry, stories, art, photos.

Kids Magazine. P.O. Box 3041, Grand Central Station, New York, NY 10017.

For kids 5 through 15. Accepts all kinds of student work.

Merlyn's Pen. P.O. Box 716, East Greenwich, RI 02818.

For grades 7 through 10. Accepts all kinds of writing.

National Council of Teachers of English. 1111 Kenyon Rd., Urbana, IL 61801.

If you are not already aware of the 8th grade and 11th grade writing competitions sponsored by NCTE, write them and find out. By the way, the *English Journal* at this same address accepts poetry from *teachers.*

On the Line. 616 Walnut Ave., Scottdale, PA 15683.

For kids 10 through 14.

R-A-D-A-R. 8121 Hamilton Ave., Cincinnati, OH 45231.

For kids 8 through 11.

Read. Xerox Education Publications, 245 Long Hill Rd., Middletown, CT 06457.

Grades 7 through 9. Runs students' jokes and poems often. Has a special feature for student writing each year.

Scholastic, 50 West 44th St., New York, NY 10036.

Scholastic publishes *Scholastic Scope* and *Scholastic Voice* magazines for students. Both accept student writing. They also sponsor the annual Scholastic Writing Awards Program for grades 7, 8, and 9.

Seventeen. 850 3rd Ave., New York, NY 10022.

For girls 12 through 18. Hard to get into. Try the "Free-for-All" column.

Stone Soup. Box 83, Santa Cruz, CA 95063.

For kids under 15. The whole magazine is student work.

Touch. P.O. Box 7244, Grand Rapids, MI 49510.

For kids 8 through 15.

Trails, Pioneer Girls, Inc. Box 788, Wheaton, Il 60187.

For kids 6 through 12.

Wee Wisdom. Unity Village, MO 64065.

To 13. Poetry and short stories.

Young Miss. 685 3rd Ave., New York, NY 10017.

Poetry and opinions accepted.

Notes

1. Thomas Wolfe. *The Story of a Novel.* Scribner's, 1936.

CHAPTER SIXTEEN

Resources

My own experience has been that the tools I need for my trade are paper, tobacco, food, and a little whiskey.

—WILLIAM FAULKNER

Paris Review, 1956

I

Judging by the number of books and articles on writing published in the last decade or so, it's obvious that teachers value the dialogue about writing instruction going on in our profession. I want to talk about books—books that have stimulated and inspired me and the teachers I've worked with. Reading helps me locate myself in current theory and practice. Reading forces me to find my way through a maze of competing theories and practices. It's just plain confusing at times to go foraging for confirmation of our best laid theories and plans. I keep reading and reading more. I keep trying to perfect my craft.

For high school teachers of writing, this dialogue becomes mind-boggling, even mind-numbing. After all, much of our energy goes into the nuts and bolts of managing 150 kids a day. It's hard to keep up. It's hard to know what to read in the little time there is to read. Dan and Tom asked me to organize this chapter any way I wished, so here's a stab at it, beginning with what I think are the "musts."

The Musts

Obviously, the list of "musts" must start with the books (and authors) referred to frequently throughout this book, works which Dan and Tom, in the Resources chapter of the first edition, praised as having "dramatically shaped [their] thinking," and which have similarly shaped mine. The second section of this chapter, "Works Consulted," includes the major works of these authors: Ann Berthoff, James Britton, Peter

Elbow, Janet Emig, Donald Graves, Ken Macrorie, Nancy Martin, James Miller, James Moffett, Donald Murray, and Stephen Tchudi (Judy). Over time, we urge you to read as much of, and as many of, these books as you can. Your thinking, too, will be "dramatically shaped" as you do.

As you begin your inquiry, look at Stephen North's discussion of major contributors and schools of investigators in the field of composition. In *The Making of Knowledge in Composition,* North gives us the premises and working methodology of the schools of thought that represent the major ways of thinking about our discipline. Also, he provides a bibliography that traces development within the field.

The following books represent further signposts that have marked, for me and for many teachers, a journey toward understanding. As I recount the values of their offerings, I compromise their breadth and depth to give you one or two starting places that might lead to new ideas or raise new questions that spur further investigations.

The philosophy, writing to learn, validates the writing process philosophy. Through writing, learning is *active.* Meaningful answers are not always at the tip of a learner's tongue. Rather, language provides a tool that helps the learner discover meaning. Hence, writing directs learning. In *The Climate for Learning,* Mike Torbe and Peter Medway recognize that teachers either foster or prevent learning through their control of language events in the classroom. The authors offer a methodology for exploring the teaching and learning of language events. They recommend strategies within this climate that help learning happen for both teachers and students.

Writing, then, represents one language event that students can use to process learning. In *Learning Through Writing* Bernard T. Harrison takes us through the writings of one group of students over a three year period. Understandably, the record of their experiences holds a general truth about how writing attends them as learners. Writing is often repetitive and convoluted until the writer makes sense of the unfamiliar, until the learner makes meaning through the writing. Harrison traces many of the thinking processes that attend such learning—telling, reflecting, identifying, organizing, and integrating—through student writing samples. We literally watch the mind work in these concrete representations of thinking.

If writing to learn emphasizes a strategy the writer might use to make meaning, another facet of our current writing philosophy suggests we learn to write by writing. In *Learning to Write/Writing to Learn,* John Mayher, Nancy Lester and Gordon Pradl bring together both writing to learn and learning to write in their discussion of writing instruction. They provide valuable suggestions and activities on how we might implement writing to learn strategies in the classroom. They offer an excellent description of writing processes that can provide students with writing practice.

The assumption that good writing is the result of good thinking exists within this philosophical framework as well. *The Writer's Mind* (Hays, et al.) explores this relationship. In this collection of essays, our most outspoken researchers raise their questions and tentative suggestions about the relationship of thinking and writing. The collection deals with the complex issues and questions within process approaches to composing. Such issues as writing development; connections among written, oral, and visual composing; and the range of heuristic strategies are discussed.

Ann E. Berthoff, in *Forming/Thinking/Writing* and *The Making of Meaning* correlates acts of discovering, interpreting, connecting, and naming with composing. Her text *(F/T/W)* and her collection of articles and talks challenge us to see more clearly the connections among philosophy, theory, and practice. From Berthoff we discover the highly speculative nature of ideas and trace ways in which the learner/writer shapes meaning. She ends with the issues that concern us most—strategies to help writers compose meaning.

Much of what we understand about language and writing comes from the work of James Britton, in particular his seminal work, *Language and Learning,* and the collection of his selected essays, *Prospect and Retrospect.* Britton's taxonomy of language use—expressive, transactional, and poetic—differentiates types of writing while allowing for the blurring of these designations. The work of James Britton moves us into the late 1980s with questions, insights, and a good deal more wisdom than we might have otherwise.

If we follow Britton's lead, we'll bring our own minds to the task of studying the crucial issues in our discipline. This notion of teachers observing, studying, and documenting their own classroom happenings shows commitment to further the knowledge in our field. As research grows, it will shape the teaching of writing. I'd like to see more teachers participating in the ongoing dialogue through further study, observation, and reading.

Two books discuss ways teachers have approached research: Miles Myers' *The Teacher-Researcher: How to Study Writing in the Classroom* and *Reclaiming the Classroom: Teacher Research as an Agency for Change* edited by Dixie Goswami and Peter Stillman. These discussions help us develop strategies and questions for research, and we learn how research can improve our teaching.

Stories from Classrooms

If you want a glimpse into other classrooms where students engage in writing, take hope. Teachers are opening their classroom doors to interested readers. *Through Teachers' Eyes,* by Sondra Perl and Nancy Wilson, moves inside the classrooms of six teachers as they face the challenges and excitement of a process approach to teaching writing. For example, Nancy creates a forty page portrait of Audre Allison, an eleventh grade teacher, as she designs, experiments, and occasionally flounders throughout one school year. We get to know the daily struggles of students engaged in writing. These glimpses into classrooms from first through eleventh grade show teachers responding to the issues in teaching writing that range from what to do about Regents Exams to the dilemma faced in keeping up with the typing of first grade books. We see through an observer's eyes the teacher teaching, pondering, and adjusting.

What's Going On? edited by Mary Barr, Pat D'Arcy, and Mary K. Healy, presents a series of teacher inquiries into learning and language. The inquiries start from questions, and these provoke new questions we all must ask if we are to sort out the issues and problems in language experience classrooms. In each chapter, we're invited to participate in the language of students and to follow teachers through an assignment or strategy—writing horror stories, journaling, keeping reader's logs. I found myself plugging in my own students and classroom experiences, constantly asking, "Will this work with the logistical constraints of operating bell to bell?" I found myself nodding affirmation as student enthusiasm slumped, or I re-energized when Lori, a bright eleventh grader, made a leap forward in understanding complex relationships among literary selections.

While Nancie Atwell's *In the Middle* is a "how to" book on designing lessons, conducting conferences, grading, and managing the minutiae of daily concerns, its power extends far beyond advice for teaching reading and writing. Engagement through active learning takes place for both Atwell and her students. She tells stories of her classroom over a ten year period to trace her experience and her growing understanding. We enter the world of Boothbay Harbor Elementary in Maine where Atwell describes her experience of growing into junior high school teaching. She traces and explains how "Every day in our writing and reading workshops, my students and I try out and test our beliefs about written language" (p. 22). We get to know eighth graders through their writing, their reactions, and Atwell's exchanges with them. We watch Amanda and Hillary and Tom, but more than that we see theory in action and Atwell's methods of testing her beliefs through classroom practices.

A slightly different approach records the research done by teachers as they observe and monitor student writers. *Seeing for Ourselves,* by Glenda Bissex and Richard Bullock, moves into the classroom with a narrow focus on one or two writers. Through close observation of those writers, the teacher-researcher attempts to explore the fundamental questions in writing instruction: What are ways of encouraging editing skills? How can I balance self selection and teacher selection of topics? How does the writing environment influence the writer? How might a learning disabled pupil benefit from a writing process approach? The individual case studies might cause you to look at your own students differently or more specifically. Each study shows unique strategies for finding out and recording information about students. You'll find more questions than answers, because this collection celebrates the search rather than the answers. Asking the questions is our first step toward growing understanding. *Seeing for Ourselves* confirms that philosophy.

For even sharper focus, you might follow the development of a single child, Susie, through third and fourth grades in Lucy Calkins' *Lessons from a Child.* You'll participate in Susie's growth as a writer, her frustrations and successes.

Tom Romano is full of stories about high school students learning to write, and about teaching writing, in describing what he has learned in his years as a teacher. That's the strength of *Clearing the Way.* Romano shares the successes and failures of his writing assignments, of his conferencing techniques, and of student product in various writing contexts. He follows student texts that demonstrate young writers moving toward powerful written language. You'll enjoy his humor and good will.

Together, all of these books that describe encounters in the classroom bring us face to face with our work and ourselves. By vicariously experiencing other classrooms, we socialize writing instruction and allow ourselves to step back and see the results of our practices. I recommend collegial visits, firsthand experiences in other teachers' classrooms, as well. Go out there and see what's happening.

Writing About Literature

Literature cannot be ingested through study and talk alone. One learns about literature by making literature, by writing reflections about literature, and by thinking through literature. Experience and experimentation with writing literature and writing about literature will lead students to a better understanding of technique and craft. Not many years ago, writing explications, essays about literature, or literary criticism were the only ways we knew to have student writers respond.

More and more teachers are suggesting avoidance of this heavy-handed approach and concentration on more personal and creative responses.

New Essays in the Teaching of Literature, edited by David Mallick, Peter Moss, and Ian Hansen, presents several essays that advocate alternatives to the traditional responses to literature. If you're interested in seeing how informal responses can guide and shape discussions of literature, Bob Probst, in *Response and Analysis,* gives advice not only on the types of responses one can elicit, but also on how to pattern the subsequent discussions.

Rosemary Deen and Marie Ponsot, in *The Common Sense* (pp. 95-117), give specific classroom assignments that bring the reading of literature and the writing about literature together. Much of their strategy involves reading and rereading, writing observations nonstop, then putting the reading and writing aside and sorting through what resonates, what holds the reader's attention. Their elemental question, "What is the turning point, and why do you think so?" (p. 107) sets the foundation for the essays on literature that students will write. A more detailed explanation of their procedure is described in their *Beat Not the Poor Desk* (pp. 154-180).

If you want alternatives to informal responses or analytical essays, take time to read about writing literature as a way of responding. We have few sources to consult, but the richness of these ideas will get you started. Richard Exton (Miller, 1984, pp. 70-79) criticizes the way in which we have kept the study of literature and the writing of literature separated. He describes two specific lessons—studies of a short story and a poem—that challenge the traditional approach. In both cases, students study the genre by writing in that genre. They learn conventions of a genre through writing.

Perhaps Tom Romano gives the clearest examples of this consolidation. He says that "[students] should be striking out on their own, creating literary artifacts of personal importance, trying just about every genre of literature they study" (p. 136). He makes recommendations for other ways to respond as well. In Chapter 10 (pp. 149-161) he tackles the subject of writing about literature through exposition. Throughout, he is articulate and strong-willed, and he leaves the teacher with the confidence to try his suggestions with students. His book is high on my list.

Revision

Most students don't think about revision in the ways we'd like them to. I asked a group of eleventh graders what the word revision means. Noel's response typifies the general attitude: "...touching up little stuff for the teacher, writing it a little neater and sometimes changing a word here and there because it sounds better."

If your kids feel that way, and you're trying to make sense of ways to get them to revise, or you want to see student drafts change in significant ways, check out Marian Mohr's *Revision: The Rhythm of Meaning*. For Mohr, revision should help a writer achieve meaning and form. Mohr emphasizes that different assignments require different revision practices. The spirit of her suggestions, at the end of each chapter, encourages students to see revision as a way to experiment with meaning and form.

Roland Huff and Charles Kline, in *The Contemporary Writing Curriculum*, recommend that peer response groups give feedback to a writer during the composing process. They provide two examples of response sheets that focus students' attention on central problems of written text. They explain that careful modeling of constructive feedback by teachers is essential to the success of peer groups (pp. 122-125). The response sheets, along with Huff and Kline's brief discussion of modeling, may whet your appetite for more information.

If so, Karen Spear's *Sharing Writing* gives detailed advice on the logistics of group work—ways to clarify group purposes, to train students to read texts analytically, to encourage collaborative work, and to monitor group activity. The early chapters set up a theoretical base for response groups. Later chapters show groups in operation and give practical suggestions for implementation.

Browsing through the first half of *Revising: New Essays for Teachers of Writing*, edited by Ronald Sudol, I'm struck by a central issue that theoretical discussions on revision raise: revision is not a step in the writing process. It is the act of discovering and shaping discovery again and again until the writer has said clearly what is on her mind. Revision does not impose artificial constraints over meaning. Revision arises from within the reader's writing to shape and reshape thought into language.

The last half of the book presents collected articles on revision techniques, but none set a model of revision process or suggest approaches to study revision as Mohr does or as Gabriel M. Della-Piana does in "Research Strategies for the study of Revision Processes in Writing Poetry." Her article (pp. 105-134) is one in the collection edited by Charles R. Cooper and Lee Odell, *Research on Composing*. We've come a long way in helping students value revision.

Toby Fulwiler, in *Teaching with Writing* (pp. 59-74), believes that the lackluster attitude many students have toward revision may result from teachers whose assignments do not reflect revision's importance. Fulwiler believes we must call attention to the role of revision in learning, and the teacher must suggest how this might be accomplished. He brings the voices of Donald Murray, Ann Berthoff, Ken Macrorie, William Zinsser and others into this chapter. Their suggested approaches might give you several different ways to bring your students face to face with the values of revision.

Mary K. Healy (Camp, 1982, pp. 226-291) gives step by step procedures for sensitizing students to effective use of language and for training response groups. Her discussion of the teacher's role in monitoring a response group's progress will give you ideas of procedural ways to keep track of how students work together.

If you want recommendations for ways to practice revision with whole classes, take a look at what Marie Ponsot and Rosemary Deen, in *Beat Not the Poor Desk* (pp. 113-119), suggest. They narrow revision practice to the smallest possible units—isolated sentences and endings. Through this specific focus, they alert writers to the strategies of revision.

Wise writers test and retest the language and structures that represent their thinking. They make choices of consequence. If students are having trouble revising, we might suspect that they have not clarified their intentions. Revision requires writers to ask many questions of themselves: What do I mean here? What tone do I want? What word best describes my feeling? Consider helping students through the hurdles of clarifying their intentions.

Grammar in Writing

Now we catch in the bramble bush. Research indicates there is little, if any, connection between formal grammar instruction and the use of such instruction in writing (Braddock, Schoer, Lloyd-Jones, 1963). So, we're stuck trying to figure out how to teach grammar through writing. I have a hunch that teachers will need more knowledge of linguistics to pull off the subtle instruction necessary in a process classroom.

We nod our heads in agreement nowadays that ideas come before correctness, but most teachers want correctness when the time arrives for a student to publish a piece of writing. Most of us don't want Mom and Dad cringing at a paper filled with errors. Most of us don't want to hear about the call placed to our principal that questioned our methods and rigor.

A process approach does provide an answer, though few teachers are speaking up to tell how they manage. One of the braver souls, Peter Forrestal (Tchudi, 1986, pp. 131-133) provides a technical focus for pieces of writing that reach the editing stage. He advocates direct instruction before students review their piece of writing to look for places where that error may be evidenced.

Ponsot and Deen work from much the same position. They limit grammar instruction to those areas that "need to be brought to writers' conscious attention" (p. 134). They teach from written product rather than through isolated rules. As they establish a hierarchy of concerns— the sentence with its graphics (capital, period, comma or semicolon for coordinate independent clauses); governing pronouns along with the implication that each clarifies point of view, focus, and references; governing tense as a conveyor of time; paragraphs as isolation points for various ideas—the focus of their discussion is always on how conscious-ness of grammar produces better writing. Ponsot and Deen recommend handbook and workbook only when writers reach the editing stage. Discussions of grammar serve as aids to strengthen the writer's power.

Traditional grammar instruction—labeling parts of speech, identify-ing forms—is of little value in writing courses. For writing, the sentence is the basic unit of grammar to most linguists. Richard Weaver (Graves, 1984, pp. 95-99) discusses the ways in which sentence form shapes meaning and intention, and introduces ways to instruct student writers to use such shapes to their advantage.

Francis Christensen (Graves, 1984, pp. 110-118) identifies the structural principles of the sentence through sentences from contemporary writers. His example sentences have made me take a closer look at layers of structure and helped me articulate the usages and effects of layering for students. His discussion of texture in sentences alerts me to the potentials of adding density and variety to writing. Christensen gives us the vocabulary to talk about texture and layers of structure with our students.

In the same collection of essays (Graves, pp. 128-132) Valerie Krishna presents her method of helping basic writers correct syntax errors. She narrows the problem to the writers' lack of understanding about the subject-verb position, and the tendency to fit central thoughts in ancillary positions. The results—"feeble structures and anemic main clauses"—tangle meaning. She recommends ways for teaching writers what to do rather than what not to do.

A word of caution. You'll want to read the finding of James Moffett in "Grammar and the Sentence" in *Teaching the Universe of Discourse* before you dive headlong into teaching composition by focusing on the sentence. Moffett leads us to consider the larger issues: what kind of grammar, what kind of instruction, and what kind of improvement do we expect in what aspect of writing?

For the most part, the advice we get for teaching grammar through writing is vague and mostly procedural. If you want a procedural guide, Toby Fulwiler, in *Teaching with Writing* (pp. 129-132), offers nine rules that help students handle the mechanics in their papers. Roy Clark, in *Free to Write* (pp. 133-156), follows a "teach grammar through writing model." His "Yucky List," an idea he adopted from Eliot Wigginton, makes sense as a way of reminding students of persistent errors. The list grows throughout the year as problems arise. You'll find his discussion of editing and editing teams helpful if you're still struggling to figure out how to do this in a writing class.

One of my favorite pieces of advice is given by Huff and Kline (pp. 125-127). It is short and to the point: students take responsibility in groups of five to clean up mechanics. They should be the janitors of their own language. Huff and Kline tell how students are held accountable for the cleanup job.

Our diagnosis of students' writing problems should be informed by our knowledge of linguistics. If you need a refresher course, several books provide help. Beware. The reading gets thick and soupy in the world of linguists' language.

In *Reading Children's Writing,* John Harris and Jeff Wilkinson present collected essays that provide detailed analyses of pieces of writing from secondary school students. The descriptions of text structures help label and clarify organizational features. The collection helps detail the aspects of language that contribute to the effectiveness of a piece of writing. With a conscious understanding of structures (grammatical, lexical, and organizational) teachers can provide help with writing.

Articles on linguistics and stylistics appear in many of our professional journals, but *The Territory of Language* (McQuade, 1986) brings many together in one volume. From Edward Corbett's article (pp. 23-32) on teaching style, we recognize diction, syntax, tropes, rhythms of sentences, and the manner of paragraphing as categories of stylistics. From Donald Freeman (pp. 165-173) we learn ways to analyze sentence flaws to suggest revisions. The collection gives us the opportunity to examine how linguistics, rhetoric, and writing intertwine so that we might use our knowledge to benefit our student writers.

The practical application of linguistics to our teaching practice requires the internalization of linguistic concepts. It takes practice to analyze discourse. One way to extend the practice beyond student papers is to analyze literary texts. Elizabeth Traugott and Mary Pratt apply linguistic concepts to literature in *Linguistics for Students of Literature.* Their discussions of particular pieces of literature sharpen our awareness of structure and use of language. The exercises at the end of each chapter provide extra challenges.

If you want to tackle M. A. K. Halliday's *An Introduction to Functional Grammar*, you'll find an interpretation of grammatical patterns that relate to text analysis. The work is systematic, full of examples, but difficult given its density. For a lighter touch, you might read Constance Weaver's *Grammar for Teachers*. She explores ways in which teachers can use their knowledge of grammar to help students improve their writing. The second part of the book reviews the essentials of grammar. Weaver's comparison of traditional, structural, and transformational grammar proves useful if you are thinking about designing a framework of grammar instruction within your writing course.

Conferencing

In most of what's being said about writing, conferencing is viewed as an effective method of teaching. The problem for most of us is how to plan and conduct conferences within the limitations posed by a classroom setting. A few folks are beginning to talk about the issues involved.

Tom Romano (pp. 85-105) traces his experiences with one student through conferencing sessions and gives us his philosophy and many of the practical implementations at the same time.

While Donald Murray, in *A Writer Teaches Writing* (pp. 147-186), describes conference teaching with college students, much of his advice for patterning conferences applies to lower levels as well. He discusses effective ways to respond to student writing during conferences and more of the nitty-gritty of the problems and their solutions in conferencing than I've seen elsewhere. There isn't much written yet, but these sources might get you interested.

What Writers Say About Writing

Some writers talk about writing, noting their own processes, the practice of their craft, and the influences that enrich them. Scavenging through their insights helps me trust the erratic processes of young writers. Many times professional writers give us ideas to encourage growth, give us insights into craft that help us see the divers ways a writer gets ideas flowing. Sharing excerpts of such insights with students helps them reflect on their strategies.

I'm always interested in where writers get ideas. Barry Lopez finds that "It's very pleasant for me to go someplace and do a story. I like that. I like seeing a different part of the landscape..." (O'Connell, p. 11). William Stafford finds the landscape in his mind. "When I write, I like to have an interval before me when I am not likely to be interrupted....I get pen and paper, take a glance out of the window ...and wait. It is like fishing" (Stafford, p. 17).

Eudora Welty details the events of her home life and Davis School days to show the influences in her fiction. "I never resisted it when, in almost every story I ever wrote, some parade or processions, impromptu or ceremonious, comic or mocking or funereal, has risen up to mark some stage of the story's unfolding. They've started from far back" (Welty, p. 37).

In *Triggering Town*, Richard Hugo suspects "that the true or valid triggering subject is one in which physical characteristics or details correspond to attitudes the poet has toward the world and himself."

Ordering the bits and fragments of ideas and performing feats of technical and artistic mastery require keenness, insight, and practice. Here is how some writers say they've apprenticed. "The great guides were the books I discovered in the Johns Hopkins library, where my student job was to file books away....My great teachers...were Scheherazade, Homer, Virgil, and Boccaccio....A beginner...needs to be taught that literature is there...(Plimpton, Interview with John Barth, pp. 231-232).

John Gardner examines the techniques in the art of fiction and reminds us that "For centuries, one of the standard ways of learning techniques has been imitation" (Gardner, p. 142). His chapter on technique (pp. 125-164) is particularly valuable in pointing out specific practices that help writers fine tune their art.

In *Falling Through Space*, Ellen Gilchrist, superb writer of fiction, gives advice that may help our students trust the starts and stops of the process. "A piece of writing is the product of a series of explosions in the mind....It is helpful to me to pretend that writing is like building a house. I like to go out and watch real building projects and study the faces of the carpenters and masons....It reminds me of how hard it is to do anything really worth doing" (p. 132).

When revising gets our students down, let them hear the words of Barry Lopez: "I rewrite a great deal. The language is very important to me and it takes a long time to get the language right....I always think of that image of making the pieces fit together more tightly" (O'Connell, p. 12). You can find such discussion of revision by Virginia Woolf, Robert Frost, and Henry David Thoreau. The words surround us; we need to bring them into the classroom for our student writers.

I've said enough. These writers say it better. Look for interviews, diaries, and journals. You have a few here to get you started. Such discussions allow us to visit the dressing rooms of a writer's mind. Many reaffirm our notions about writing but many more add new facets that deserve our close attention.

Writing Personal Narrative and Fiction

Understandably, many of us are looking for one great book that explains how we can teach fiction writing. I haven't found it either, but, in combination, several sources provide a patchwork and it is through such bits and pieces that a pattern develops.

James Moffett provides a rough fictional sequence of student work in the *Active Voices* Series, I-IV. The hierarchy established interrelates assignments according to structure and/or language principles. What Moffett has in mind delineates the range of discourse into teachable segments. You'll want to look at *Active Voices II* (grades 7-9) and *Active Voices III* (grades 10-12) to see the student product.

For a specialized look at storytelling, oral and written, consult Harold Rosen, who explains the structures and significances of narrative in *Stories and Meanings*. Put Meredith Sue Willis's *Personal Fiction Writing* into Rosen's larger framework, and you'll begin to see how fiction grows from the fabric of personal experience and knowledge. Willis brings her firsthand experience as a fiction writer to the methods and exercises in this book. Along with specific assignment suggestions, Willis includes student and professional writing. You can find her explanations of and reactions to certain pieces of writing as you read. Through her responses, you might see a model for ways to respond to students' fiction as well.

Two other writers, Robie Macauley and George Lanning, combine their resources in *Technique in Fiction* to probe the problems of getting pieces of a story to work together as story. They discuss technique by presenting the crafting of the most virtuoso performers, dozens of writers from divers times and places, then relating these pieces of writing to successes and failures in practice.

Rust Hills, in *Writing in General and the Short Story in Particular*, discusses techniques of fiction, presenting how each technique functions. Behind his discussion, I hear him saying over and over again that good writers are readers of literature. Read and continue reading. Keep up on the contemporary short story writers—Ellen Gilchrist, Raymond Carver, Gloria Naylor, Charles Johnson, Michael Ondaatje, and Wallace Stegner among the hundreds that deserve mention.

John Dixon and Leslie Stratta, in *Writing Narrative—and Beyond*, offer thoughtful readings of students' narratives. They help us educate ourselves as sensitive readers. Equally important, they generalize on features produced in these texts that might signal development. Within this discussion, specific strategies are recommended to promote progress.

Eventually my search for advice and ideas leads me back to writers' interviews and to personal narrative and fiction written by those authors. I try to match up what they say with what they write. Many times a sequence of classroom assignments grows from that. So, *Writers at Work* or any collection of interviews will get you started. When you find something interesting that Raymond Carver has to say, turn to his stories to see what you can make of his ideas in his fiction.

Take Italo Calvino's discussion of "Levels of Reality in Literature" in his *The Uses of Literature*. His formula will lead us to a discussion of point of view and authorial interference in a text. Armed with that perspective it is valuable to turn to Calvino's fiction. Let's say we open *if on a winter's night a traveler* and check out the levels of reality there. Then we might design assignments from our growing knowledge of how fiction "works." If we turn, then, to James Moffett and Kenneth McElheny's *Points of View: An Anthology of Short Stories* we can connect their definitions with the levels Calvino recognizes. All of our study and growing expertise reenters our classrooms in significant ways.

Two books that have helped me understand structures and techniques in fiction are by John Gardner. *The Art of Fiction* presents Gardner's theory of fiction, an articulate and incisive commentary. The second part of his discussion helps us identify specific techniques and exercises. Anyone teaching fiction should keep this book on her desk. Gardner's *On Becoming a Novelist* teaches what he values in fiction and the techniques of fiction. The work sets a context for our classrooms: What is a writer and how is a writer trained? Typical of Gardner's optimism, the last chapter is titled "Faith." I try to read it each year when school starts.

When you are ready to tackle the theoretical background, three works come to mind. Dorrit Cohn's *Transparent Minds: Narrative Modes for Presenting Consciousness in Fiction* presents a study of narrators of fiction and narrative perspective. The modes identified include: third person-psycho-narration, quoted monologue, narrated monologue; and first person-retrospective techniques, narration to monologue, and autonomous monologue. The discussion carries us into stylistic and linguistic considerations that help sharpen our sensitivities. I keep thinking this background helps us when we come face to face with the writing of our students. *Narrative Fiction,* by Shlomith Rimmon-Kenan, suggests a description of the system underlying the structure of narrative fiction. The discussion sets up theoretical bases through detailed illustrations of particular cases. The diversity of narrative forms from story to film to painting come under close scrutiny in a collection of essays, *On Narrative* (Mitchell, ed., 1980). Nelson Goodman's "Twisted Tales" (pp. 99-115), through pictorial example, tells the whole story of flashbacks and foreflashes in narrative. I've taken the art lesson into the classroom when students are writing stories. The concrete examples help them see the ways of ordering occurrences.

Have faith. Someday, somewhere, somebody will write that book.

Writing Poetry

For some time I've believed that the best ways to prepare myself to teach poetry writing are fourfold: write poetry, read poetry, read interviews with poets, and read books describing theoretical or pedagogical issues. I can't say much about writing poetry except to admit that I set time aside, then practice. I can tell you that the experience has helped me talk with students about writing poetry, and I believe the responses I give to their poetry are more genuine and insightful.

Reading poetry fits in the cracks of a busy school schedule. I always carry a chapbook by some new name with me. I read the knowns as well. It is true that such reading consistently points to things I've not observed before—the highly specialized use of language, the repetition and condensation, or the sound image. I've spent the past five years trying to hear the voices of contemporary poets and I've barely scratched the surface with my relentless reading. A few of my favorites are worth mentioning: Jonathan Holden, Jorie Graham, David St. John, Richard Hugo, Tess Gallagher, Donald Hall, Donald Justice, Rita Dove, Kathleen Fraser, and Ann Deagon. Read anything you can by these people.

A collection like *The Morrow Anthology of Younger Poets* (Smith and Bottoms, eds., 1985) brings many fine American poets together in one volume. Of the numerous collections available, *19 New American Poets of the Golden Gate* (Dow, ed., 1984) presents a particularly interesting format. The nineteen poets provide collected poems that span their writing careers. An essay by each poet accompanies the poems—"Real Nouns," "Making Us Speak," "Interview from a Treehouse," "O Come All Ye Faithful: a brechtian oratorio in five acts." Sound interesting? The collection is informative, entertaining, and instructive. Dedicated to the memory of Richard Hugo, *Singular Voices* (Berg, ed., 1985) includes poets who present one poem and an accompanying essay they wrote about that poem. The essays explain difficulties, tell stories, elaborate on technical matters—a whole range of topics. We get to know the poet—the frustrations, elations, and intellect involved in creating that one poem.

Essays, interviews, journals all provide insights. When Wendell

Berry notes "Structure is intelligibility" (1983, p. 82), I nod my head and take his words into the classroom where students learn to confirm the simplicity of structure's effect. When John Wain, in *Professing Poetry,* gives "Homage to Emily Dickinson" (pp. 76-90) for her beautifully chosen words and her continuing influence on our consciousness, I remember the lines "Because I could not stop for Death" and carry them into the classroom to define terms of our existence. And M. L. Rosenthal *(Poetry and the Common Life)* reminds us of the sources of poetry in our daily lives. He guides us to hear and to see the poetry present in the voices of people around us. Passion to retain what is transient in life—the shadings and depths we might lose—is the motivation for writing. Rosenthal takes us on a journey through our surroundings and explains how our awareness speaks through language. Rosenthal guides and coaches. Through his example, we can do the same for our students.

These poets teach us much about the writing of poetry. Two additional sources deal specifically with the techniques that poets master. In *The Intimate Art of Writing Poetry,* Ottone M. Riccio's extended metaphor—anatomy likened to the creative process—brings the structural elements and the meaning of the poem into one well-tuned and highly efficient body. The bone and muscle of poetry include the stanzas, rhyme patterns, rhythm, and line breaks among others. Riccio details these various dynamics in his prologue to poetry. His subsequent discussions offer extended examples of crafting devices as well as provide exercises for application. In conjunction with Riccio, Barbara Drake, in *Writing Poetry,* discusses the basics of poetry through examples of particular poems. Her explication of each poem sets a backdrop before she focuses on issues that are covered in detail—use of memory, variations of voice, form, and use of archetype and myth. Each of the fourteen chapters contains suggestions for writing. Her book supports a synthesis of reading and writing poetry as an undeniable must to understanding poetry.

The study of poetry no longer appears to be a frill in our schools, or something different to do on Fridays. A historical view of this changing attitude is traced by Peter Benton in *Pupil, Teacher, Poem.* Worrying about how to teach students to read and write poetry triggers anxiety in teachers. Avoidance is an obvious response. Benton articulates strategies for engaging students after he spends a chapter discussing what some teachers are doing with poetry and their subsequent frustrations. This look at pedagogy leads Benton to believe less time should be spent teaching poetry and more time experiencing it. He describes many ways of doing that as he describes students and teachers "doing" poetry.

Another book with sound, practical advice and exercises, *Getting from Here to There: Writing and Reading Poetry,* advocates diving into the reading and writing simultaneously. We've talked with many teachers who find Florence Grossman's challenging book a must for their libraries.

If you want to look at more philosophical or more technical discussions consult Martin Heidegger's *Poetry, Language, Thought,* Philip Dacey and David Jauss's *Strong Measures: Contemporary American Poetry in Traditional Forms,* and Barbara Smith's *Poetic Closure: A Study of How Poems End.* Heidegger gives us a highly philosophical look at aesthetics through his thoughts on the art of poetry. Dacey and Jauss collect contemporary poems in traditional forms. If you are looking for form poems to share with students, you'll find a wealth of examples in this collection. My students often query: How do I end this? I've said just about everything, but the poem falls flat at the end. Barbara Smith can help you answer the question. The study is not light reading, but the application of her insights is invaluable.

The struggle to teach, to write, and to read poetry overwhelms us at times. But we do have resources to guide our thinking and our practice.

II

Works Consulted

Atwell, Nancie. *In the Middle: Writing, Reading, and Learning with Adolescents.* Portsmouth, NH: Boynton/Cook, 1987.

Barr, Mary, Pat D'Arcy, and Mary K. Healy. *What's Going On? Language/Learning Episodes in British and American Classrooms, Grades 4-13.* Upper Montclair, NJ: Boynton/Cook, 1982.

Benton, Peter. *Pupil, Teacher, Poem.* London: Hodder & Stoughton, 1986.

Berg, Stephen. *Singular Voices.* New York: Avon, 1985.

Berry, Wendell. *Standing by Words.* San Francisco: North Point, 1983.

Berthoff, Ann E. *The Making of Meaning: Metaphors, Models, and Maxims for Writing Teachers.* Upper Montclair, NJ: Boynton/Cook, 1981.

————. *Forming/Thinking/Writing.* 2d ed. Portsmouth, NH: Boynton/Cook, 1988.

Bissex, Glenda L., and Richard H. Bullock. *Seeing for Ourselves; Case-Study Research by Teachers of Writing.* Portsmouth, NH: Heinemann, 1987.

Braddock, Richard, Lowell Schoer, and Richard Lloyd-Jones. *Research in Written Composition.* Champaign, IL: NCTE, 1963.

Britton, James. *Language and Learning.* Harmondsworth, England: Penguin, 1970.

————— . *Prospect and Retrospect: Selected Essays of James Britton*. ed. Gordon M. Pradl. Upper Montclair, NJ: Boynton/Cook, 1982.

Britton, James, Tony Burgess, Nancy Martin, Alex McLeod, and Harold Rosen. *The Development of Writing Abilities (11-18)*. London: Macmillan Education, 1975.

Calkins, Lucy. *Lessons from a Child*. Portsmouth, NH: Heinemann, 1983.

Calvino, Italo. *The Uses of Literature*. New York: Harcourt Brace Jovanovich, 1986.

Camp, Gerald, ed. *Teaching Writing: Essays from the Bay Area Writing Project*. Upper Montclair, NJ: Boynton/Cook, 1982.

Clark, Roy. *Free to Write*. Portsmouth, NH: Heinemann, 1987.

Cohn, Dorrit. *Transparent Minds: Narrative Modes for Presenting Consciousness in Fiction*. Princeton: Princeton University Press, 1978.

Cooper, Charles R., and Lee Odell, eds. *Research on Composing: Points of Departure*. Urbana, IL: NCTE, 1978.

Dacey, Philip, and David Jauss, eds. *Strong Measures: Contemporary American Poetry in Traditional Forms*. New York: Harper & Row, 1986.

Deen, Rosemary, and Marie Ponsot. *The Common Sense: What to Write, How to Write It, and Why*. Upper Montclair, NJ: Boynton/Cook, 1985.

Dixon, John, and Leslie Stratta. *Writing Narrative—and Beyond*. Ottawa: The Canadian Council of Teachers of English, 1986.

Dow, Philip, ed. *19 New American Poets of the Golden Gate*. New York: Harcourt Brace Jovanovich, 1984.

Drake, Barbara. *Writing Poetry*. New York: Harcourt Brace Jovanovich, 1983.

Elbow, Peter. *Writing Without Teachers*. New York: Oxford University Press, 1973.

————— . *Writing with Power*. New York: Oxford University Press, 1981.

————— . *Embracing Contraries: Explorations in Learning and Teaching*. New York: Oxford University Press, 1986.

Emig, Janet. *The Web of Meaning: Essays on Writing, Teaching, Learning, and Thinking*. Upper Montclair, NJ: Boynton/Cook, 1983.

Esbensen, Barbara Juster. *A Celebration of Bees: Helping Children Write Poetry*. Minneapolis: Winston, 1975.

Fulwiler, Toby. *Teaching with Writing: An Interdisciplinary Workshop Approach*. Upper Montclair, NJ: Boynton/Cook, 1987.

————— . *The Journal Book*. Upper Montclair, NJ: Boynton/Cook, 1987.

Fulton, Len, and Ellen Ferber, eds. *The International Dictionary of Little*

Magazines and Small Presses. Paradise, CA: Dustbooks, published annually.

Gardner, John. *On Becoming a Novelist.* New York: Harper & Row, 1983.

_____ . *The Art of Fiction.* New York: Knopf, 1984.

Gilchrist, Ellen. *Falling Through Space.* Boston: Little, Brown, 1987.

Goswami, Dixie, and Peter Stillman, eds. *Reclaiming the Classroom: Teacher Research as an Agency for Change.* Upper Montclair, NJ: Boynton/Cook, 1987.

Graves, Donald. *Writing: Teachers and Children at Work.* Portsmouth, NH: Heinemann, 1983.

Graves, Richard, ed. *Rhetoric and Composition: A Sourcebook for Teachers and Writers,* 2d ed. Upper Montclair, NJ: Boynton/Cook, 1984.

Grossman, Florence. *Getting from Here to There: Writing and Reading Poetry.* Upper Montclair, NJ: Boynton/Cook, 1982.

Halliday, M.A.K. *An Introduction to Functional Grammar.* England: Edward Arnold, 1985.

Harris, John, and Jeff Wilkinson. *Reading Children's Writing: A Linguistic View.* Boston: Allen & Unwin, 1986.

Harrison, Bernard T. *Learning Through Writing: Stages of Growth in English.* Atlantic Highlands, NJ: Humanities, 1983.

Hays, Janice, et al. *The Writer's Mind: Writing as a Mode of Thinking.* Urbana, IL: NCTE, 1983.

Heidegger, Martin. *Poetry, Language, Thought.* trans., Alfred Hofstadter. New York: Harper, 1971.

Hills, Rust. *Writing in General and the Short Story in Particular.* New York: Bantam, 1977.

Huff, Roland, and Charles R. Kline, Jr. *The Contemporary Writing Curriculum: Rehearsing, Composing, and Valuing.* New York: Teachers College Press, 1987.

Hugo, Richard. *Triggering Town.* New York: W.W. Norton, 1979.

Irmscher, William F. *Teaching Expository Writing.* New York: Holt, Rinehart & Winston, 1979.

Koch, Kenneth. *Wishes, Lies, and Dreams: Teaching Children to Write Poetry.* New York: Vintage, 1970.

_____ . *Rose, Where Did You Get That Red?* New York: Vintage, 1973.

Macauley, Robie, and George Lanning. *Technique in Fiction.* New York: St. Martin's, 1987.

Macrorie, Ken. *Uptaught.* New York: Hayden, 1970.

————. *Writing to Be Read,* 3d ed. Upper Montclair, NJ: Boynton/Cook, 1984.

————. *Telling Writing,* 4th ed. Upper Montclair, NJ: Boynton/Cook, 1985.

————. *The I-Search Paper,* 2d ed. of *Searching Writing.* Portsmouth, NH: Boynton/Cook, 1988.

Mallick, David, Peter Moss, and Ian Hansen, eds. *New Essays in the Teaching of Literature.* Norwood, S.A.: The Australian Association for the Teaching of English, 1982.

Martin, Nancy, Pat D'Arcy, Bryan Newton, and Robert Parker. *Writing and Learning Across the Curriculum 11-16.* London: Ward Lock, 1976.

Mayher, John, Nancy Lester, and Gordon Pradl. *Learning to Write/Writing to Learn.* Upper Montclair, NJ: Boynton/Cook, 1983.

McQuade, Donald, ed. *The Territory of Language: Linguistics, Stylistics, and the Teaching of Composition.* Carbondale, IL: Southern Illinois University Press, 1986.

Miller, James E., Jr. *Word, Self, Reality: The Rhetoric of the Imagination.* New York: Dodd, Mead, 1972.

Miller, James E., Jr., and Stephen N. Judy. *Writing in Reality.* New York: Harper & Row, 1978.

Miller, Jane. *Eccentric Propositions: Essays on Literature and Curriculum.* London: Routledge & Kegan Paul, 1984.

Mitchell, W.J.T., ed. *On Narrative.* Chicago: University of Chicago Press, 1981.

Mohr, Marian M. *Revision: The Rhythm of Meaning.* Upper Montclair, NJ: Boynton/Cook, 1984.

Moffett, James. *Teaching the Universe of Discourse.* Boston: Houghton Mifflin, 1968.

————. *Active Voice: A Writing Program Across the Curriculum.* Upper Montclair, NJ: Boynton/Cook, 1981.

————. *Active Voices,* vols. I-IV. Upper Montclair, NJ: Boynton/Cook, 1986-87.

Moffett, James, and Kenneth R. McElheny. eds. *Points of View: An Anthology of Short Stories.* New York: New American Library, 1966.

Murray, Donald M. *Learning by Teaching.* Upper Montclair, NJ: Boynton/Cook, 1982.

————. *A Writer Teaches Writing,* 2d ed. Boston: Houghton Mifflin, 1985.

Myers, Miles. *The Teacher-Researcher: How to Study Writing in the Classroom*. Urbana, IL: NCTE, 1985.

North, Stephen M. *The Making of Knowledge in Composition: Portrait of an Emerging Field*. Upper Montclair, NJ: Boynton/Cook, 1987.

O'Connell, Nicholas, ed. *At the Field's End*. Seattle: Madrona, 1987.

Perl, Sondra, and Nancy Wilson. *Through Teachers' Eyes*. Portsmouth, NH: Heinemann, 1986.

Plimpton, George, ed. *Writers at Work*. 7th Series. New York: Knopf, 1984.

Ponsot, Marie, and Rosemary Deen. *Beat Not the Poor Desk*. Upper Montclair, NJ: Boynton/Cook, 1982.

Probst, Robert. *Response and Analysis: Teaching Literature in Junior and Senior High School*. Portsmouth,

Riccio, Ottone M. *The Intimate Art of Writing Poetry*. Englewood Cliffs, NJ: Prentice-Hall, 1980.

Rimmon-Kenan, Shlomith. *Narrative Fiction: Contemporary Poetics*. New York: Methuen, 1983.

Romano, Tom. *Clearing the Way*. Portsmouth, NH: Heinemann, 1987.

Rosen, Harold. *Stories and Meanings*. England: The National Association for the Teaching of English, 1984.

Rosenthal, M.L. *Poetry and the Common Life*. New York: Schocken, 1983.

Smith, Barbara. *Poetic Closure: A Study of How Poems End*. Chicago: University of Chicago Press, 1968.

Smith, David, and David Bottoms, eds. *The Morrow Anthology of Younger American Poets*. New York: Quill, 1985.

Spear, Karen. *Sharing Writing: Peer Response Groups in English Classes*. Portsmouth, NH: Boynton/Cook, 1988.

Stafford, William. *Writing the Australian Crawl*. Ann Arbor: University of Michigan Press, 1978.

Sudol, Ronald A., ed. *Revising: New Essays for Teachers of Writing*. Urbana, IL: NCTE, 1982.

Tchudi, Stephen, N., ed. *English Teachers at Work: Ideas and Strategies from Five Countries*. Upper Montclair, NJ: Boynton/Cook, 1986.

Torbe, Mike, and Peter Medway. *The Climate for Learning*. Upper Montclair, NJ: Boynton/Cook, 1981.

Traugott, Elizabeth, and Mary Pratt. *Linguistics for Students of Literature*. New York: Harcourt Brace Jovanovich, 1980.

Wain, John. *Professing Poetry*. New York: Penguin, 1978.

Weaver, Constance. *Grammar for Teachers: Perspectives and Definitions.* Urbana, IL: NCTE, 1979.

Welty, Eudora. *One Writer's Beginnings.* Cambridge, MA: Harvard University Press, 1984.

Willis, Meredith Sue. *Personal Fiction Writing.* New York: Teachers and Writers Collaborative, 1984.